"*Angel investing is not easy, nor is it*
shares in a publicly traded compan
in startups are illiquid and not easy
great deal; mistakes in terms can m
successful investment and one where
but your investment is not. The auth ... the legal
matters in this book, but also give many angel investors a framework to
think about both individual deals and a long-term portfolio approach.
They provide options for many complex issues that confront angels and
help you decide what is important in a deal."
— Dan Rosen, Chair of the Alliance of Angels

"*When both sides approach fundraising with transparency, empathy*
and respect, outcomes are better for everyone. Angel Investing, Start to
Finish gives you the knowledge and tools to achieve more successful
investor-investee relationships. My advice to everyone who is new to
investing, fundraising, advising, or a combination of all: take this
book and make it your cheat sheet."
— Lelsie Feinzaig, CEO, Female Founders Alliance

"*Joe and Pete have put together a very comprehensive, modern,*
relevant work on angel investment. This is the book I wish I'd had 10
years ago. It's all the bits and pieces of angel investment perfectly
structured for angel and entrepreneur consumption. The details on
terms and term sheets are particularly focused and critical. A must-
read for anyone involved in early-stage investment."
— Burton Miller, Co-Founder, Startup206, Bliip Networks, Roost

"*This book is an excellent review of angel investing. It is complete and*
thorough so that, even after 10 years as an active angel investor, I
learned some insights. It is clearly written and the links provide easy
references so that it is perfect for a novice angel investor."
— Dan Delmar, Chief Mentor and Board Director, Harvard Business
School Alumni Angels of New York

Other Books Available at Holloway.com

The Holloway Guide to Remote Work
Katie Womersley, Juan Pablo Buriticá et al.
A comprehensive guide to building, managing, and adapting to working with distributed teams.

The Holloway Guide to Equity Compensation
Joshua Levy, Joe Wallin et al.
Stock options, RSUs, job offers, and taxes—a detailed reference, explained from the ground up.

The Holloway Guide to Technical Recruiting and Hiring
Osman (Ozzie) Osman et al.
A practical, expert-reviewed guide to growing software engineering teams effectively, written by and for hiring managers, recruiters, interviewers, and candidates.

The Holloway Guide to Raising Venture Capital
Andy Sparks et al.
A current and comprehensive resource for entrepreneurs, with technical detail, practical knowledge, real-world scenarios, and pitfalls to avoid.

Land Your Dream Design Job
Dan Shilov
A guide for product designers, from portfolio to interview to job offer.

Founding Sales: The Early-Stage Go-To-Market Handbook
Pete Kazanjy
This tactical handbook distills early sales first principles, and teaches the skills required for going from being a founder to early salesperson, and eventually becoming an early sales leader.

Angel Investing

Angel Investing

START TO FINISH

Joe Wallin and Pete Baltaxe

A practical and detailed guide to angel investing that is essential for beginners and seasoned investors, as well as founders raising an angel round. Covers fundamentals, finding deals, financings, term sheets, example documents, and common pitfalls.

RACHEL JEPSEN, EDITOR

HOLLOWAY

Published in the United States by Holloway, San Francisco
Holloway.com

Cover design by Order (New York) and Andy Sparks
Interior design by Joshua Levy and Jennifer Durrant
Print engineering by Titus Wormer

Typefaces: Tiempos Text and National 2
by Kris Sowersby of Klim Type Foundry

Print version 1.0 · Digital version e1.0.2
doc a272cf · pipeline d040a0 · genbook fb7d96 · 2023-08-29

Want More Out of This Book?

Holloway publishes books online. As a reader of this special full-access print edition, you are granted personal access to the paid digital edition, which you can read and share on the web, and offers commentary, updates, and corrections. A Holloway account also gives access to search, definitions of key terms, bookmarks, highlights, and other features. Claim your account by visiting: **holloway.com/print20046**

If you wish to recommend the book to others, suggest they visit **holloway.com/ang** to learn more and purchase their own digital or print copy.

The authors welcome your feedback! Please consider adding comments or suggestions to the book online so others can benefit. Or say hello@holloway.com. Thank you for reading.

The Holloway team

LEGEND

Some elements in the text are marked for special significance:

◇ **IMPORTANT**	Important or often overlooked tip
⚠ **DANGER**	Serious warning or pitfall where risks or costs are significant
◈ **CAUTION**	Caution, limitation, or problem
⚘ **CONFUSION**	Common confusion or misunderstanding, such as confusing terminology
❯ **EXAMPLE**	An example or illustration
✿ **FOUNDER**	Considerations for founders

Web links appear as numbered footnotes in print.

References to other related sections are indicated by superscript section numbers, prefixed with §.

x

OVERVIEW

TABLE OF CONTENTS

INTRODUCTION

1 About Us

Joe is a Seattle-based attorney who has been working in the early-stage company space since the late 1990s. He has worked with hundreds of founders and investors on too many financing and M&A transactions to count. Okay, maybe he hasn't seen it all. But he has seen *a lot*. Joe represents startups, investors in startups, and founders and executives of growth companies. He is a member of the Angel Capital Association's public policy advisory council, where he is actively involved in trying to make the law better for investors and founders.

Pete has played many roles in the startup ecosystem, and has been an angel investor for 10 years. As a serial entrepreneur, he raised over $25M in seed financing and venture capital, and had two successful exits, an acquisition for 2Market and an IPO for RedEnvelope. For 25 years, Pete has advised startups on fundraising and product strategy, both individually and as part of accelerators like Techstars. He has the dubious distinction of losing most of his first $200K in angel investments, in part because he didn't have the knowledge and wisdom in this book. He strongly believes that one learns more from the failures than from the successes, and his goal is to give you the benefit of those hard lessons without the financial (and emotional) pain.

2 About This Book

After his first two years of angel investing, Pete had the equivalent of a bad hangover. $200K had disappeared into companies that had looked very promising but had failed. He had invested too fast, committed too much to a single investment, failed to do thorough enough due diligence in one case, and committed one or two other angel investing mistakes. It can be gut wrenching to watch a company you have invested in fail, and take with it a couple years of your kid's college tuition, or more.

Angel investing can be fun, financially rewarding, and socially impactful. But it can also be a costly place in terms of money, time, and missed opportunities. This book is intended to help you optimize your experience as an angel investor and avoid some pain by learning from those who have gone before you.

If you want to read a book about "How to make millions in angel investing without even trying," this is not it. In this book you are going to learn from our successes, failures, and collective experience working on angel deals. We are going to talk about how to be good and thorough at the often rewarding work involved, how to increase your chances of success in a world where 80%-90% of startups fail,[1] how to position yourself to stay involved with your companies, how to increase your payout when your investment succeeds (we'll show you how VCs do it), and what to do if things go sideways. In short, we want to help you improve how you go about angel investing so that you make the most of your money and your time.

If you invest in a successful startup, your economic return will be driven by the legal arrangements you have with the company. You don't want to miss out on a great economic return because you failed to ask for an important legal term when you made an investment. It is a terrible thing to find a great company, make an investment, but ultimately miss a great financial outcome because you overlooked something important. To that end, we discuss many of the legal and business issues investors face when evaluating deals, negotiating terms, and working with entrepreneurs in good and bad situations. This knowledge should allow you to engage in angel investing with more confidence in every aspect of the process. This book will reduce your need to seek expensive legal advice; and when you do need to talk to a lawyer, you will have the context that will make those conversations more efficient.

Whenever possible, we have included conventional wisdom about being a successful angel investor, based on the experience of successful investors and data about angel investing outcomes. When it comes to legal matters, we have tried to be as accurate and up to date as possible, but you should know that in some cases there are multiple definitions for

---

1. https://fortune.com/2014/09/25/why-startups-fail-according-to-their-founders/

some commonly used terms. We endeavor to always explain the ones we use. Additionally, angel investing isn't a science, it's situational—for every piece of specific advice, someone will have a counter example. Every company and investment opportunity is unique, which is part of what keeps it interesting. We don't pretend that every piece of guidance applies in every case, but have endeavored to give you the context that will help you make your own decisions.

This book will help **both new and seasoned investors** gain confidence. If you are interested in angel investing or already actively engaged as an angel investor, this book is for you. We do not assume any prior knowledge of how to find or evaluate companies, or investment techniques or terms. But we do go deep enough that even a seasoned investor can learn something new, and we have endeavored to organize the book as an easy reference for many of the common investment forms and terms.

♣ FOUNDER This book will also be helpful for **founders raising an angel round**. The content covered here will help you understand the point of view of the investors, where they can be found, and how to meet them. It will also help you understand the term sheet when you negotiate one with an angel or angel group. We explain what all the terms mean, how they work, and why they may exist in your term sheet and investment documents. (In this book, material with a founder perspective is marked with this icon.)

We also explain how investors (and entrepreneurs) should think about due diligence and what should be covered. This can be a handy reference as you prepare to make an investment or seek funding.

3 Special Thanks

We had the feedback of a lot of our friends in writing this book. To give thanks to just some of who helped us, and not in order of importance: Thank you Mary Baker Anderson, Bryan Brewer, William ("Bill") Carleton, Barnaby Dorfman, Jeff Greene, Mitchell Hymowitz, Mike Koss, Adam Lieb, Josh Maher, Brandon Nett, Dave Parker, Gary Ritner, Dan Rosen, and Nancy Thayer. If we have forgotten anyone, please forgive us.

Pete would also like to thank The Academy, and his lovely wife Carol and charming daughter Katelyn for putting up with his long hours of writing when he should have been mowing the lawn or waxing the skis or baking bread. And, of course, he would like to thank the book's editor, Rachel, who made the whole process fun.

All errors are entirely ours.

4 Disclaimer

Although this book contains a lot of legal information and is intended in part to be a guide to frequently encountered legal issues, it does not constitute legal advice, nor the establishment of an attorney–client relationship with any reader. Nor does this book constitute financial advice. You should always consult with your own legal and financial advisors before investing in a startup or early-stage company.

PART I: ANGEL INVESTING OVERVIEW

5 What Angels Do

Angels invest typically in very early-stage companies, providing capital for growth in exchange for equity—partial ownership—in the company. That equity can translate into enormous rewards, or nothing at all—angels tend to have an appetite for risk, and the means to take risks with confidence.

An angel investor might consider herself a patron of experiments, the first outsider tasked with judging a company's real potential for success.[2] That outside money can become, for those who choose to let it, a path to the inside, where an angel becomes an advisor and confidante, helping founders make good business decisions and supporting them when things get tough. Other angels will choose a less involved path, staying out of the company's way after making their initial investment.

Angel investing is different from other types of investing. Like venture capitalists, angels typically invest in companies they hope will grow rapidly and eventually reach a liquidity event. But as the earliest outside investors who do not invest through institutions like VC firms (though individuals may invest as part of an angel group), angels take on more risk. Their investments are also typically smaller than those that VCs make; while VCs can invest tens of millions of dollars (or a *lot* more), angel investments are typically $25K–$50K and top out at $100K, though they can go higher. To make an investment, an angel must be deemed an accredited investor (which we'll discuss in detail[§8.1]), meeting income and asset thresholds set by the Securities and Exchange Commission.

---

2. The term "angel" is taken from Broadway, where wealthy individuals would drop in to fund new productions to get them off the ground.

Angels usually *don't* invest in companies that are expected to stay private and generate an ongoing cash flow for their investors,[3] the way an LLC might be organized to start or grow a real estate business or chain of grocery stores.

Angel investing is also different from investing in public companies, where you can turn around the day after you invest and sell the securities you purchased to someone else on a public market. In angel investing, once you invest you are generally "stuck" holding your investment for some indefinite period of time, until the company in which you invested is sold or goes public—which could be years away or never happen. In most investment classes an investor can cut their losses when things go badly. Even in less liquid assets like real estate, an investor can sell a piece of property, even one in bad shape or in a bad market, for some residual value; in angel investing, you are generally investing in companies which, if they don't succeed, have very little in the way of assets to distribute to shareholders.

Angel investing might sound like gambling, but it is not entirely a game of chance. Angels have the chance to spot a company early that's going to change the world. With robust resources and best practices for conducting thorough due diligence on a company, and making smart decisions around financings and term sheets, you can increase your odds of a great outcome, for both your investment and the company's trajectory.

5.1 *The Rewards of Angel Investing*

While there are many risks to angel investing, the rewards, both financial and personal, are real. If you like spending time with entrepreneurs and learning about new technologies and methods, if you want a ringside seat at the ongoing disruption of industries, if you want to flex your knowledge and experience, or if you want the chance to make an impact, angel investing can be fun, educational, and exciting.

---

3. Though as we will see, this is not always the case. Some angels and institutional sources of capital like to invest for cash flow in steadily growing business with revenue loans.

5.1.1 FINANCIAL RETURN

Maybe you bought this book after reading that Peter Thiel made a billion dollars from Facebook out of a $500K investment.[4] You might even have friends who invested $25K in a business to see it return 18 times that amount. But beware—the majority of angel investments return nothing to investors.

As a benchmark for purely financial return, large portfolios of well-screened angel investments either aggregated by so-called "super angels" or across active angel investing groups can generate internal rates of return of 20% or more.

If you have a large investment portfolio, angel investing can provide diversification, as it represents another asset class. But it is high risk and requires patient capital. Your investment advisor may be able to provide you with suggestions on what proportion of your overall portfolio to allocate to private, early-stage deals.

◇ CAUTION Because angel investments are extremely risky and illiquid, the common wisdom is that you should not invest more than 10% of your assets in angel investments, and you should be able to withstand the loss of all of that money.

5.1.2 SHARING WHAT YOU KNOW

Many angel investors are successful entrepreneurs or business people who have benefited from the mentoring of others and now want to give back to the entrepreneur community. You might have knowledge and experience that you want to share with the next generation of doers. That might be general management wisdom, industry specific knowledge (domain expertise), or functional expertise in marketing, business development, or technology. Angel investing frequently involves mentoring or advising founders of companies, so you will have ample opportunity to share your knowledge.

5.1.3 MAKING AN IMPACT

◇ IMPORTANT Entrepreneurs want to change the world; angels can make that possible. Your investment could help bring a new medical device to market, help people stop smoking with a mobile app, increase food safety

---

4. https://www.reuters.com/article/us-facebook-stake/
peter-thiel-sells-most-of-remaining-facebook-stake-idUSKBN1DM2BQ

with organic blockchain barcodes, reduce food waste with AI-driven produce inventory management systems, or make the great American game of football safer with impact-reducing helmets.

Explicitly mission-driven investments aren't the only path to making a positive impact as an angel. You could help create new social media marketing tools for small businesses, support building a social network for grade school kids, bring an end to the paper business card, make trucking more efficient for truckers, or create augmented reality video game platforms. Whatever the industry, your investment may lead to the development of a company that employs thousands of workers at good wages.

Angel investing is a unique experience, and the field is constantly changing. There are a lot of smart, creative, highly motivated people involved, not just building new technologies and companies, but also building new financial legal innovations (such as SAFEs and revenue loans). There is also increasing activity around combining mission-driven startups with angel investing and mentoring, where as an angel investor you can become a force multiplier for good. Fledge[5] is an example of a conscious company accelerator that mentors both angels and startups focused on social good.

5.1.4 GETTING INVOLVED

Being an angel investor is a meaningful way to get involved in your community and to meet other successful business people. Angels love talking about startups and technology and industry trends. As you participate in the angel investing community you will have the opportunity to get to know the local startup incubators, accelerators, and venture capitalists, and to generally participate in your area's startup ecosystem. If you have time on your hands, helping to grow your local startup ecosystem can be a very rewarding way to spend your time.

5.1.5 CONTINUED LEARNING

As an angel investor, you will hear a lot of company pitches, and review many slide decks. Each company presents a unique learning opportunity, and you will get insight into industries you didn't even know existed.

If you focus your investing in a specific domain or industry, you can gain insight into the trends and technologies that are going to be impact-

---

5. https://www.fledge.co/

ing that industry. How are new technologies getting applied, how might related industries get disrupted? When you hear how someone is thinking differently about customer acquisition or service levels or product delivery in a related industry, there is often something you can learn that might be applicable to a business you're involved in.

By talking with entrepreneurs and following startups you will learn about the general processes, tools, and techniques enabling companies to quickly build and test products, inexpensively acquire customers, and the metrics they watch to manage their businesses. If you do not have it already, you will acquire a respect for how difficult it is for someone to build a company from nothing.

Angel investing will test your business acumen, ability to judge character, negotiation skills, research skills, intuition, and discipline. Many of these skills are put to the test in the due diligence phase.^{§11} If you make some investments, you will have the opportunity to learn from your wins and your losses.

5.1.6 THE THRILL

Angel investing is exciting. Have you invested in the next Facebook? Will your friends envy your foresight? Will you kick yourself for passing on a deal that would have made you spectacularly wealthy, or on an idea that could have improved people's lives?

Part of the fun of angel investing is following the progress of the companies in your portfolio. It is a ticket to the emotional rollercoaster of the entrepreneur—the excitement of the big customer deal, the disappointment of the partnership that got away, the thrill of the payout from an acquisition, or the sting of one of your companies shutting down and winding up.

5.2 *The Perils of Angel Investing*

Angel investing can be challenging for a number of reasons. It can be time-consuming and may require you to quickly come up to speed on industries or technologies you know little about. It can involve negotiating investment terms and dealing with unfamiliar legal issues. Additionally, once you invest you may have very little insight into what is happening to your investment and very little (if any) control over what the company does.

You will also be impacted by the rights and valuations the company negotiates with any follow-on investors, which can have a dramatic impact
on your return. The goal of this book in part is to help you understand
the legal issues, deal terms, rights, and limited controls that will have an
impact on your outcomes. Ultimately an angel investment is a gamble,
and your goal is to try to increase your odds of winning before you place
your bet.

5.2.1 TIME COMMITMENT

Angel investing can be time-consuming if you are actively involved in
selecting your investments. A typical active angel investor may see 50–100
investment opportunities in a year. They attend angel group meetings,
meet with individual entrepreneurs who reach out to them, and see deals
from within their network of other angels. They may be interested enough
to look into ten of those deals and engage in serious due diligence on a
handful or more. On the deals they decide to move forward with, they
will spend time negotiating terms and reviewing legal documents. All that
work might result in three or four investments in a year.

Your degree of involvement and time commitment is up to you, especially if you are part of an angel group (formal or informal) where members split up a lot of the work. So while it is possible to take a "free rider"
approach and jump in on deals someone else recommends and has negotiated, your colleagues may eventually ask you to share some of the workload.

As an angel investor you will get a lot of requests from entrepreneurs
who are beginning their fundraising journey. And once you have some
investments, you might make time to meet occasionally with the entrepreneurs you're backing and respond to requests for advice or introductions
to potential customers or follow-on investors. If meeting with entrepreneurs (think long hours in coffee shops) and doing due diligence sounds
fun and exciting, then you will enjoy the time you commit to angel investing. If you are really committed, you can aspire to be a lead investor,$^{§7.4}$
which can be quite time consuming and might enable you to sit on the
board of the startup^{§26} (more time commitment), which has its own set of
perils and rewards.

◇ IMPORTANT Every angel investor's situation is different. Some are retired
or semi-retired, and angel investing is a great hobby and source of social

engagement for them. Other angels are working full-time and have families and other commitments, but can fit in angel group or diligence meetings when they come up. Necessarily, they will be less involved. But the nature of the startup world—where founders are often working days, nights, and weekends on their companies—means you'll likely be able to fit in founder meetings and other angel investing responsibilities outside of your normal work hours.

5.2.2 LACK OF LIQUIDITY

◇ CAUTION In general, you should think of your angel investments as almost always completely *illiquid*, meaning you should not expect to be able to sell your convertible note or your restricted shares to get your money out unless there is some sort of liquidity event. Sometimes a secondary market[6] for a company's stock develops before an IPO, but this is rare. By definition, angel investors are putting in their money very early in a company's life, and it will typically take five to eight years or more for the company to see a liquidity event;[7,8] even then, the company may be acquired by another private company whose shares could also not be sold for cash in a public market. It is possible to have an investment return a profit within a year or two through an acquisition by a public company, but that case is an exception.

5.2.3 FUTURE ROUNDS

The terms of the follow-on rounds of investment have a big impact on your investment outcome and can determine to a large extent whether you make a lot of money or none on your angel investment. We will cover the deal terms that you can use to influence how follow-on rounds may affect your investment.

5.2.4 FINANCIAL RISK

The SEC rules exist to protect consumers by trying to ensure that the investor is financially savvy enough to broadly understand the implications of investing in private equity, and that they can afford to lose the investment.

---

6. https://www.holloway.com/g/equity-compensation/sections/can-you-sell-private-stock

7. https://venturebeat.com/entrepreneur/
   vc-investing-still-strong-even-as-median-time-to-exit-reaches-8-2-years/

8. https://about.crunchbase.com/blog/startup-exit/

◇ **IMPORTANT** To the latter point, you must be able to afford to lose your entire investment! To be a successful angel investor, you should build a portfolio of investments over time and be able to afford to see those investments fail—hoping that the success of one or more investments outweighs the losses on the rest. Ideally, you are placing multiple educated bets and hoping you hit the jackpot.

⚠ **DANGER** Angel investing can be a great portfolio diversification strategy (in addition to more liquid assets like public stocks and bonds and real estate), but it should not be your retirement strategy.

This book is designed to make sure you deeply understand the terms and implications of your investment in addition to helping you be selective about those investments. But people without a high appetite for risk will find that angel investing isn't for them. The thrill of the risk should be a draw to you.

5.3 *Joining an Angel Group*

There are a number of reasons it is beneficial to join an angel investing group.

An **angel investing group (or angel group)** is a syndicate of angel investors that collaborate on deals. These groups can be large and formal (like Seattle's Alliance of Angels, which has over 140 members as of this writing), or small and informal (especially when not based in a major metropolitan area). They can help green investors learn the ropes of angel investing, improve access to deals, and share the work and potential costs of due diligence and negotiations.

There are over 400 angel groups spread across the U.S. and Canada according to the Angel Capital Association, which maintains a directory[9] on its website. You might also be interested in the Angel Capital Association's FAQs About Angel Groups.[10]

◇ **IMPORTANT** If you want to educate yourself before joining a group, or if you can't find a group that aligns with your interests or investing goals, then this book will go a long way towards getting you up to speed on the

---

9. https://www.angelcapitalassociation.org/directory/
10. https://www.angelcapitalassociation.org/faqs/

process, terms, and other topics that will give you the confidence to move forward with your angel investing!

You may also decide to invest as part of an AngelList syndicate.[11] Make sure to do your due diligence on the syndicators.

5.3.1 ACCESS TO DEALS

It is easy for entrepreneurs to discover the local angel groups, so being part of one means you will likely get exposure to a regular flow of deals. Angel groups tend to be known in their community and entrepreneurs will seek them out because it is an efficient way to get in front of a large number of angels. As a member, it will be easier to see a lot of deals if you attend the angel group's regular meetings where some number of entrepreneurs will pitch their companies to the assembled group of angels. Additionally, most groups have a screening process, so the main membership group will only invest time in looking at deals that have passed the initial filtering process. If you're not a member of an angel group, there are still lots of ways to see deals, which we cover in Finding Opportunities.§9

5.3.2 SHARING DUE DILIGENCE

20–40 hours of due diligence per company is recommended;[12] it's nice to be able to share that workload among a group of interested angels. Within a larger angel group there is almost always someone who is an expert in the specific field that a startup is engaged in, whether that is a medical device or a social media marketing tool. Having that domain expertise in the diligence team brings insight into customer pain points and behaviors, competition and the ecosystem generally, distribution and pricing, and a host of other topics that would otherwise take significant effort to understand.

5.3.3 DEAL NEGOTIATION

There will almost always be experienced angel investors in a group, and you can benefit from their knowledge and wisdom if you let them lead the terms negotiation for your first investment or two. They will have a sense of what is customary in the terms and which terms are worth fighting for. Those angels can act as mentors when you are ready to lead a deal and

---

11. https://help.venture.angel.co/hc/en-us/sections/360009504072-Syndicates
12. https://willamette.edu/~wiltbank/seattle_angel_conference_may_2012.html

negotiate terms yourself. This book will bring you up to speed on the deal terms for the most common types of investments, but it is still useful to have guidance on the ground when going through the process.

5.3.4 EDUCATION

An angel group is a great opportunity to network with other successful business people who have a passion for angel investing, and you can learn from their experience. You will see a lot of deals, which will provide a valuable perspective on the range of investment opportunities. You will begin to learn what a great opportunity looks like versus a more risky one, what a complete team should look like, how much traction is an indication of product/market fit, and so on. You can participate in due diligence to learn that process even if you do not plan to invest in the company. Some groups check in on the companies that pitched a year or two ago and present updates to the group. This provides great insight as to why some companies fail[§27.1] to reach their goals and the types of pivots[§27.4] that may happen. This learning enables you to ask the right questions the next time you are doing due diligence on a similar company.

6 Startup Fundraising and the Road to Liquidity

Startup CEOs spend a surprising amount of time trying to raise money. Over the course of five to ten years they will likely raise many rounds of financing from many different sources, including angel investors. Each round of financing impacts the value and rights associated with the previous rounds of investors, and as we will discuss later on, many of the terms negotiated in an angel round will deal with the impacts and opportunities regarding these future rounds of financing. A company may not go through all of the stages laid out below, and it is also possible that they will do multiple rounds of investment in any one stage. Your goal as an angel investor is to get to an exit—a liquidity event—in order to realize a return on your investment.

6.1 *Stages of Startup Funding*

6.1.1 BOOTSTRAPPING

Bootstrapping refers to the entrepreneurs self-funding, typically through a combination of savings and debt. In the bootstrapping phase, founders are doing their initial research, testing their hypotheses about product demand and features, and perhaps creating a minimum viable product (MVP) to get early customer feedback. The founders may be working full or part-time elsewhere and are drawing no salary for their work on the startup. Hopefully they have engaged a startup attorney and have executed the standard set of legal formation documents, invention assignment agreements, and so on.

Minimum viable product (or MVP) refers to the product that the company has built which it believes it can sell and monetize. The product is far enough along to gauge whether customers will pay for it.

6.1.2 FRIENDS AND FAMILY

Sometimes companies accept funding from friends and family. There are many stories of founders receiving very early investments from family or friends as they pursue their startups. Jeff Bezos received an investment from his parents to start Amazon (they are now fabulously wealthy). "Friends and family" rounds can be a few tens of thousands of dollars or even a few hundreds of thousands of dollars, and might be used to pay for a designer on contract, a part-time engineer, or some costs related to prototyping.

◇ CAUTION You should be aware that friends and family rounds are frequently not done in compliance with the law. While this very early funding may have helped a company come into being, it frequently represents what could be called "legal/regulatory debt." We cover this in more detail in Fundraising and Securities Law.§8

6.1.3 INCUBATORS AND ACCELERATORS

The term **incubator** generally refers to a company that generates its own startup ideas in-house. Using a resident team that is deeply versed in startup techniques, they will typically research the market, prototype the product or service, and test customer demand. If they see an idea getting traction, they look for a full-time CEO and help to build the core team of early employees. That team is then sent out to raise money as an independent entity. Incubators, which often refer to themselves as "labs," retain a significant ownership stake in the startups they help create.

IdeaLab,[13] founded by Bill Gross, was one of the famous early incubators and spun out such companies as CitySearch, Cooking.com, Shopping.com, Twilio, and eToys. Looking at their historical portfolio companies[14] is like a walk down internet memory lane.

Venture capital firms are increasingly founding early-stage incubators in the hopes that they will be able to reduce the risk of investment by vetting business ideas early and advising founders early on. Firms with their own incubators can buy equity in these companies at the lowest possible price, at the very beginning. Madrona Venture Labs,[15] associated with the venture capital firm Madrona Ventures, is one example based in Seattle. Many incubators will also accept entrepreneurs who have their own ideas but lack a team or other resources to test and validate those ideas efficiently.

Accelerators are institutions that take in cohorts of a dozen or so very early-stage startups, which go through a structured three or four month intensive program of education and mentoring. At the end of this period, there is typically a "demo day," where all the startups pitch to potential angel and institutional investors. These demo days may be how you find some of your deals.

The better-known accelerators include: TechStars,[16] Y Combinator,[17] and 500 Startups.[18] In addition to mentoring and a structured program, accelerators often provide a certain amount of cash to the company, taking a percentage of equity in return. Many of these accelerators are active in introducing their cohort companies to angel investors. They often have standard term sheets that they use as starting points for the financing rounds of their startups, like Y Combinator's entrepreneur-friendly SAFE documents.

---

13. https://www.idealab.com/
14. https://en.wikipedia.org/wiki/Idealab
15. https://www.madronavl.com/
16. https://www.techstars.com/
17. https://www.ycombinator.com/
18. https://500.co/

6.1.4 ANGEL OR "SEED" ROUND

Whether or not a startup company comes out of an incubator or accelerator, the **angel round or seed round**, as it is usually called, is typically the first tranche of outside funding—that is, money from people the founders don't know. There is a tremendous range in the amount of money raised at this stage. Investments can take the form of debt (typically convertible notes) or a priced round in which the founders are selling shares of stock in the company. Seed rounds can vary from $100K to several million dollars.

If the round is a priced equity round, then it is often called the series seed round. A company typically raises an angel round when they have full-time employees and have built a product; they may also have early customer traction. They need money to improve the product, hire key people in engineering or sales, and engage in marketing. Ideally they are raising enough money that they can last at least a year before they need to raise again.

6.1.5 VENTURE CAPITAL ROUNDS

Venture capitalists (or VCs) generally invest $1M or more (sometimes, *a lot* more) in a round of financing for a startup. They typically invest through a VC firm. Most VCs are looking to make $3M–$10M initial investments, with that number rising in follow-on rounds. They typically look for companies that have real traction with paying customers, though occasionally they will back successful serial entrepreneurs who have only an idea. They often like to invest when the company has achieved product/market fit, thereby dramatically reducing the risk of early failure. They invest when the company needs cash to accelerate its sales and marketing and scale up its engineering team to flesh out the early product. A company may raise many rounds of venture capital, and many VCs keep money aside to invest again in subsequent rounds for the winners in their portfolio (the "follow-on" investment).

Currently, the first VC round is commonly called the Series A round (although there are seed stage VCs as well). Each subsequent round adds another letter: Series B, Series C, and so on. If things are going well, each of those subsequent rounds is a bigger investment at a higher valuation.

Venture capitalists raise their funds from outside limited partners, or LPs.[19] VCs have a duty to those partners to do rigorous due diligence. VCs make their living (and reputation) from the returns on their investments, so tend to seek advantageous terms when they invest, and often sit on the boards of directors of their portfolio companies in order to monitor progress and exercise more control where they can; VCs can be quite aggressive in protecting their interests when things go sideways.

VC funding is typically the first money founders will raise from institutional investors.

Institutional investor refers to an entity that is in the business of investing either its own money (like a family office) or other people's money. They are usually sophisticated in their legal knowledge and are savvy negotiators of early-stage deals, because they are in the business of making investments. In some cases they might be quite aggressive in the terms they seek from entrepreneurs.

6.2 *Liquidity Events: How Angels Make Money*

In a **liquidity event (or exit)**, the company in which you invested is sold or the company goes public, allowing investors to cash out of their investment.

6.2.1 ACQUISITION

Acquisition is a kind of liquidity event that occurs when a company buys at least a controlling interest in another company, for cash or stock of the acquiring company or a combination of the two. Being acquired by another company is the most common outcome for startups, excluding total failure. In 2018, 90% of the exits were acquisitions, while 10% were IPOs.[20]

Often startups—which are all private companies—are acquired by public companies, in which case the startup's investors will get either cash or shares in the public company. But the investor may not be able to cash out on those shares right away—they may be subject to a lockup agreement.

19. https://www.holloway.com/g/venture-capital/sections/vc-firms-and-funds

20. https://nvca.org/wp-content/uploads/2019/08/NVCA-2019-Yearbook.pdf

A **lockup agreement** is an agreement with the issuer of the securities (the company) that you will not sell your shares for some period of time, sometimes for as long as a year.

If the shares in the public company are not subject to a lockup agreement, then the shares will be tradeable on the public markets.[21] If the acquiring company is another private company, and they use their shares rather than cash to buy the stock of your portfolio company, then after the transaction you will own different shares that you still cannot sell. You will have to wait for the acquiring company to be sold or go public.

6.2.2 INITIAL PUBLIC OFFERING

Acquisition is not the goal of every startup—many hope to eventually make it to an IPO.

An **initial public offering (IPO)** is the first sale of a company's stock to the public where the sale is registered with the Securities and Exchange Commission, specifies an initial trading price for the stock, and is generally financed by one or more investment banks.[23] This type of liquidity event is colloquially referred to as "going public."[24]

Early investors may have a lockup period of three to six months post-IPO, after which they will be able to sell their shares and reap the rewards of their early-stage angel investment.

◇ IMPORTANT While IPOs typically represent the largest multiple in terms of return on investment for an angel investor, it is almost always a long wait to get there—11 years on average[26] in 2020. Companies typically need to be of significant scale (hundreds of millions of dollars of annual revenue) with robust, profitable businesses to be able to bear the burden of the significant regulatory, legal, and accounting expenses of being a public company, and to be able to engage the investment bankers who will underwrite the offering and guide the company through the rigorous IPO process.

---

21. Subject to the rules for doing so (see SEC Rule 144[22]).

22. https://www.investopedia.com/terms/r/rule144.asp

23. https://www.sec.gov/files/ipo-investorbulletin.pdf

24. This definition has been adapted from the *Holloway Guide to Raising Venture Capital*.[25]

25. https://www.holloway.com/g/venture-capital/sections/exits-and-returns

26. https://www.nytimes.com/interactive/2019/05/09/business/dealbook/tech-ipos-uber.html

6.2.3 SECONDARY MARKETS

There has been some movement in recent years toward trying to make shares in private companies more easily saleable even in the absence of a public market transition. For example, in 2015 Congress enacted Section 4(a)(7) of the Securities Act of 1933, enabling secondary transactions in non-generally solicited exchanges with an accredited investor buyer.[27] However, secondary market transactions[28] in private company shares are still rare, and you should not expect that this will be a ready source of liquidity for you.

7 The Process of an Angel Investment

For entrepreneurs, raising capital from angels is frequently a grueling process that takes months of pitches, meetings, document preparation, and negotiation—all while trying to build a company.

In a best-case scenario, an entrepreneur may be able to close a round in a month or two. In a more challenging scenario, they might be pitching to and negotiating with multiple angel groups and super angels and smaller VCs for a year to get the round closed. There are no hard rules about this process, and an entrepreneur may be finalizing terms with one angel or group while still preparing to pitch to others.

7.1 *The Back of the Napkin*

As an angel investor, you will see some really early companies and have a chance to be the first money in. But there is a huge range in the how far along these companies will be as they raise their first outside investment so before we talk about the angel's investment process, it is worth a brief discussion about what expectations you should have.

Years ago, when it was expensive to build websites and set up servers in data centers to host a website and license layers of software, founders who didn't have deep pockets themselves (or rich uncles) had to raise money on little more than an idea and a business plan. If you were creating a

---

27. https://techcrunch.com/2016/03/10/
    new-law-changes-the-liquidity-game-for-tech-company-founders-workers-and-investors/
28. https://www.holloway.com/g/equity-compensation/sections/can-you-sell-private-stock

physical product, you needed significant cash for molds and prototyping. That was then.

The environment has improved dramatically in this regard. Startups don't have to buy servers and rack space in data centers now, they rent servers by the hour from Amazon Web Services or Microsoft's Azure. There are many existing software services that can be leveraged to create a software prototype, including drag-and-drop website builders and mobile app prototypers. There are dozens if not hundreds of low-cost offshore app development companies that can build version-1 products. In the physical product space, one can buy desktop laser cutters and 3D printers. There are simple computers like Arduino and Raspberry Pi that are designed to be embedded in hardware as controllers. It's a golden age for innovation![29]

All that said, how far an entrepreneurial team can get before needing to raise money depends on *what they are doing*. The more fundamental a company's innovation is, the more money it may take to get to a working prototype or functional product. Artificial intelligence is a hot investment area, for example, but it can take a lot of processing power to develop and test and train new algorithms. The last AI startup that Pete worked at was spending sometimes over $100K a month on cloud processing costs to support its customers and development! Quantum computing is another example of an extremely expensive industry. Rivian, the electric vehicle startup that built a completely new and innovative electric vehicle platform, raised $1.3B[31] without a product to take to market.

♟ FOUNDER However far along a company's product is, the team should be following Lean Startup principles. Lean Startup had its origins in Steve Blank and Bob Dorf's book, *The Startup Owner's Manual*,[32] and was then popularized in Eric Ries' *The Lean Startup*.[33] (Here is a quick primer.[34]) The basic idea is that startups are a series of experiments and need to be managed very differently than more mature businesses; and most importantly, that before you build anything, you should be validating every iteration of the idea with potential customers—even if it is drawing on the

---

29. If you want to get a sense of what is possible, check out this amazing product.[30]

30. https://www.wired.com/story/justine-haupt-rotary-phone/

31. https://www.nytimes.com/2019/12/23/business/rivian-truck-investment.html

32. https://www.amazon.com/Startup-Owners-Manual-Step-Step/dp/0984999302

33. https://www.amazon.com/Lean-Startup-Entrepreneurs-Continuous-Innovation/dp/0307887898

34. https://2000books.com/the-lean-startup-pdf/

back of a napkin. This process is called customer discovery or customer development. So at a minimum, even if the entrepreneurial team has not written a line of code or printed their first plastic widget, they should have done dozens, ideally hundreds, of potential customer interviews. (There is even a book called *Lean Customer Development*[35] you can check out.)

So in short, given the time, entrepreneurs should be able to make quite a bit of progress in terms of understanding and gathering data around whether customers really want this product or service, and building a prototype or MVP before they need to raise money. Again, exclusions apply, but this context will be helpful if you run into one of those exclusions.

Not all startups you meet will be at this MVP stage. Entrepreneurs who are just getting started on their idea may approach you for advice on when they should start raising money. Wise entrepreneurs may start meeting casually with angels long before they need to raise money in order to build those relationships for when the time comes. Investing in very early-stage companies (that have no paying customers) is a bit like speed dating. You are betting on the entrepreneur him or herself almost exclusively, with very little else to go on. You have to be passionate about the idea, ideally know a lot about the industry, and really click with the entrepreneur.

At the other end of the spectrum, you may be approached by companies that have been around for years, are on their third or fourth generation product, have dozens or hundreds of customers or hundreds of thousands of consumer users. You will see companies raising their first external round who have self-funded for years because the founders had prior exits or other resources that allowed them to pursue their idea. You will also see entrepreneurs who need the validation and external money to be able to quit their day jobs and engage full-time in their startups.

Finally, as an angel investor, you will see deals where the company has a sizable team and has raised several rounds of investment prior to pitching to you. These opportunities often have higher pre-money valuations and can require more due diligence, but they can be great investments too if they have executed on the prior money and decreased a lot of the risks.

As an investor, you will find your comfort zone, whether that is getting in very early when there are the biggest risks and biggest rewards, or waiting until there is more evidence of potential success.

---

35. https://www.amazon.com/Lean-Customer-Development-Hardcover-version/dp/1449356354

7.2 *The Investment Process Flow*

Below, we will walk through what an idealized process looks like when an angel group is investing in a preferred stock funding round.[16] (We discuss the types of financings and the relevant terms in Part III, but you don't need to know all those details now.)

A preferred stock round is usually closed in one or more coordinated "closings" when, after months of pitching, due diligence, and negotiation, the formal documents[14.2] for all investors are signed and the funds delivered to the company at the same time. At that point the entrepreneur and team pop a bottle of champagne and collapse in exhaustion.

In contrast, convertible note rounds are often much simpler than priced rounds, and the process is typically much faster. The time between first meeting with an angel and the writing of the check can be as little as a couple of weeks (or even less). If the company is raising a large round through convertible notes, say $500K, and is pitching to angel groups, then the process will look much more like the process outlined here:

- **The pitch.** A presentation by the CEO to an individual or group of angels using a slide deck to cover the key points of the business and often the top-level fundraising terms. The terms typically include the amount of money the company is hoping to raise and the pre-money valuation if it is a priced equity offering, or the valuation cap if it is a convertible note offering. In most settings, the pitch is followed by a question and answer session, where investors seek clarification on any aspects of the business or team. This whole process may take 20 minutes if there are multiple entrepreneurs pitching to a gathering of angels, or it could take an hour over coffee if you are meeting with an entrepreneur one-on-one.
- **The follow-up meeting.** If there is investor interest from the pitch, the investor(s) will have a much longer meeting with the startup where the founder(s) provides more detail on many aspects of the business and perhaps demonstrates the product in detail. The investors have a chance to meet the other members of the team and ask detailed questions[10] about the company's technology, go-to-market strategy, customer traction, et cetera.
- **Selecting a lead.** If after the follow-up meeting(s) there are interested investors, and they agree that the high-level deal terms offered by the

company are acceptable (or likely to be negotiable), they will coordinate to select a lead investor among themselves and then start to plan the due diligence and more detailed negotiations of the term sheet. If the investors feel that the investment terms offered by the company are not acceptable, there is often an effort to negotiate the valuation and other key terms to an agreeable place before investors are willing to engage in time-consuming due diligence.

- **Commencing due diligence.** The investors within the group will divide up the due diligence tasks. Typically over some number of weeks, the investors complete their diligence tasks and share their findings with the group.

- **Negotiation of the term sheet.** If the early due diligence is looking favorable and enough investors signal their continued interest in investing, the lead investor will negotiate the primary terms of the investment. The terms of the deal depend on the type of financing, and are covered in Part III.

- **Agreement on the term sheet.** If the investors and the entrepreneur cannot agree on the principal investment terms to be captured in the term sheet, the deal could fall through. The purpose of the term sheet is to ensure that all parties are in agreement on the principal terms before the costly work of preparing the definitive documents gets underway. A signed term sheet, usually contingent on a final round of due diligence, is a major milestone for all parties.

- **Final due diligence.** A company may not want to let you talk to their big customers or take up a lot of their engineers' time with a technical deep dive or review their employee contracts until they are pretty confident that a deal is going to get done on reasonable terms. That is why some diligence items may have to wait until after a term sheet is agreed upon to conduct an in-depth technical review, customer contract or customer number reviews, and review of some important legal items.§12

  - At any point in the due diligence process, red flags may emerge which cause some or all of the investors to drop out. More commonly, if investors discover issues that give them concern, they may try to negotiate for more favorable terms (such as a reduced pre-money valuation) that more accurately reflect the state of the company's progress or its risk factors.

For example, a B2B company may represent that it has six customers. Reviewing the contracts or talking to those customers may reveal that only two are paying, three are in free trials evaluating the product, and one is in negotiation but has not signed the purchase order. Investors may decide that the situation represents significantly less customer traction than they were led to believe and warrants a lower pre-money valuation.

- In many cases, especially when a fund or other "institution" is among the investors, the lead investor will coordinate the results of the due diligence efforts into a final report summarizing the findings of the diligence team.

- **Investor commitments.** Once due diligence is complete and the term sheet is negotiated, the lead investor will typically ask for firm commitments from the investors, including how much they will invest and contact details of the angel or the legal entity through which they are making the investment. This information will be included in the final documents along with the number of shares being issued and other key items.

- **Preparation and negotiation of draft definitive documents.** The drafting of the definitive documents can start while due diligence is still ongoing. This is where the lawyers on both sides earn their money. The definitive documents for each deal type are covered in Part III.§14

- **Agreement on the definitive documents.** If you have confidence in your lead investor and the law firm representing the investors, you may not need to invest the time in reading all of the definitive documents, though we recommend that you do, as it is often educational and generally prudent to understand the terms of your investment.

- **Closing.** On the closing date, you should be prepared to sign and return documents (usually by email) and deliver checks or wire funds to the bank account specified by the company. You will typically know the closing date a few days in advance, though sometimes it can be a moving target as issues come up during the final document negotiation and preparation.

7.3 *When Are You Committed?*

Legally you are not committed to the investment until you sign the definitive documents and send in your check. Typically both the entrepreneur
and the lead investor will be checking with investors throughout the diligence and negotiation process to gauge the level of interest and commitment of each investor. An entrepreneur will want to know whether he or
she is negotiating over $100K or $500K of collective angel investment, so
they will likely also be checking with investors. It is normal for investors
who expressed initial interest to drop out because they discovered issues
in due diligence that make them less enthusiastic, or because they do not
like where the terms negotiation ended up, or because of other time or
financial commitments that arise for them during the weeks or months
that the process takes.

Angels are free to increase or decrease their intended level of investment as they go through the diligence process and term sheet negotiation.

◇ IMPORTANT No one should complain if you decide anywhere in the
process that you will not invest or will invest less than you had initially
indicated, until you are asked for your firm commitment from either the
entrepreneur or the lead investor. Firm commitments are used to generate
the definitive documents, so pulling out after those are generated likely
requires more work and legal costs for the parties involved and would
be viewed as very bad form. If you are making a verbal commitment or
"handshake deal," we suggest following Y Combinator's handshake deal
protocol.[36]

7.4 *The Lead Investor*

Almost always in priced equity rounds, and often in convertible note
rounds, there is a lead investor.

The **lead investor** is typically an experienced angel investor (or institutional investor) who negotiates the detailed terms of the deal with the
entrepreneur, including the valuation. They also often have the thankless
task of coordinating the due diligence efforts, working with the lawyer(s)
representing the investors (including hiring and paying them, to be reimbursed later by the company), and reviewing the final documents. They

---

36. https://www.ycombinator.com/handshake/

may also be coordinating with other angel groups or investors on the closing date.

◇ **CAUTION** This is time-consuming work, and it can feel like herding cats at times—wealthy, busy, sophisticated cats. Investment rounds can bog down if no one is willing to step up and be the lead. We would not recommend that you take on this role until you have invested in a couple of deals and have some experience with the process.

7.5 *Being a Good Investor*

If everyone is motivated, the deal is priced attractively, and there are few if any red flags, getting through this process can take as little as four to six weeks. Unfortunately, this process can often drag on for several months or more, in which case it becomes a big time and energy drain for the entrepreneur who is trying to build a company.

◇ **IMPORTANT** It behooves angels to move as quickly as is prudent to get the deal done if they want to maintain the momentum of the company they are investing in. As an angel, be respectful of the lead investor's time, and be responsive to their inquiries and requests, as they have taken on the extra work and responsibility for no additional gain.

Paul Graham, in his essay "How To Be an Angel Investor,"[37] writes that being a "good" investor is defined by the following traits:

- Decide quickly whether you want to dig in on a deal.
- After you have done your diligence, be decisive about whether you are going to invest. Stringing entrepreneurs along while you are waiting for their company to make progress is bad for them and will not lead to your getting deals referred to you.
- Don't get too aggressive on deal terms, as there is plenty of room for a win-win if the company is successful.
- Be helpful where you can, whether or not you invest.

---

37. http://www.paulgraham.com/angelinvesting.html

7.6 *What to Watch Out For*

7.6.1 NON-DISCLOSURE AGREEMENTS

Sometimes a company will ask you early on to sign a nondisclosure agreement.

A **nondisclosure agreement (or confidentiality agreement or NDA)** is an agreement in which you agree to keep a company's confidential information confidential. In the broader business world, companies consider almost all their information confidential unless it is publicly available on their website, for example, or has been made public through press releases or financial filings. The startup world is a more specialized context, in which the investors will need to know a lot about a company before they consider investing, and will likely be pitching to groups of potential investors and sharing key details of the business in the process.

⚘ FOUNDER It would be atypical to sign a confidentiality agreement as part of the early conversations with an entrepreneur. Unless you are truly accessing and reviewing company confidential information, such as full customer lists, source code for a patentable software algorithm, chemical formulas, or other intellectual property that represents the core innovation of the company. That typically wouldn't happen until you were deep in due diligence. Business ideas, early revenue numbers, and other elements that you would expect to find in a company's pitch are not normally what an investor would sign an NDA to gain access to. Unsophisticated founders may ascribe a lot of value to their idea. Experienced investors know that there are very few unique ideas and that the largest determinant of success is whether the team can execute the idea quickly and effectively.

⚠ DANGER You should be wary when asked to sign an NDA, especially if the request is made early. If you sign one, and the company then shares its "business idea" with you, and you decline the investment—but then decide to invest in another company with a similar idea—the first company may threaten suit, claiming you violated the NDA and "stole" their idea. As absurd as this may sound, people have been sued in situations like this.

If you are asked by a company to sign an NDA early on in your discussion, you should politely decline. In general, tell the company that it is not typical for a prospective investor to sign an NDA when discussions are still at a very high level. If there is pushback but you are still interested, you can refer the company to one of the many resources on this topic, such as those by Paul Graham, who wrote:

> *"If you go to VC firms with a brilliant idea that you'll tell them about if they sign a nondisclosure agreement, most will tell you to get lost. That shows how much a mere idea is worth. The market price is less than the inconvenience of signing an NDA."*
> — Paul Graham, "How To Start a Startup" [38]

If you proceed into more detailed due diligence, *then* it might be appropriate and reasonable for you to sign an NDA. For example, if a company wants to begin sharing detailed intellectual property information and wants to protect its intellectual property rights and ability to patent its inventions, then an NDA may be called for. Down the road, if you are going to receive information rights from the company and receive its financial statements, or board observer information, it is typical to sign a confidentiality agreement with respect to that information.

⚠ DANGER If you are going to sign an NDA, ensure that it doesn't include any type of covenant that will prohibit you from investing in any other deal that you find. Make sure it doesn't include any sort of non-compete or non-solicit clause, and that it has the standard exclusions (see section 3 of the example NDA$^{\S30.5}$ included in the appendix).

7.6.2 **INDUCEMENTS TO INVEST EARLY**

Sometimes companies will offer an incentive to invest before a certain date. For example, you might see incentives like these:

- An investor who invests before a certain date may get warrant coverage, *or*
- An investor who invests before a certain date may get a better price per share (this could be done, for example, by selling the shares at a discount to the price per share for investors who invest before a certain date).

◇ CAUTION These promises are not necessarily problematic from a legal point of view, but we would caution not to permit these inducements to

---

38. http://www.paulgraham.com/start.html

cause you to jump into an investment in haste. It's not worth getting a good price on a bad deal.

8 Fundraising and Securities Law

There are a lot of rules and regulations governing how companies can solicit and raise capital from investors. These rules exist at both the federal and state levels. At the federal level, the Securities and Exchange Commission is the primary regulatory body. Each state also has its own securities division in charge of regulating the issuances of securities in its jurisdiction.

The term **security** is defined very broadly under U.S. securities law.[39] In general, a security is an investment in a common enterprise purchased with the expectation of profit, the value of which depends on the efforts of others.[40]

⚠ **DANGER** If a company is not following SEC rules around securities, it can lead to serious problems, such as investor rescission demands or government investigations,[41]—and the money to respond to such problems can come out of your investment. While these scenarios are not common, it is worth understanding the law so that you can avoid investing in companies that are flaunting it.

---

39. The Securities Act of 1933, as amended, states that a security is "any note, stock, treasury stock, security future, security-based swap, bond, debenture, evidence of indebtedness, certificate of interest or participation in any profit-sharing agreement, collateral-trust certificate, preorganization certificate or subscription, transferable share, *investment contract*, voting-trust certificate, certificate of deposit for a security, fractional undivided interest in oil, gas, or other mineral rights, any put, call, straddle, option, or privilege on any security, certificate of deposit, or group or index of securities (including any interest therein or based on the value thereof), or any put, call, straddle, option, or privilege entered into on a national securities exchange relating to foreign currency, or, in general, any interest or instrument commonly known as a 'security,' or any certificate of interest or participation in, temporary or interim certificate for, receipt for, guarantee of, or warrant or right to subscribe to or purchase, any of the foregoing."

40. https://en.wikipedia.org/wiki/SEC_v._W._J._Howey_Co

41. That is, demand to undo the transaction and get money invested back. Rescission demands usually include statutory interest, and sometimes attorneys' fees; there is also a risk of personal liability.

Understanding the rules will also help you understand why in some environments companies do not discuss fundraising as part of their pitch, and why in other circumstances companies might ask you for specific documentation on your income or assets. There are red flags to watch out for here as well, such as third parties soliciting funds for a startup for a commission.

8.1 *Accredited Investors*

◇ **IMPORTANT** As a general rule, you cannot be an angel investor unless you are accredited.

Startups raise money from **accredited investors**: either individuals or entities who meet the qualifications set by the Securities and Exchange Commission. According to the SEC, investors must meet a minimum level of income or assets (either high net worth or high income) in order to be accredited. The SEC rules make it challenging for companies to raise money from **non-accredited investors** who do not meet these standards.

For individuals, an accredited investor is someone who falls into one of the following categories:[42]

- income of at least $200K a year for the two years prior to the year of investment with the expectation of the same in the the year of investment, or $300K with spouse; or
- net worth of at least $1M (excluding equity in primary residence, but taking into account debt on that residence to the extent that the debt exceeds the fair market value of the residence); or
- any director, executive officer, or general partner of the issuer of the securities being offered or sold, or any director, executive officer, or general partner of a general partner of that issuer.

In addition, a family trust or family partnership may invest in a private company as an accredited investor so long as that family trust or family partnership qualifies as an accredited investor. However, entities such as these must meet different tests to qualify as accredited investors. For an

---

42. The SEC proposed to expand[43] the definition of accredited investor in 2019.

43. http://dodd-frank.com/2019/12/19/
sec-proposes-to-update-the-definition-of-accredited-investor/

entity to be an accredited investor, it must fit within one of the following categories:

- an entity of which all of the equity owners are individual accredited investors (per the qualifications above)
- a trust, with total assets in excess of $5M, not formed for the specific purpose of acquiring the securities offered, whose purchase is directed by a sophisticated person as described in 230.506(b)(2)(ii),[44] or
- any organization described in section 501(c)(3) of the Internal Revenue Code, corporation, Massachusetts[45] or similar business trust, or partnership, not formed for the specific purpose of acquiring the securities offered, with total assets in excess of $5M.

By definition, therefore, one cannot form a limited liability company or another type of business entity to make an angel investment as a means of avoiding the "accredited investor" requirement.

⚜ FOUNDER   In general, under federal law, if a startup accepts even one non-accredited investor in their round, they have to provide what is essentially an IPO-level of disclosure to all investors, which is very costly. In contrast, if a private company limits its securities offering solely to accredited investors, there is no specific information the company has to provide to investors.

You can find an explanation of this dramatic dichotomy in the law on the SEC's website,[46] which provides:

> *Companies must decide what information to give to accredited investors, so long as it does not violate the antifraud prohibitions of the federal securities laws... [B]ut companies must give non-accredited investors disclosure documents that are generally the same as those used in registered offerings.*

---

44. https://www.law.cornell.edu/cfr/text/17/230.506

45. "A Massachusetts Trust" is an informal term used to describe an unincorporated business organization or an arrangement where the investor serves as the grantor of the trust and gives management authority to a trustee. The investor's liability is limited to their investment.

46. https://www.investor.gov/introduction-investing/investing-basics/glossary/rule-506-regulation-d

8.2 *Exemptions*

The Securities Act[47] (also known as the Truth in Securities Act) states that "every offer and sale of securities be registered with the Securities and Exchange Commission (the 'Commission'), unless an exemption from registration is available."

An **exemption (or exempt offering)** is an offer and sale of securities that does not have to be registered with the SEC because the SEC has adopted an exemption from registration that you can qualify to use.

The two most common ways for private companies to sell securities are through the following exemptions:

- an "All Accredited Investor Rule 506(b) offering"
- a Rule 506(c) offering

We'll get into the details below, but the primary difference between Rule 506(b) and Rule 506(c) is that if a company generally solicits its offering it is taking the 506(c) exemption and must take "reasonable steps to verify" that its investors meet the criteria of accredited investors, while under 506(b), companies can solicit only to people who affirm beforehand that they are accredited investors, and there is no verification requirement for the company.

General solicitation (or general advertising or public advertising) means using radio, TV, the unrestricted internet, and other means of soliciting investors. General solicitation and general advertising are defined in Rule 502(c) of Regulation D.

8.2.1 "ALL ACCREDITED INVESTOR RULE 506(B) OFFERINGS"

The **All Accredited Investor Rule 506(b) offerings (or Rule 506(b))** is the most common way for private companies to raise money. Under Rule 506(b), companies cannot "generally solicit" or "generally advertise" their securities offerings. In a Rule 506(b) offering:

- A company can raise an unlimited amount of money from accredited investors.
- The company can't generally solicit or advertise the offering.

---

47. https://www.investopedia.com/terms/s/securitiesact1933.asp

- The company is required to file a Form D with the SEC and state securities divisions within 15 days of its first sale of the securities in the offering.
- Each investor has to check a box averring that they are an accredited investor, and the company does not have to take any further action to verify that the investor is accredited as long as the company's belief that the investor is accredited is reasonable. This means you will not have to provide any personal financial information to the company to prove you are accredited.
- State securities regulators cannot "merit review" or condition the offering on any basis.

⚒ FOUNDER By following the 506(b) rules—only soliciting accredited investors and only allowing accredited investors to invest—a company dramatically reduces their securities offering requirements. Rule 506(b) offerings are popular because the rules are easy to follow. There are no specific information requirements, meaning companies don't have to spend weeks preparing expensive disclosure documents. A company can raise money on a term sheet and an executive summary and pitch deck. And the company doesn't have to prepare the definitive legal documents until it has commitments on its term sheet. This means that the legal fees for preparing the definitive documents come due at or after the money committed has come in (which is a nice timing coincidence). Finally, the company does not have to file anything with securities regulators until after it has closed the deal.

⚒ CONFUSION Under Rule 506(b), it is also possible to sell to up to 35 non-accredited investors, but if a company does this it has to provide registered offering level disclosure to all of the investors. This is why companies usually limit their offerings to accredited investors only.

8.2.2 RULE 506(C) OFFERINGS

A Rule 506(c) offering is an exemption under Regulation D in which companies can generally solicit, but they have to take additional steps to verify the accredited status of their investors. Rule 506(c) offerings are less common than Rule 506(b) offerings primarily because of the verification requirement.

In a Rule 506(c) offering:

- A company can raise an unlimited amount of money from only accredited investors.
- The company *can* generally solicit and advertise the offering, which means:
  - posting on unrestricted websites
  - advertisements published in newspapers and magazines
  - communications broadcast over television and radio
  - seminars and meetings where attendees have been invited by general solicitation or general advertising
- The company has to take reasonable steps to verify the accredited investor status of each investor.

🔥 CONFUSION Until recently, general solicitation in (the public advertising of) private company securities offerings was illegal. If you generally solicited a private company securities offering, you risked jail time. This changed with the JOBS Act[48] in 2012. Now it is not illegal to generally solicit your private company securities offerings, but if a company generally solicits or generally advertises its offering, then it is conducting a 506(c) offering and it must take reasonable steps to verify the accredited investor status of its investors before it can accept their investments.

Reasonable steps to verify means that a company might ask to see your Form W-2 or Form K-1 or Form 1099 to verify that you meet the income test. Alternatively, the company might ask to see your personal financial statements and ask to run a credit report on you to confirm your liabilities and verify that you meet the net worth test. This is a process many investors are not familiar with and is an additional burden to closing an investment. For this reason, many companies choose not to generally solicit or generally advertise their offerings.

Conveniently, service providers do exist that provide verification services (meaning verifying that the investors are accredited). Therefore, it is not necessary that the investors provide their personal financial information directly to a company; they can provide it to a third party[49] instead,

---

48. https://www.investopedia.com/terms/j/jumpstart-our-business-startups-act-jobs.asp
49. https://www.verifyinvestor.com/

who would then provide a certification to the company, which the company could rely upon.

8.2.3 CROWDFUNDING AND OTHER LESS COMMON EXEMPTIONS

Though 506(b) is by far the most common exemption for private companies to raise money, followed by 506(c), there are others you may run into. are other ways for private companies to raise money other than Rule 506 of Regulation D. If you would like to review a comprehensive list of all of the exemption available, you can find one starting on page 11 of this 2020 SEC release.[50] They include:

- **Title III equity crowdfunding (Regulation CF).** Under this exemption, companies can raise up to $5M during any 12-month period. But they have to use either a registered broker-dealer or registered crowdfunding platform, such as Wefunder.[51] Title III is becoming more popular, but right now the amount of money raised in Title III equity crowdfunding offerings is a small fraction of what is raised in Rule 506 offerings. However, the SEC has recently adopted new rules that not only raised the amount companies could raise in a Title III equity crowd raise to $5M in a Title III equity crowd raise. These favorable regulatory changes might make the use of Title III much more common in the future.
- **Regulation A+.** Regulation A+ is an exemption that allows companies to raise as much as $50M during any 12-month period. But the exemption is expensive to use, and thus not used very frequently by the overall startup community. It might become more popular in years to come, however.
- **State crowdfunding laws.** Some states have laws allowing companies to raise money in crowdfunding-type offerings. For example, Washington State has a crowdfunding exemption allowing companies to raise up to $1M during any 12-month period, provided certain conditions are met.
- **Various state exemptions.** Each state typically has its own rules as well. But for the most part, companies tend to raise funds from investors from a number of different states, and tend not to rely on state-specific exemptions.

---

50. https://www.sec.gov/rules/proposed/2020/33-10763.pdf

51. https://wefunder.com/

8.2.4 IS THERE A FRIENDS AND FAMILY EXEMPTION?

It is very common to hear an entrepreneur say that their first round of investment was "friends and family." This is understandable: when the company is little more than an idea, it is likely only to be able to get money from people who are betting on the entrepreneurs based on a pre-existing relationship.

Many states have exemptions allowing companies to raise money from non-accredited investors with whom they have a pre-existing, substantive relationship under Rule 504 of Regulation D.[52] It is beyond the scope of this book to provide a state-by-state analysis, but, for example, California has such a law,[53] as does Washington State, where companies can raise up to $1M during any 12-month period from both accredited and up to 20 non-accredited investors.

◇ CAUTION As an investor, you do need to be careful about this. There is no "friends and family" exemption from registration under the federal securities laws. There are federal securities law exemptions pursuant to which companies can raise money from unaccredited investors (Rule 504, Title III, Reg A+, Rule 506(b)), but none of these exemptions have as exempt a category of purchasers identified as "friends and family." For the most part, the federal securities law exemptions require either that the purchaser of the securities be "accredited" or the company provide registered offering level disclosure so that the purchasers of the securities had access to the same information they would have had if the company had registered the securities.

---

52. https://www.sec.gov/education/smallbusiness/exemptofferings/rule504
53. https://www.bendlawoffice.com/2016/07/07/the-friends-and-family-investment-round/

8.3 *Impacts of Securities Law on Pitching Events*

8.3.1 PITCHING TO ANGEL GROUPS

You might wonder, do companies engage in general solicitation if they pitch to an angel group? The SEC has provided specific guidance around angel groups and how they can facilitate companies meeting angels without triggering the general solicitation rules:[54]

> *Question 256.27*
>
> *Question: Are there circumstances under which an issuer, or a person acting on the issuer's behalf, can communicate information about an offering to persons with whom it does not have a pre-existing, substantive relationship without having that information deemed a general solicitation?*
>
> *Answer: Yes. The staff is aware of long-standing practices where issuers and persons acting on their behalf are introduced to prospective investors who are members of an informal, personal network of individuals with experience investing in private offerings. For example, we acknowledge that groups of experienced, sophisticated investors, such as "angel investors," share information about offerings through their network and members who have a relationship with a particular issuer may introduce that issuer to other members. Issuers that contact one or more experienced, sophisticated members of the group through this type of referral may be able to rely on those members' network to establish a reasonable belief that other offerees in the network have the necessary financial experience and sophistication. Whether there has been a general solicitation is a fact-specific determination. In general, the greater the number of persons without financial experience, sophistication or any prior personal or business relationship with the issuer that are contacted by an issuer or persons acting on its behalf through impersonal, non-selective means of communication, the more likely the communications are part of a general solicitation. [August 6, 2015]*

---

54. https://www.sec.gov/corpfin/securities-act-rules

8.3.2 **PITCHING OUTSIDE OF ANGEL GROUPS**

Many startup incubators and accelerators have demo day events in which friends and supporters of the startups as well as angel investors are invited to attend. At these and similar events, entrepreneurs will pitch their startup but not disclose any fundraising terms—because not everyone in the audience is an accredited investor, they want to stay within Rule 506(b) guidelines and avoid any general solicitation. By including deal terms in their pitch, like, "We're raising $500K at a $3M valuation," they could be deemed to be soliciting the audience and thereby engaging in general solicitation. The SEC has issued rules[55] with respect to demo days.

8.4 *Disclosure of Investment*

In general, the law does not require that private companies disclose the names of their owners or investors, with the exception of what is required to be disclosed on the SEC's Form D.[56]

If you accept a board seat, or if you become an executive officer of a company, the fact that you are a member of the board or an executive officer of a company may be disclosed on the Form D the company files with the SEC. Companies are required to file the Form D with the SEC when they raise money in a Rule 506 offering, and they are required to list on the Form D the directors and executive officers of the company. You can review the Form D from the SEC.[57] Filed Forms D are publicly available on the internet, and many media outlets watch these filings so that they can report any interesting news.

◇ CAUTION Though they are not required to do so, a company may want to issue a press release or otherwise publicly disclose the fact that it has closed its investment round, and in those releases, the company may want to disclose the names of its investors. If you do not want your name disclosed in this process, you should take special care to require the company to agree to keep your name confidential.

---

55. https://www.sec.gov/rules/final/2020/33-10884.pdf

56. This is from time to time an issue that is politicized and legislation is introduced to require public disclosure of private company stockholders, but to date these efforts have not succeeded.

57. https://www.sec.gov/about/forms/formd.pdf

8.5 *What To Watch Out For*

⚠ DANGER A few important pitfalls when it comes to securities law and fundraising:

- Make sure the company is complying with the law in regard to its fundraising. When you are evaluating a company, you should make sure the company is following the rules of whichever securities law compliance path it chose.

  For example, if the company is telling you that it is conducting a Rule 506(b) offering, but it is advertising its securities offerings on its website, that is a red flag. It means that the company is not complying with the law. The company may not be getting good legal advice, which is a signal that other things might be amiss as well.

- While you're investigating the company's fundraising history, note that many angel investors are leery of companies that have crowd-funded or taken money from friends and family, partly because there may be a large number of non-accredited and potentially naïve investors on the cap table, which can complicate future fundraising.

- If you run across a company with a large number of non-accredited investor shareholders, this may make it more difficult for the company to receive venture capital funding. The presence of a large number of non-accredited investors on the cap table can also indicate the company has not received good legal advice, and other things in the company's corporate records are not correctly done either.

- Sometimes companies are not careful in how they conduct their securities offerings. You want to make sure that the company you are investing in is well advised and scrupulous about its securities law practices. If a company violates the rules, your money may well be used to clean up the mess. You don't want your funds used in this way.

- Don't inadvertently become a VC. Unless you are in the business of investing other people's money, and you have all of the required licenses and credentials, complied with all legal requirements, and have insurance, do not invest other people's money, charge other investors a fee for investing in your deals, or take a carry on other investor's investments.

  - It is not uncommon for angel investors to want to follow a well-known investor who has access to deals that they might not have access to, because of their reputation or prior experience. You might run into someone who asks you to start investing their money in your deals. This might be alluring to you if you would like to have more negotiating power.

- The problem is, the law in this area is onerous and easy to run afoul of. For example, if you charge other investors a fee to invest in your deals, you might have to be registered as a broker-dealer or an investment advisor. If you form a fund, even if you don't charge any fees, you have to worry about compliance with the Investment Company Act.[58]

- You never want to be sued by another investor in a deal based on the claim that you advised that person to make the investment. Each investor in any deal should make their own independent decision whether to invest.

- In general, securities regulators are hostile to non-registered broker-dealers (so-called "finders") receiving a commission on the sale of securities. In general, if someone is receiving a commission on the sale of a security, the securities regulators will take the view that the person should be registered as a broker-dealer. Some states, such as California, provide investors with a statutory rescission right if a company paid a commission to a non-registered broker-dealer. You should be aware that finders and broker-dealers must be disclosed on the Form D that the company is required to file with the SEC, which is a public filing anyone can access.[59]

- The key advice here is: don't act as a finder for a fee. Meaning, don't help raise money for a startup in a way that provides you any kind of payment or commission or other remuneration such as additional stock.

58. https://www.sec.gov/investment/laws-and-rules
59. https://www.sec.gov/about/forms/formd.pdf

PART II: FINDING AND EVALUATING DEALS

In this section, we will look at finding potential investment opportunities and how to determine if they are interesting enough to warrant investing time and effort in due diligence. Many angels will engage in due diligence on less than 10% of the companies whose pitches they hear. The goal of due diligence is to investigate and validate all the aspects of the pitch that got you excited.

Legal due diligence will follow. This effort is focused on making sure there are no red flags in how the business was formed and structured, how it has been funded to date, and whether the founders and early employees have assigned their inventions and innovations to the company and are properly motivated to stay with it.

9 Finding Opportunities

To have the opportunity to make a good investment, you have to see a lot of deals.

Deal flow refers to the number of potential investment opportunities you review during a particular period. Ideally, if you are active, you will have the chance to review, if not all, a substantial portion of the investment opportunities in your particular area.

⚹ FOUNDER If you're new to angel investing—or a founder looking for ways to get in front of investors—here we include some recommendations on how to get access to deal flow.

9.1 *Get to Know the Local Startup Ecosystem*

There are a number of benefits to investing in local startups. When considering making an investment, you may want to visit the startup's office, talk to key team members, and perhaps see a demo of a not-yet-released version of a product. You will want to get to know the CEO over the course of several meetings. Many of these activities are more easily done if the company is within an easy drive.

Once you've decided to move forward with the investment process, being physically close to the company makes it easier for you to stay in touch with the CEO over the occasional lunch, and perhaps introduce them to potential local hires or customers. In the event that things go poorly with the company after you invest, or they are unresponsive to your inquiries, you will be able to just go to their offices and talk to them. Finally, by investing locally, you will be helping your local startup ecosystem.

You can learn more about investment opportunities in your community through the following channels:

- **Angel investing groups.** Angel investing groups are a great place to get exposed to potential investment opportunities. We discuss this in detail in Joining an Angel Group.[§5.3]

- **VCs.** Introduce yourself to the early-stage VCs in your town. Let them know you are looking to invest and ask them who the prominent local angels are.

- **Accelerators and incubators.** Research the local startup accelerators and incubators and introduce yourself to them. You can offer to be a mentor if you have the time, but at a minimum let them know that you are an accredited investor looking to make investments and ask to be invited to their demo days.

- **Universities.** Many universities now have entrepreneurship programs, and they may be open to having local angel investors attend their demo days or meet with their student teams to provide feedback and advice.

- **Meetups.** Meetups are a good place to get to know entrepreneurs. There are a surprising number of meetups focused on startups. In addition to searching Meetup.com[60] for "startups" or "entrepreneurs,"

---

60. https://www.meetup.com/

try some of the hot topics in the startup community such as "lean startup" or "lean analytics."

- **Co-working spaces.** Co-working spaces are also an excellent place to find startups. In many cities there has been a proliferation of co-working spaces targeted specifically at founders. Check the calendars of these spaces, as they often have events where you can begin to network into that community. In many cities you can find local chapters of startup-centric organizations like Startup Grind[61] that put on regular events that cater to entrepreneurs.

9.2 *Be Public About Your Interests (Or Not)*

If you don't live somewhere with a robust startup ecosystem, or if you are looking for startups in quite specific technologies, you may have to look more broadly.

Let your network know that you are interested in making angel investments. Mention angel investing on your LinkedIn profile. You will be surprised at how many people reach out to you. You can also join investor-centric networks like AngelList,[62] where many entrepreneurs may be looking for investors who share an interest or expertise in their industry.

Whether you are interacting with the local startup community or creating a profile on a national site like AngelList, it will be helpful to have an elevator pitch about the types of deals you are interested in. You might be interested in a particular industry or technology focus or a stage of company. Communicating your desired focus will help get the right deal flow while minimizing the noise.

Alternatively, many angels prefer to remain as anonymous as possible. That is fine too. There is really no wrong way to go here.

9.3 *Stick Close to Your Area of Expertise*

Do you know what the key success factors and milestones are for a medical device startup? How about a messaging app targeted at teens? Do you

---

61. https://www.startupgrind.com/
62. https://angel.co/

know how long it takes to sell an enterprise software solution to Fortune 500 company CIOs? You will be a more effective investor if you understand the market and/or technology that is the focus of the startup.

◇ **IMPORTANT**   In 2011, Rob Wiltbank of the Angel Resource Institute[63] completed a study of angel investments made by members of angel groups.[64] He found that angels had a 60% better return on their investment when they invested within their area of expertise. So stick to your knitting!

Why? If you have had a career in enterprise software sales, you will understand intuitively the challenges in selling in that market. You'll know how potential customers evaluate solutions, allocate budget, calculate ROI, what their risk tolerance is, who the influencers are, how long the sales cycle takes, what supporting proof is required, what marketing techniques are effective, and so on. You will have colleagues and friends in the industry that you can contact to litmus test some of the assumptions being used by the startup you are considering. You will be in a much better position to evaluate an idea, scrutinize the team, gut check the financials and perform effective due diligence if you are looking at companies in an area you know something about.

If you do decide to evaluate companies in areas outside your expertise, it makes sense to do so with the support of an angel group or someone in your network who does know the industry well. You can lean on the knowledge of other angel investors, but it will always be easier if yourself know—or are at least willing to learn—what questions need to be asked and can converse with a founder intelligently.

10   Evaluating Opportunities

Of all the opportunities you're likely to come across, how do you narrow your list down to the companies you're willing to spend the time and effort of due diligence on? There is an ongoing debate among venture capitalists and angel investors about what is most important in determining the likelihood of a startup's success: a strong team, a big market, or a compelling

---

63. https://angelresourceinstitute.org/
64. https://willamette.edu/~wiltbank/seattle_angel_conference_may_2012.html

idea? They are *all* important, so we will cover how to evaluate all three below.

10.1 *Evaluating the Team*

Ideas are everywhere, and there are very few unique ones. There is a long road between the idea and an actual compelling product, and longer still to a revenue-generating business (and longer still to profits!). It is the team that is going to build the business out of the idea, so you should be as confident as possible that the people pitching to you are going to be able to execute. Many believe that one of the best predictors of success is an entrepreneur who has built *and exited* one or more successful companies. Absent that scenario, below are some key things to consider after hearing the pitch. (We'll address team issues in more detail in Business Due Diligence for Angel Investments.[§11])

Your goal here is to figure out whether the team is particularly well-suited to tackle the problem that they have set out to solve because of their skills, background, and experience.

10.1.1 DOMAIN AND FUNCTIONAL EXPERTISE

A good team generally has *domain expertise* in the industry that they are now planning to disrupt, and ideally in the *functions* that are core to succeeding with that disruption.

Domain expertise (or domain knowledge) means a thorough understanding of a particular field of study. In the context of angel investing, a deep knowledge of a particular industry's inner workings, including the ecosystem, market, competitors, and customers. Domain expertise can also refer to **functional domain expertise**, such as a deep understanding of social media marketing or iOS app development.

> ⟩ EXAMPLE
>
> If a company is bringing an internet of things (IoT) solution to the managing of railroad cars, it's important that someone on the team has a thorough understanding of IoT technical architectures (has built IoT systems before) and someone has spent time working in the railroad industry or has specific insight into that industry.

In addition to domain knowledge, is there enough functional domain
expterise—practical experience—among the team to tackle the problem
they've chosen? You might ask it this way: How *functionally complete* is
the team? Is it two engineers with no experience in marketing, sales, or
operations? Ideally, each key area of functional expertise required for success is represented by someone on the team. Often, each member of a
small startup team is wearing many hats, and so they need to convince you
that they can execute those roles or be clear that they will use the money
they are raising to hire to fill the gaps. It can be challenging for a very
early-stage company to hire a great marketing person, or a great engineering leader, so if a key function is lacking, it creates extra risk for the company.

10.2 *Evaluating Market Size*

The other aspect of an investment opportunity that can sway an investor
is the sheer size of the market opportunity presented. Angels and venture
capital investors frequently focus on the size of the market for the company's product to evaluate the potential return on investment.

◇ IMPORTANT It is important that the company can convince you that they
can be a $100M-revenue company while owning only a small fraction of
their target market. That suggests that the company needs to be targeting
a $1B market or larger. Angel investors typically do not want to invest in
a lifestyle business[65] that tops out at less than $10M in revenue, because
there are fewer exit possibilities,[§6.2] and it is hard to achieve the levels of
returns that VCs and angels seek if the company is going after a small market.

A typical scenario for a startup is that they are targeting a large market,
but are starting with a very focused market entry strategy. This is a smart
approach: create a beachhead[66] and initial traction with a very focused

---

65. A **lifestyle business** is a business that provides the founder a nice lifestyle (income),
    but it is not a business on a growth trajectory that is likely going to result in a sale for
    the benefit of the investors. A founder of a lifestyle business will have no motivation to
    sell the business to provide liquidity to the investors.
66. https://exec.mit.edu/s/blog-post/
    launching-a-successful-start-up-3-the-beachhead-market-MC7FUMDZ6IU5AIPP4WGIPN2PZ
    JI4

product in a very specific market and then expand to the broader market as their resources for engineering and sales grow. So while the initial market may be small, the total addressable market (TAM) in which they believe their product, service, or approach will be superior, should be large.

10.3 *Evaluating the Idea*

Angel investors will often categorize an idea as a *painkiller* or a *vitamin*. A vitamin is something that makes the customer's life a little easier or a little better, whereas a painkiller is something that solves a real pain point for the customer. The assumption is that if you are addressing an actual problem a customer has, they will have a greater urgency to purchase your product or service and will more readily take on the risk of buying and using a product or service from a startup.

B2B startups have a particular challenge in that they are asking their customers to take a chance on the product *and the company*. If a customer buys a startup's product, invests in setting it up and training their employees on it, and then the company disappears in a year because they ran out of money or pivoted, then the customer is up a creek, and that purchasing manager has some explaining to do to his or her boss. The product has to be really compelling for the buyer to take that chance. It is often not enough that it has better features than existing products or that it saves the customer 10%-20% on their costs.

Even for B2C companies, it can be challenging to get consumers to change their behavior. The product has to be significantly better than the alternatives to get consumers to switch and stick around.

10.4 *Evaluating Traction*

Sales to paying customers is the greatest validation of an idea, and the product that delivers on the idea. Traction is a term that most often refers to a startup's progress in getting customers.

A company's **traction** with customers indicates that there is actually demand for the product or service. This is sometimes referred to as (or as an important part of) **product/market fit**,[67] meaning that there is a validated market for the product at the stated price. Traction also shows that the company has actually built a working version of their product, and that they can sell it to businesses or generate consumer demand, for B2B or B2C offerings respectively.

In many cases you, the angel investor, will not be the intended customer for the startup's product, and without interviewing lots of potential customers it can be challenging to assess the appeal of the product. Traction tells you unequivocally whether the intended customer is willing to use and pay for the product. You do not need to be an expert in the domain or up to date on the competition, because the customers are making rational decisions with all that information.

◇ CAUTION   Keep in mind that traction with a free product is not necessarily indicative of customers' willingness to pay.

◇ IMPORTANT   As we have said elsewhere in this book,[§7.1] the stages companies are at when seeking angel investment vary radically, and every angel has a different level of comfort around risk. Some companies you might choose to invest in won't have reached product/market fit, but can demonstrate how they plan to get there. As you proceed on your angel investing journey, you'll have a better sense of what are deal-breakers for your investment, and what you're willing to forego.

10.5 *Evaluating Competition*

A little bit of competition—especially from other early-stage companies—is a good thing: competition validates that a market exists. Hopefully, the company in question has some well-articulated advantage over the competition. Crowded markets are more challenging for investors and companies because it is harder to define a clearly superior product or differentiated value proposition when there are lots of products in the mix. Even if it is a clearly better widget, it is hard for new entrants to rise above the noise and gain significant mindshare.

---

67. There are a few schools of thought around what defines product/market fit. Holloway has a great post[68] about this, part of the *Holloway Guide to Raising Venture Capital*.

68. https://www.holloway.com/s/rvc-fundamentals-of-product-market-fit

In addition to looking for a first-to-market advantage, investors often look at whether the company can build barriers to competition. If the idea proves great and the company begins to get traction, they will also gain the attention of potential competitors who could move to address the same market:

1. Can the company lock up key customers, distributors, or vendor relationships?
2. Do they have intellectual property that will act as barriers to competition?
3. What hard problems has this company solved that will be hard for competitors to duplicate?

We'll talk more about competition in Business Due Diligence for Angel Investments.§11

10.5.1 INTELLECTUAL PROPERTY ASSETS

We mentioned intellectual property as a barrier to competition above. Intellectual property may include traditional forms such as patents or trademarks or even a particularly effective domain name. Often an early-stage company will only have filed provisional patents, but this can be an indicator that there is some real innovation in the company's technology or approach. While an early-stage company would likely not have the resources to defend their patents, a strong patent portfolio might make them an attractive acquisition target for a company that could leverage and defend those patents.

11 Business Due Diligence for Angel Investments

Business due diligence is where things start to get a bit more serious. You've evaluated opportunities and chosen a handful of companies that might merit an investment. Due diligence digs deeper and sometimes wider to validate whether the story told by the entrepreneur stands up under scrutiny.

Due diligence (or business due diligence) refers to the process by which investors investigate a company and its market before deciding whether to invest. Due diligence typically happens after an investor hears the pitch and before investment terms are discussed in any detail.

◇ IMPORTANT Due diligence is arguably *the most important* part of the angel investing process. The amount of due diligence that is done on a company is the factor most correlated with investor return; the more due diligence you do, the more likely you are going to invest in companies that make you money. Rob Wiltbank looked at the amount of due diligence completed by angel investors, and found that the number of hours of due diligence performed on a company was one of the key success factors in angel investing outcomes.[69] In fact, investors got a 2X better return on an investment when they did more than 20 hours of due diligence versus when they did less than 20 hours. We cannot overstress the importance of due diligence.

⚘ CONFUSION You may know of active angel investors making investment decisions with little due diligence. These are likely angels investing alone, and making those investments based on prior relationships or the recommendation of a fellow experienced angel. In part, this is because they have more money and less time. They can afford to lose the money on some percentage of investments more than they can afford to spend the time doing rigorous due diligence on all their investments.

Angel groups and institutional investors tend to have more formal processes and do more due diligence. This reflects some of the benefits of investing as part of a group. Because groups often invest more in the

---

69. https://willamette.edu/~wiltbank/seattle_angel_conference_may_2012.html

aggregate than individuals, they can justify the time investment of more diligence. Groups may also be investing money on the part of members who are not actively involved in the process and who expect some level of due diligence to be performed.

Our goal in this section is to help you focus your business due diligence efforts, and to give you some insight into what to look for and how to think about what you find out. We will focus on business risk due diligence in this section. *Legal* due diligence is also important, and is addressed in its own section.§12

In addition to what's included here, there are many other areas that may merit due diligence, depending on the nature of the business. In general, understand the key sources of value in the company and what its key challenges on the road to success might be, and dig into them. The answers will not all be perfect, but at least you will better understand your risks and what you are getting when you invest.

⚒ FOUNDER Most startups will know that their pitch deck[70] should include slides representing the following: team, customers, competition, product, market size, and finances. If they are missing any of these, that may be a red flag that the founders are underprepared. Regardless, angels should expect to dig deeper into each of these through the due diligence process.

⚠ DANGER When a founder dismisses your concern about a particular issue or is not forthcoming with data that you have requested (be it customer names, founder references, customer counts, or something else) it may be tempting to let it go as there is lots of other work to do. Experienced angels take this as a sign to be persistent. If data is not forthcoming that may be where the skeletons lie.

It is easy to see how it can take more than 20 hours to perform even just the business due diligence on a company! Ideally you are sharing that load across a team. Some angel groups and many websites offer due diligence checklists. We're happy to be able to share the due diligence checklist from Alliance of Angels[71] with our readers, which can supplement what you learn here.

---

70. https://www.holloway.com/g/venture-capital/sections/designing-your-pitch
71. https://docs.google.com/spreadsheets/d/1NpHUWKPunKr_
9aeTJJKnpqIv4-StuPokb2rMkSBMUBs/edit?usp=sharing

11.1 *Diligence on the Team*

As we discussed in Evaluating Opportunities,[10] the startup team may be the most important determinant of a company's success. While you should have gotten a good sense of the team's potential when you were first evaluating the opportunity, digging deeper into the makeup of the company during due diligence will help you gain certainty on your initial impressions.

There are also legal considerations when it comes to diligence on the company team; we discuss employee assignment agreements and vesting of founders' stock in Legal Due Diligence for Angel Investments.[12]

11.1.1 PERSONALITY

Below are a few personality traits to consider. Throughout the diligence process you will likely have multiple conversations with the founding team. Try to assess some of these important traits:

- **Hustle.** Hustle is shorthand for a team's tenacity, resourcefulness, and passion. The team needs to be able to make decisions and meet goals quickly, overcoming obstacles again and again. In short, they need to be able to *execute*. Talking to the key members of the team about challenges they have run into, how they solved hard problems, how long it took them to build the prototype or get their first sale, how they convinced their first key hires to take the risk, can all give you a sense of how they are able to get things done.

- For example, Pete worked with one CEO who was pulling all-nighters reviewing and negotiating key partner contracts in the early days of his startup, while having his infant daughter strapped to his chest with a Babybjörn carrier. At the other extreme, Pete was mentoring a first-time CEO who kept discussing their vision and the technology research they were doing, but who never built even the most basic prototype. The first CEO built a company and raised over $80M, the latter was never able to turn their vision into reality.

- **Commitment.** Building a successful company requires the ability to work steadfastly for years through sometimes extremely difficult circumstances. The core founders should be committed to the enterprise. They might talk passionately about how they want to change their industry. Try to get a sense of their motivation. You are looking for someone who will stick to it when the going gets tough. Be wary of an entrepreneur who mentions a plan B if this venture doesn't work out: "If I can't get this to $1M in revenue in a year, I'll just go back to work for Microsoft."

- **Compatibility.** What about the strength of the team bonds? Is the team likely to fracture and break up? Can you sense tension when different members answer questions or discuss challenges or decisions? It's a good sign if several members of the team have worked together before, as they will know each other's personalities and capabilities well. If it is unclear from their backgrounds that they have worked together, feel free to ask questions about how they know each other, whether they have collaborated in any capacity, how they became convinced that the other could take on key management roles beyond their existing experience. The breakup of the founding team is one of the leading reasons early startups fail,$^{§27.1}$ so don't overlook this issue.
- **Coachability.** Finally, it is important that a CEO is coachable, especially a first-time CEO. A wise CEO will seek guidance from investors, advisors, and experts in their network. They will face many new challenges and you want them to be willing to benefit from the experience of others. Pete can attest that there is nothing more frustrating than a young first-time CEO who will not heed the collective advice of the board of directors and advisors!

11.1.2 TEAM EMPLOYEE STATUS

In Evaluating Opportunities,^{§10} we touched on functional coverage of the team, meaning the degree to which the key functions required for success (product development, sales, marketing, customer success, design, finance, et cetera) are represented in the team. The critical functions will vary to a degree according to the type of company, and certain functions will often be outsourced, like legal and often the CFO role.[72] Beyond those roles, look carefully at who is employed, and who is contracted or outsourced.

The entrepreneurs feel pressure to show a complete team in their presentation, but as you dig in you will often find that there is a mix of full-time and part-time employees or contractors, and even friends chipping in for just an equity stake in the dream. This mix is not uncommon, but

---

72. Though there should be someone on the team who can do financial modeling of the business.

you will want to know who you are investing in, who will be full-time when the money is in, and what has been promised to whom.

◇ IMPORTANT It is highly recommended that you interview each of the key team members called out on the team slide (the ones you are investing in), and ask them directly about their level of commitment. You may find that some are never planning on committing full-time. In that case, you have a functional gap to fill on the team, and a potential red flag as to why this person is not excited about the venture.

◇ CAUTION There can be liabilities associated with deferred wages or vague undocumented promises of equity to people who have made contributions over time. Understand the personnel history of the company as early founders or contributors may have already exited, but still own a stake. Furthermore, anyone who is contributing to the company in some capacity should have signed an invention assignment agreement$^{§12.3.4}$ acknowledging that their work is owned by the company. We will discuss liabilities and employee issues in more detail in Legal Due Diligence for Angel Investments.$^{§12.3}$

You should also determine whether the technical development team is in-house or outsourced.[73] Outsourcing software development teams is increasingly popular among startups because it can be significantly cheaper if the coders are offshore; and because building a good in-house development team[74] is hard, expensive, and time-consuming. For an entrepreneur, it can be challenging to convince a great software developer to commit to an idea and work full-time for little or no salary while they build the first version of a product. It is often easier to find a team of developers in Eastern Europe or South Asia to build the first version of the product for a few tens of thousands of dollars.

◇ CAUTION As the investor, you want to know what you are getting into, and make sure that whoever is managing offshore teams, if that is the case, has done that before. If there is no one technical enough on the team to vet the offshore team, provide architectural guidance, and vet the code coming in, that might be a cause for concern. As the business grows, it will

---

73. For some startups raising angel funding, there may not be any engineers employed at the company or outsourced, beyond one or two technical co-founders.

74. https://www.holloway.com/g/technical-recruiting-hiring/about

likely have to backfill the technical roles locally, which will take energy and resources.

11.1.3 REFERENCE CHECKS AND OTHER THIRD-PARTY INSIGHTS

Beyond interviewing the team members yourself, it is highly recommended to get some reference checks on the team. In addition to checking the references supplied by the company, you'll want to track down your own. Use LinkedIn to see if you have any way to get an introduction to other people who know them or have worked with them. It is not uncommon for entrepreneurs to amplify the scope of their responsibilities in their last role as an employee. That's understandable to a degree, since they are trying to convince you that they can be an effective CEO of a soon-to-be-huge company. So it is important to dig in on this.

There are other ways to get some additional information on the founders and key team members:

- **LinkedIn.** LinkedIn provides job history information and also can show references provided by former bosses, partners, or direct reports. Increasingly, LinkedIn is a publishing platform as well, and many entrepreneurs may have written articles about their industry.
- **Twitter.** If team members are active on Twitter,[75] you may be able to get a sense as to whether they are actively consuming articles and commenting with insight on the domain of the startup, and whether they are attending or speaking at conferences. Not everyone is active on Twitter, however, and eschewing Twitter (in our honest opinion) should not be a strike against the entrepreneur.
- **Google.** Google searches will bring up all kinds of information about an entrepreneur. Conference appearances, blogs, articles, or scientific papers they have written, and more.

While it may seem creepy to some people to be scouring the web for information on your startup founders, remember that the internet is largely how the startup is going to generate awareness and promote itself. If they are effectively doing that already across social media, that's a positive signal of their marketing savvy.

---

75. https://www.holloway.com/g/using-twitter/about

Finally, you can pay services to verify employment or education, but these may be an unnecessary expense if you can find what you need through basic web searches.

11.2 *Diligence on Market Size*

In Evaluating Opportunities[§10.2] we discussed why you want to make sure the startup in question is targeting a large market. In performing due diligence, you may want to do a quick check on that market size calculation.

Let's start by defining what we mean by market size. A common mistake entrepreneurs make is to use the value of the target industry they are selling into, rather than the value of the product or service they are selling. Using a fictitious example:

> ❯ EXAMPLE
>
> A startup wants to sell an IoT tire pressure sensor that costs $10 and is compatible with 19" wheels. The total addressable market is not the value of cars sold, or even the value of wheels sold: it is the value of sensors sold.

Jared Sleeper at Matrix Partners has written a useful article[76] about different ways to calculate the TAM (total addressable market), including "top-down" and "bottom-up":

- **Top-down market sizing.** The entrepreneur, and later the investor in due diligence, will Google around trying to find some research company or government estimate on market size for the product in question. This may or may not exist, and if the product in question does not exist, they, and later, you, will have to look for proxy markets. If there is no report on the tire pressure sensor market size, then you would need to find an analogous market size.
- **Bottom-up market sizing.** This is more about estimating the number of likely customers, which forces the entrepreneur to go through a more useful exercise around product/market fit.

> ❯ EXAMPLE
>
> Continuing with our example above, we would want to look at how many new cars are sold with 19-inch wheels, or perhaps how many

---

76. https://www.forentrepreneurs.com/calculating-tam/

existing cars on the road have 19-inch wheels. Right away you can see that this brings up clarifying questions about the market. Is this product meant to be a retrofit product for existing car owners? Is it a way for new car buyers to save on expensive options like factory tire pressure sensors? Is it going to be sold through tire dealerships, or car dealerships? Is the value proposition that it is cheaper than alternatives? In that case, you need to cut down your estimate of the market to those buyers who are price sensitive—Ford buyers versus BMW buyers, for example.

- If there is a clear existing alternative for the startup's product, like the tire pressure sensor, then you can check some of the numbers on car sales or tire sales with your own searches. It can be a little trickier if the product doesn't yet exist. If electronic tire pressure sensors didn't exist, you could think about who the target customer is. Early customers might be performance car owners and wealthy families who care about safety, such as luxury SUV buyers.

Every market sizing exercise will be different. Have the entrepreneur walk you through how they did it. Ideally their approach reflects some solid thinking about what existing products they are substituting (for Uber it was taxis), and the breadth of product/market fit for a new product category.

Ideally the target market should be growing; it is always easier to build a company in a growing market. Just being in a rapidly growing market will generate some sales even if the initial product is not dramatically superior to the competition. The company will also have more pricing power in a fast-growing market. In a slowly growing market, the startup will have to steal its customers from the competition.

11.3 *Diligence on Customer Traction*

Because traction is such a critical indicator of potential success, it is important to do diligence on the stated customer count and customer engagement and motivation.

> ❯ EXAMPLE

Pete once got excited about a company that claimed to have 85K customers. This was a consumer and small business product. After a few probing questions, it became clear that these "customers" were acquired when the company's product was an add-on to a large ecosystem. These customers were on a free tier of the product, and the company determined that it could not monetize them, so it pivoted to a different value proposition. Entrepreneurs know how important customer traction is to investors, so the pressure to present numbers in a positive light can be extreme.

◇ CAUTION Early-stage companies may end up signing very unfavorable contracts to secure key deals or early customers that they need to move the business forward. If the company or its valuation is heavily dependent on a particular distribution contract or customer letter of intent (LOI),[77] ask to see it.

11.3.1 B2B COMPANIES

B2B companies (or business-to-business companies) sell their product or service to other companies, not individual consumers. B2Bs sell things like an inventory tracking app to restaurants, or a loyalty system for retail stores. A subset of B2B is **enterprise sales**, where companies sell to larger organizations like Microsoft, Intel, HP, or Procter & Gamble. B2B companies will usually have a list of existing customers, a number of trialing or beta customers, and a pipeline of deals.

⚓ FOUNDER The hardest part of B2B startups is selling to businesses, especially enterprises. There was an old saying that "nobody gets fired for buying IBM"; meaning, go with a big name and reliable provider. A manager or executive takes a big risk when they buy a software system from a startup, since the company may not be around in a year, or could suffer operational problems when they try to scale, or fail to deliver software or training support. As a result, it is often the case that entrepreneurs' first sales are to companies where they have a personal connection, such as a former employer. This is not a red flag. However, entrepreneurs need to be realistic about how they can expand their sales beyond their personal network.

❭ EXAMPLE

---

77. https://www.jumpstartinc.org/wp-content/uploads/2016/09/
     Non-Binding-Letters-of-Intent-9616.pdf

While Pete was performing due diligence on a startup that had created a software system for managing police staffing and the use of police department vehicles for events (such as football games), he asked the founder how he had gotten the first sales. The founder was a former police commander himself and used to manage this process on pieces of paper and chalk boards; so he had both great domain expertise and credibility with police departments. His first sale was to his former employer, the town's police department, and his second sale was to the township next door, where he had a strong relationship with the head of the department. He had a few more sales in the state after that based on relationships and referrals. His challenge, he admitted, was finding sales people who would have credibility with police departments with whom he had no personal connection.

So, what's the takeaway? The founder's first sales were based on personal relationships, which is common. But if in his pitch he had said that the company had closed the first four sales within 30 days and had modeled accelerating sales rates in the first year, you now have reason to discount the next few months' sales velocity. The entrepreneur is now having to sell outside of his personal network, so things will likely slow down until there is a good list of referenceable happy customers that the sales team can point to (ideally with case studies published on the company's website.) Scrappy entrepreneurs very often tap their personal networks for early traction. Make sure you know where in the company's story that ends and the sales to cold customers take over.

Enterprise Sales

◇ **IMPORTANT** There are many specialized markets in the B2B space, which is one reason that domain expertise is so important. Schools, governments, medical practitioners, and many other markets all have their own sales calendars and hurdles that entrepreneurs must navigate. Perhaps none is more daunting than enterprise sales, where the sales person has to navigate to find who in a large organization is the actual customer, who has purchasing authority, who has veto authority, and how the procurement department factors in.

The enterprise sales process can be very long and taxing. Because the sales process is long, and companies that sell to enterprises need to know how they are doing relative to sales expectations and cash forecasts, they track a sales pipeline, also called a sales funnel. The specific steps in that sales pipeline may vary by company, but it's usually something like the following:

1. **Leads.** Leads are prospective customers that came to the company's website and requested a demo.
2. **Qualified leads.** Prospects that someone has talked to in order to confirm that they have a budget, are looking to purchase a solution soon, and the contact has the authority to purchase.
3. **Proposals or requests for proposals (RFPs).** Some sales person has sent the prospect a proposal.
4. **In-negotiation deals.** There is active negotiation on a contract.
5. **Trials or proofs of concept (POCs).** This may be appropriate for some software products, but typically means that the product is being used on a test basis often for free within a prospective company.
6. **Closed deals (or lost deals).** Signed customer contracts, or definitive *no's* from prospects.

FOUNDER An entrepreneur should be able to tell you about their sales pipeline, even if it is in the very early stages, and ideally their win/loss ratio. If they have a few sales, they should also be able to tell you about their annual contract value (ACV), that is, how much is the average customer paying per year for the product/service.

FOUNDER The entrepreneur's financial model should reflect the length of time they need to close deals (three months? six months?) and the cost of sales people. Remember, those "in-network" sales we discussed in the example above will often reflect a shorter sales cycle than what the company will see as it tries to expand sales.

B2B Customer Interviews

Ideally, you should speak to a handful of paying customers, if the company is far enough along to have any. If you spend a couple of hours talking to three or four customers you will be much more enlightened about the prospects of the company's product, price point, and marketing. You may also learn who the key competitors really are in the eyes of customers. Ask them:

- How did they hear about the company or product?

- What are they using the product for?
- What problem is it solving and how much is that worth to them?
- What product were they using before, or what other solutions did they consider?
- How do they like the product so far? Does it meet expectations?
- How do they like working with the company? Is the company responsive, competent, et cetera?
- Are they actually paying for the product?

Companies may resist giving you actual customers to call as they may worry that it will make their customers nervous. Keep in mind that all startups are trying to punch above their weight, meaning they want to appear to their customers in many cases as mature businesses that are not in need of money.

This can be a valid concern, but there is usually a way to work through this. For example, you could let the entrepreneur know that you'll position the financing round as "expansion capital," and will follow a script like this when you talk to customers:

> *"We love the team and the product. It seems to solve some real problems and have some real advantages. We are interested in investing in the company, and part of our investment process is to talk to a few customers."*

That sort of a script should ease most of the concerns of an entrepreneur.

⚠ **DANGER** If a company *refuses* to let you talk to customers or drags their feet in giving you contact information, that could be a red flag. It may be that the entrepreneurs have claimed that a company is a "customer" when they are in fact just evaluating the product and have not committed to purchasing it or even trialing it.

Early-stage companies may not have paying customers or even trialing customers or beta customers. In that case they are very early in the traction stage and likely much more risky. If they are following best startup practices, they have done a lot of potential-customer interviews and demos of a minimum viable product to gain confidence that they are working on a product that customers will buy. Ask to talk to some of the potential customers they interviewed.

For very early-stage investments, it is all the more important to work your own network and angel group to find people who are familiar with the company's product category so that you can validate the customer pain point, and the fit of the product as a solution. Ask them what they think of the product, the value proposition, and the solutions that already exist in the market. Is the startup really solving an urgent pain point? Is there really a gap in the solutions available?

If a company is not selling to large enterprises but is selling to small or medium-sized businesses, then many of the B2C metrics below should also be examined. Finally, make sure that the revenue generated from a customer aligns with the marketing and sales effort to acquire that customer. For example, if the product is going to generate less than $1K per year in revenue, it should likely not be sold via a sales team; it should be largely self-serve for the customer, with little support required. If a product sale requires the customer's CTO or CEO approval and it involves a six-month sales cycle, it needs to generate thousands or tens of thousands of dollars a month in revenue from that sale to justify the costs of sales people, contract negotiations, and any on-boarding and support costs.

11.3.2 B2C COMPANIES

B2C companies (or business-to-consumer companies) are offering a product or service to the general public.

B2C companies at the early stages will typically not provide a list of customers to talk to (imagine downloading a yoga app and then getting a call from an angel investor ☺) but if the company has an app or product in the marketplace you can hear the voice of the customer by reading customer reviews (see Usability$^{\S11.5.1}$). Beyond that, there is still work you can do to better understand the company's relationship with any customers it may have.

Many companies are building products that will be profitable only if customers use them over a period of time and come back fairly frequently. This includes gaming companies, online services businesses like on-demand food delivery, online marketplaces, fitness apps, and so on. In this case, digging into what Dave McClure brilliantly popularized as the "pirate metrics" (AARRR![78]) is really important:

- **Acquisition.** How many new customers is the company acquiring and at what cost?
- **Activation.** Are those new customers engaging in the product? Having customers downloading an app and then never using it will not result in a profitable business.
- **Retention.** How engaged are those users? Learn what percent are coming back daily, weekly, monthly, never.
- **Referral.** Do the customers refer other customers? This is often key to scaling profitably.
- **Revenue.** What percentage of customers are generating revenue, often in the form of upgrading from a free product to a paid version? What percentage of customers are delivering more margin than it costs to acquire them?

The entrepreneur should be able to show you charts with actual numbers pulled from a database of how many customers are signing up per week or month, the number of daily or monthly active users, and the level of attrition (leaving, quitting, cancelling).

If the company's revenue model is purely transactional, like selling widgets, then many of the same metrics apply, with the exception of *activation*. The *retention* metric is about repeat purchases, which is often critical to profitability.

Customer acquisition cost (CAC) is a critical metric of the B2C startup. The company should be able to tell you about their most effective marketing channels, and what it costs on average to acquire a customer.

- For example, they might be acquiring customers through Facebook ads at $5, and through Google Adwords at $6. They may also be getting referrals from existing customers, sometimes tracked as the viral "k" factor. Having a free tier and a paid tier is extremely common in con-

---

78. https://www.slideshare.net/dmc500hats/startup-metrics-for-pirates-long-version

sumer and SMB products, and is often referred to as the "freemium" model.

- ◇ CAUTION It should also be clear whether the customer numbers refer to free or paid versions of a product. A startup's profitability model will likely have some assumptions about what percent of free customers they can convert to paid. Sometimes those assumptions are very rosy. Any conversion assumptions in the double digits should give you pause unless they are actually seeing this.

Customer lifetime value (or CLTV or CLV) is another critical metric. Entrepreneurs should understand (or at least have a model with assumptions around) the customer lifetime value and how long it takes for them to recover the cost of acquisition. For the company to be profitable, their CLTV has to dramatically exceed their customer acquisition cost (CAC). That may not be the case initially while they are experimenting and tuning their marketing mix and retention and pricing strategies—but they should have a hypothesis of how they are going to get there.

⚠ DANGER If a company cannot provide the data discussed in this section, that might be a red flag. If some of the numbers don't look good, that is not a deal killer as long as they are tracking the right KPIs (key performance indicators) and working and testing diligently to improve the ones that are not working.

11.4 *Diligence on Competition*

In every pitch deck there should be a slide about competition.

⚠ DANGER If a company says there is no competition it may be a red flag that they don't understand their customers or their market. If you were the inventor of the first car, for example, you might have been tempted to say that there was no competition; but in fact the competition was horses and carriages and trolleys and trains and bicycles and human feet.

⚘ FOUNDER Most entrepreneurs know that they have to be better than the competition or at least differentiated to get funded, but their products are early and as a result are often lacking in features. This creates a temptation for founders to be dismissive of certain competitors or to leave them out of the competitive slide in their pitch altogether. They shouldn't—again, these are key indicators of how well a founder understands her market, customers, and product. Evaluating competition is very company-specific, but the following are some general guidelines for angels to follow when doing diligence on competition:

- Start with the list of competitors provided by the company and look at those products closely.

  - Look at each company's website. Who are they selling to? How are they positioned? What do they cost?
  - If it's possible for you to try out their product, do so.
  - Read reviews of those products.
  - You may even want to call up a salesperson from one of the competitors to hear their pitch and their counterargument to the "weaknesses" identified by your entrepreneur.

- Do your own search for competitors.

  - Google the type of product or pain point (try searching, "best solutions to X" or "comparison of X-type products).
  - When you discover new companies not mentioned by the entrepreneur, bring those products to their attention and judge the reaction. If the entrepreneur was really unaware of clearly competitive products (unless they are very niche) that might be a red flag that they have not done enough homework on their own market.

11.5 *Diligence on Product and Technology*

11.5.1 USABILITY

At a minimum, you should get a thorough demo of the company's product (if it has one$^{\S 7.1}$). If it is a product that you can use yourself, then use it as much as you can even if you are not the target customer. Is it elegant and effective or confusing and buggy?

It is not uncommon for an entrepreneur to show a very polished demo of their product using a very specific scenario, and it may turn out that the product only works elegantly under quite specific constraints.

Let's say the startup you're considering has an app that finds adventure activities for travelers, and the demo shows someone going to Belize looking for a scuba diving trip. The demo shows five options with pricing information, and everything else you'd need to know. Great. Now you should try the app yourself and search for glacier walks in Iceland, rock climbing in Patagonia, whatever you can think of. Are the results just as good?

If the product is live in the marketplace, look for reviews. The Apple app store has reviews, as does the Android Play store. There are review sites for enterprise software as well, though it often takes longer for a startup's product to show up in those listings. When in doubt, just Google for reviews and often sites you have never heard of will have written about the app or service in question. Reading reviews is a great way to get a sense of whether actual users are happy with the product, where it falls short of expectations, and whether there are real limitations to how well it works.

11.5.2 TECHNOLOGY STACK

Hopefully you or someone on your diligence team has the skills to do some technical due diligence. Understand what technology choices they have made and why. How will they scale? If it is a hardware or manufacturing company you are considering investing in, then take a look at their manufacturing and/or prototyping facilities. Venture capitalists often hire technical experts to do thorough technical diligence and talk in depth to the company's engineering leader(s). If you do not have the requisite technical knowledge on your diligence team, consider asking a friend or colleague with the skills to help you.

It is beyond the scope of this book to do a deep dive on technology due diligence. It is common that the initial implementation of a product is a little rough around the edges because startup teams are trying to build a lot of functionality quickly. That said, in the case of a company with a software product there should be the capability, or at least a clear plan, for user scalability, meaning the ability to support 10X or 100X more users. There is nothing more heartbreaking than seeing a huge surge in demand for the company's product only to have the application or service collapse under the load. Even if you are not technical you can ask questions like "What will it take to support 10X your current user base?" The wonderful advantage the current startups have over those of years ago is that with modern web services like AWS, the answer in a properly architected system is often just more money.

11.5.3 REGULATORY COMPLIANCE

Depending on the company's product, there may be many regulatory requirements it needs to meet. That can vary from UL underwriting[79] to HIPAA compliance.[80] If you are staying within a domain you know well, you will likely know the regulatory compliance issues and can gauge the management team based on their approach to them. If you are not familiar with the regulatory compliance issues, make sure someone on your diligence team or perhaps your lawyer can help you.

There are some new compliance issues that have been introduced over the last few years around consumer privacy and the obligations they place on any companies that store consumer data. These include the EU's General Data Protection Regulation[81] and the California Consumer Privacy Act.[82]

11.6 *Diligence on Finances and Key Assumptions*

11.6.1 FINANCIAL MODEL

Every pitch deck has a financial projections slide showing that in 3–5 years the company will have millions or tens of millions of dollars in revenue and be profitable. Those projections come from a financial model built on a set of assumptions about growth rates, customer transaction size, customer acquisition costs, attrition rates, and others more specific to the type of business.[83]

The model and the assumptions will be very specific to the type of business. Especially in B2C businesses, the profitability will be very sensitive to some of those assumptions. Any of the pirate metrics mentioned above will likely have big impacts on profitability. The entrepreneur

---

79. https://en.wikipedia.org/wiki/UL_(safety_organization)

80. https://www.hhs.gov/hipaa/for-professionals/security/laws-regulations/index.html

81. https://en.wikipedia.org/wiki/General_Data_Protection_Regulation

82. https://en.wikipedia.org/wiki/California_Consumer_Privacy_Act

83. For example, for an ad revenue business, you might focus on page views per visit, while for a gaming business you care more about the percent of gamers who buy virtual products and the average price of those products; for freemium models you care about what percentage of customers upgrade from free to paid.

should be able to defend any critical assumptions in the model by point-
ing to comparable businesses. For B2B businesses, some of the critical
assumptions will be conversion rates in the sales pipeline we mentioned
above, attrition rates (how many customers don't renew their contracts),
length of the sales cycle (impacts growth rate and cost of customer acquisition), contract size, and how much revenue a single salesperson can generate.

Ask for a copy of the model and work with it until you understand what
the key drivers of growth and profitability are. Test the impact of the key
assumptions:

- What if the conversion rate of customers upgrading from free to paid
  is 2% instead of the assumed 5%? Does the business become wildly
  unprofitable?
- What if the transaction size is $50 instead of $100?
- What happens to profitability if the attrition rate is 15% a year instead
  of the 5% represented in the model?
- What if it takes on average six months to close a big customer instead
  of three?

♣ FOUNDER Another thing to check in a financial model is how the entrepreneurs are thinking about staff growth. Pete has seen B2B models where the
number of customers grows 100X over three years, but the operations and
support staff only double. If that seems optimistic to you too, you can plug
in a few more headcount to some of those functions, grow the engineering
staff to account for product complexity and support, and see how far out
that pushes profitability.

Many venture capitalists will build their own financial models from
scratch to make sure they understand the drivers. If you can't get the
model from the founders or it is too convoluted for you to be able to
test the assumptions, then you may want to build a simple one yourself.
Remember entrepreneurs may not be experts at financial modeling,
which is fine, but you don't want that to lead you to a poor investment
decision.

◇ IMPORTANT At the end of the day, it is important to keep in mind that three
or four-year financial models almost never pan out per the plan. The most
common scenario is that sales and/or profitability progress more slowly

than the plan projects. What you are checking for when doing diligence on these models is two primary things:

- Does the entrepreneur have a realistic idea about what will drive the unit economics (how much money does each customer make or lose for the company under a given set of assumptions) and what revenue level and cost structure are required to be profitable overall?
- If things do not turn out like the rosy assumptions in the model, does it just take slightly longer to become profitable, in which case it means the company has to raise more money than expected over time and you will have a lower return on your investment; or will it be a complete financial disaster requiring some change of course and much more risk?

11.6.2 FINANCIAL STATEMENTS

You should also look at a company's financial statements. For one thing, you want to make sure that they don't have a lot of debt that has to be paid or a large accounts payable list. If they owe tens of thousands of dollars to prior contractors for engineering or design or legal work, then your investment may go toward paying old debts rather than moving the company forward.

You may also discover that there were prior employees or founders whom you will need to dig into on the legal side.§12.3 You will want to make sure that the company has been paying any taxes, especially payroll taxes. Looking at the financial statements will also help you get a handle on the company's burn rate.

Burn rate is the amount of money a startup is spending every month. For a startup that is pre-revenue, this is considered the "monthly burn." For a startup with revenue, the burn rate is the monthly spend less any reasonably expected revenues.

◇ CAUTION If a company that has been around for a year or more and is not using the services of an accounting firm or has not engaged a part-time CFO or equivalent service, that can cause some heartburn on the part of angels. It may be difficult in such cases to get financial statements to understand where they stand in terms of any existing financial liabilities or to get a handle on their ongoing expenses. We will talk more about why this is important below in the following two sections.

11.6.3 RUNWAY

It is important to understand whether a company is about to run out of money or not—and, when you are putting new money in, how long that money will keep the company going.

In startup lingo, **runway** refers to how much time in months the company has before it runs out of cash, calculated by dividing the amount of money they have in the bank by the burn rate (the amount of money they spend each month). For example, if the company is spending $25K a month and has $100K in the bank, it has four months of runway left.

Raising money is very time-consuming, and a company should always raise enough to keep it going for at least a year, preferably 18–24 months. Due diligence on the financial statements should get you the figures you need. Keep in mind that the burn rate often increases after a company raises money. They may hire additional personnel, or the founders may start to take a small salary, or they may increase their marketing spend.

11.6.4 USE OF FUNDS

It is worth understanding how the company is planning to use the money it is raising in the current financing round. In the ideal scenario, that money is being used to pay for the existing team's salary, for hiring new engineers or sales people, to execute a marketing strategy, to file patents, to pay for ongoing office rent and for other key expenses. If that is the case, then you can run the burn rate calculation we talked about above with the existing expense level ramping up to the higher expense level if they are growing staff. This will give you the expected runway that the new financing is buying.

⚠ **DANGER** In the worst case scenario, the company has been deferring salaries, and accruing significant credit card and other debt, including running up accounts payable with its suppliers. If half the funds raised are going to pay existing debts, for example, then you will be buying half the runway you thought you were, and the company will soon be out raising money again.

❯ **EXAMPLE**

Pete was asked if he wanted to invest in a company where he knew one of the founders and had been following the company's progress for a while. It was a $750K fundraising round. When he dug into the documentation for the round, he was surprised to see that $450K was going to pay deferred salaries. Another $100K was to pay three months of component suppliers invoices. Pete politely passed on the round, and the company was out raising money again from its existing investors three months later.

Some amount of debt may be normal, and there are no hard and fast rules. Ideally, you don't want it to exceed a month's worth of expenses. If the company still has cash in the bank when you invest, then at least your investment will be used for moving the company forward.

⚑ FOUNDER Make sure you ask the founders whether they are taking a salary and whether that will change for them or any other employees when they raise this round. It is common that founders take no salaries very early on while they are bootstrapping, and then typically take a below-market salary after they raise an angel round. Founders typically have huge amounts of equity, and that will be their big reward if they are successful. That is how billionaires like Mark Zuckerberg and Jeff Bezos are made. Until they raise a significant amount of money, say $5–$10M, they should not be taking market rate salaries. Beware of any founder who expects you to pay for their $250K a year salary while they are taking angel investments. You want their equity to be their skin in the game. That said, not all founders have the same circumstances. A founder may be paying a mortgage and supporting a family, and it may be challenging for them to survive on a $75K salary. They may need $125K. That may be legitimate and should be a point of discussion and negotiation, and can be documented as part of the deal as appropriate.[84]

》 EXAMPLE

Pete was approached with a very early-stage deal—essentially two guys with an idea for something cool, and a bit of paperwork. They had no validation of the idea and no traction. In reviewing the business plan, Pete noticed that they were each planning on taking salaries of $150K from day one. The proposed investment was a $500K round. Essentially they wanted to be paid $300K to figure out if this idea had any legs. They were not putting in any of their own money, so in this case, the investors were taking all the risk,

---

84. There are a number of different ways to mechanically set the founder salaries. This can be done in a use of proceeds schedule, with an ongoing covenant that the salary won't be increased without two independent members of the board approving.

and the entrepreneurs have little or no skin in the game. Where would their sense of urgency come from?

If a founder(s) has spent $50K or $100K to get the company off the ground, should they expect to be paid back with investors' money? We would say "no." That is the cost of their initial 100% equity ownership. When they are raising money and valuing the company at $1M, they have already made a hypothetical 10–20X return on their investment.

11.7 *Don't Fall For Vanity Metrics*

⚠ DANGER Whether listening to a pitch or conducting due diligence, beware of vanity metrics.

> ❭ EXAMPLE
>
> Pete was doing due diligence on a consumer mobile app startup a few years ago that said in their angel pitch that they had achieved 30K downloads from the Apple App Store in their first week. That sounds impressive, but how many of those downloads turned into real engagement that could eventually be monetized? A few probing questions revealed that the founder knew one of the editors of the App Store and was able to get the app featured. It turns out that 30K downloads is pretty typical for a featured app, and that once that visibility was gone, the download rate fell precipitously. The entrepreneur was not lying, they were just touting a vanity metric. While downloads are necessary, they are not sufficient or directly indicative of potential profitability.

Vanity metrics are numbers that may sound exciting but don't translate in any direct way to the health of the business.[85] In a B2B scenario, a vanity metric would be how many people came by the sales booth at the conference. The meaningful metric is how many qualified sales leads came from the conference.

> ❭ EXAMPLE

---

85. Thinking about vanity metrics always reminds Joe of this old article: "The Surprisingly Large Cost of Telling Small Lies."[86]

86. https://boss.blogs.nytimes.com/2014/03/11/
   the-surprisingly-large-cost-of-telling-small-lies/

Pete invested very early (pre-launch) in a company that had locked down a vendor contract allowing them to be the sole consumer sales channel for a very desirable subscription mobile communications product. On one of the first investor reports, the company touted how many different states they were getting web traffic from. Not how many unique users were visiting the site, or the cost of that traffic, or the conversion rate to purchase. There are likely hundreds of web crawlers on the internet working continuously to visit and index every website. How many states the traffic came from means absolutely nothing. Even website traffic means nothing until you can convert it at a reliable rate to a registration or a transaction. One can always spend money to buy traffic to a website via paid advertising. What matters is the *cost of acquiring paying customers* and for how long they continue to pay.

12 Legal Due Diligence for Angel Investments

Legal due diligence refers to the process of reviewing a company's legal documents to ensure that the company has not made and is not making any legal errors that will put the investment at risk.

Legal due diligence is separate and distinct from business due diligence; its purpose is to make sure that there is no reason from a legal perspective that an investment should not proceed. You typically turn to legal due diligence after you have completed your initial business due diligence and have come to terms on the transaction.

Should you hire a lawyer to help you with legal due diligence? This depends a lot on the circumstances of the company you intend to invest in, and your own comfort level. We discuss when it might be appropriate to hire a lawyer a bit later§13—whether or not you do, it's wise for the person making the investment to have some familiary with the topics and issues that might need to be looked into during this stage.

You may find it helpful to take a look at the legal and financial due diligence checklist[87] from the Angel Capital Association.

---

87. https://www.angelcapitalassociation.org/data/Documents/Resources/
AngelCapitalEducation/Angel_Guidebook_-_Due%20Diligence_Checklist.pdf?rev=C7C4

12.1 *Legal Diligence on Corporate Formation and Stock Documents*

It is a typical part of legal due diligence to review a company's charter documents.

In the corporate context, **charter documents** are a company's articles or certificate of incorporation, bylaws, and any other corporate agreements, such as shareholder agreements, voting agreements, and so on.

⚠ DANGER　Make sure the company is in "good standing"—that is, the company has not let its corporate charter lapse. You can usually find out if a company is in good standing by reviewing the Secretary of State's website in the state in which the company is formed. Similarly, if you wanted to, you can check that the company has the appropriate business licenses.

12.1.1 WHERE IS THE COMPANY INCORPORATED?

Most startups incorporate in Delaware as C corporations, if not in the state in which they are headquartered. Delaware is a common choice because of its corporate law history and business-friendly laws.[88] In fact, many VC firms require that companies be incorporated in Delaware or reincorporate[89] as a Delaware company.

⚠ DANGER　Beware of companies that are incorporated in places other than either Delaware or their home state. For example, if a company is headquartered in California but incorporated in Nevada, it might be a red flag that the corporation is trying to avoid California income tax. State taxes do not depend on where you are incorporated, and so this is a fruitless strategy. Companies incorporated in unusual places may also incur additional legal cost and expense as a result of their bespoke domicile choice.

12.1.2 CAP TABLE AND STOCK LEDGER

Cap tables are critical in understanding a business.

The **capitalization table (or cap table)**, is a document showing each person who owns an interest in the company. Usually this is broken out by the name of each equity holder, and shows what type of equity instruments they hold. It is set up as a ledger, so that all share issuances and

---

88. https://www.firstbase.io/blog/why-do-most-startups-incorporate-in-delaware
89. http://www.calstartuplawfirm.com/business-lawyer-blog/
reincorporation-in-delaware-conversion-reverse-merger.php

transfers can be tracked. Many companies use Excel or services like Carta to keep their capitalization table. They will create a worksheet for each type of equity security outstanding, such as common stock, Series A Preferred Stock, Series B Preferred Stock, and so on, including convertible debt and equity instruments that are issued. Included in the cap table is the **stock ledger**, showing all issuances of equity from the company to equity holders and all transfers of equity from one equity holder to another. There may be multiple ledgers for each type of stock or convertible security the company has ever issued.

⚡ FOUNDER The company's cap table should show you everything having to do with the equity structure of the company—not just who owns how many shares, and what type of shares they own. If the company has issued convertible notes, there should be a note ledger; if the company has issued SAFEs, there should be a SAFE ledger. Done correctly, the ledgers will tell the complete story of the company's life, including all of the company's stock issuances from inception, and all of the stock transfers of all shareholders, for the entire life of the company. For example, the first entry on the stock ledger would be the company's first stock issuance, to the founder who received stock certificate number 1.

It can be enlightening to see how the company has allocated stock among its founders. You can also get insight into whether all the key personnel are adequately incentivized.

◇ CAUTION One cause for concern may be a large amount of stock that is owned by an early founder or employee who is no longer with the company. This suggests that the company may not have had a stock vesting plan in place for founders early on. You will want to make sure at a minimum anyone who has already left has signed an IP Assignment Agreement. We'll discuss employee issues later.§12.3.4

⚠ DANGER If the company has not maintained its cap table appropriately, it is a red flag. You need to know how much of the company you are going to own after you invest. You can't know this unless the company's cap table is complete and correct and reflects all outstanding ownership. Many, many companies have wound up in protracted and expensive lawsuits because they did not carefully document stock ownership, and then someone made a claim that they were owed a certain amount of the equity of the company.

12.1.3 SECURITIES LAW COMPLIANCE

⚜ FOUNDER Every time a company issues stock or options or warrants to anyone, it has to either register the securities with the SEC or a state securities regulator (a very expensive process), or it has to find an exemption from registration, as we discussed in Fundraising and Securities Law.§8.2 In addition to those exemptions used to raise money from investors, there are a number of exemptions available to companies when it comes to giving stock or options to employees, but they each come with their own limitations and conditions.

> **❯ EXAMPLE**
>
> If a company issues stock options to employees, it should comply with federal securities Rule 701 with respect to those option issuances. Rule 701 has mathematical limitations on how many options can be granted to services providers during any 12-month period. A company issuing options to employees also has to comply with state securities law requirements, and may have to make a filing with a state securities administrator (as is required in California, for example).

Ideally, the investor would learn in diligence that the company is not self-administering its stock option plan, but relying on competent legal counsel to administer the plan.

⚠ DANGER If a company has issued securities for which no exemption is available, the company may have to make a rescission offer to the recipient of the securities. This can be true even if the recipients of the securities didn't pay anything to receive them (as is the case for optionees). This is a very expensive and time-consuming thing you never want to see one of your portfolio companies go through.

⚠ DANGER If a company has not been working with competent securities counsel, this is a red flag. The company may have issued securities to prior investors or service providers that might have to be rescinded, with the money you invest funding those repurchases.

12.2 *Legal Diligence on Stock Options and Vesting*

12.2.1 COMPENSATORY EQUITY AWARDS

One of the ways startups conserve cash and attract talent is to pay employees lower cash salaries but reward the risk they're taking on the startup by promising them a portion of ownership in the company—equity. Typically, employees are not given ownership directly, but the option to purchase stock in the company, an option that can be exercised not right away but over time, referred to as vesting.

Equity can be awarded in different ways, most typically through stock options, but also through warrants and restricted stock awards.[90]

Compensatory equity awards are awards of stock, options, restricted stock units, and similar awards issued to service providers of a company. Under the securities laws, companies may issue compensatory equity to service providers without those service providers being accredited if they comply with another exemption, such as Rule 701.

⚘ FOUNDER You will want to make sure that if you are investing in a company that is granting compensatory equity awards, typically in the form of stock options to employees and contractors, that they are doing so correctly. All option grants must be approved by the Board, and priced[§19.1] at the time of board approval. To avoid adverse tax consequences to the optionee (in the case of options), the options must be priced at no less than fair market value as of the date of grant. Companies do not have to obtain independent third party valuations of their common stock, but if they do, the burden of proof is on the IRS to challenge a valuation. For this reason, many companies start obtaining third party valuations of their common stock for option grant purposes as soon as they have closed their first fixed price financing. As mentioned above, they should all be recorded in the stock or options ledger and included in the cap table.

12.2.2 FOUNDER VESTING

Founder vesting refers to a legal mechanism whereby founders have to continue to provide services for some period of time or have their shares potentially repurchased by the company. Founder vesting may follow a similar pattern to employee vesting, where the founder gains permanent

---

90. Read more about the different kinds of equity and how it all works in the *Holloway Guide to Equity Compensation.*[91]

91. https://www.holloway.com/g/equity-compensation

ownership of their stock over the course of typically three or four years, with potentially a one-year mark for 25% ownership and monthly increases thereafter.

☆ FOUNDER Since founders have typically purchased their stock up front as part of the corporate formation, the mechanism for founder vesting is typically a repurchase right of the shares by the company for the lesser of the fair market value of the shares or the price they paid for them. Since founders usually acquire their shares for a very small purchase price (a tenth or hundredth of a penny per share), being at risk of having those shares repurchased at the price is effectively a forfeiture condition.

As an investor, you will want the founders as well as the employees to be on a vesting schedule.

In the majority of cases, vesting occurs incrementally over time, according to a **vesting schedule**. A person vests only while they work for the company. If the person quits or is terminated immediately, they get no equity, and if they stay for years, they'll get most or all of it.[92]

Let's run through an example of why this is important.

》 EXAMPLE

Suppose a company has three founders. When the company was founded, each founder owned a third of the company, or 1M shares each. What happens if, after you invest your money, one of the founders leaves? Does that founder continue to own 1M shares? That might be painful for both you as an investor and the other co-founders, especially if that founder's expertise is going to have to be replaced by another founder who is going to want to receive 1M shares (this will dilute the value of the shares you and the remaining co-founders hold, an issue we'll discuss in detail).

How do you solve this problem? Make sure the company has a repurchase right to buy back unvested shares at the lower of the cost or fair market value of the shares, which will lapse over a service-based vesting period. In other words, make sure founders are on a vesting schedule.

You would prefer companies you invest in to have provisions in their founder stock repurchase agreements that cause unvested shares to be

---

92. This definition comes from the *Holloway Guide to Raising Venture Capital.*[93]

93. https://www.holloway.com/g/venture-capital/about

"automatically" repurchased unless the company takes an affirmative action to not repurchase them.

⚡ CONFUSION If you are investing in a company and are insisting on founder vesting, be careful to give some thought as to who will enforce these provisions against the company when and if they come due. For example, suppose you are investing in a "solopreneur"—your founder vesting agreement may as a practical matter not be meaningful if it is the founder who has to enforce it against him or herself.

12.2.3 **THE FULLY VESTED FOUNDER**

If you have founders whose shares were issued vested, or who have already vested, or have substantially vested, you can re-start their vesting schedule by having them execute a new vesting agreement.

> ⟩ EXAMPLE
>
> Two founders set up a legal corporate entity early in their work and have been pursuing a startup idea for three years. They have finally made enough progress to go out and seek their first outside funding. If they had put themselves on a four-year vesting schedule, they would be 75% vested. As an investor in a very early-stage company with two key founders, you want to make sure that they are motivated to stick around going forward. If the vesting schedule is not addressed, one founder could leave the day after the investment with a substantial portion of the company.

⚡ FOUNDER Investors may require that vesting on founders' shares be reset at the time of the investment. The reason for this is that investors might not want founders who are fully vested or nearly fully vested to lose motivation for staying in the company long-term. This is accomplished by having the founders execute a new Founder Stock Vesting Agreement, which gives the company the right to repurchase the unvested shares at the lesser of fair market value or the founder's cost, which less of FMV or at-cost repurchase right lapses over the vesting period. This is not problematic from a tax point of view for the founders involved. In fact, the Internal Revenue Service has issued guidance that in some circumstances it is not even necessary for founders in this situation to file Section 83(b) elections,[94] since they will have already owned the shares when the vesting conditions were placed on them.[95]

⚜ FOUNDER Founders may resist having their vesting schedules reset. From their perspective, they have worked hard for those three years (in the above example), and in many cases have invested their own money or foregone salary. Founder vesting will then become a point of negotiation and will likely be incorporated in the term sheet.

12.2.4 EMPLOYEE VESTING

Employee vesting refers to vesting on employee stock option grants. Sometimes investors will require that all employee option grants have to vest over a specified schedule (such as monthly over a 48-month period, but with a one-year cliff), unless approval is given by the investor's designee on the board or a majority of the investors.

All employees should be on vesting agreements for the stock or stock options that are part of their compensation. The most typical vesting schedule is four years with 25% vested after the first year of employment, often referred to as the one-year cliff, with vesting monthly after the first year.

12.2.5 CHANGE OF CONTROL VESTING

◇ CAUTION Sometimes companies provide in their documents that upon a sale of a company, holders of unvested shares or unvested options have their vesting accelerated. This is favorable for employees, but from an investor perspective you would want to make sure that such a program is well thought through.

> **⟩ EXAMPLE**
>
> A startup wants to hire an experienced enterprise software sales executive. That executive is willing to take the significant risk of joining this early startup because she is being offered 5% of the equity. If the company gets acquired in a year, and she gets fired because the acquirer does not need another head of sales, she will have only 1.25% of the equity. Being a savvy salesperson, she negotiates an acceleration provision in her employee agreement, that if

---

94. https://www.holloway.com/g/equity-compensation/sections/83b-elections

95. https://web.archive.org/web/20200218002537/www.startuplawblog.com/2009/04/13/imposition-of-vesting-on-stock-in-a-financing/

the company gets acquired, she vests 50% of her unvested stock, and if within three months she gets fired by the acquirer for no cause or is asked to move more than 100 miles away, she vests the rest immediately. Without these provisions, the sales executive may not be excited about an acquisition opportunity that is otherwise good for the startup and its investors.

◇ CAUTION You will want to look out for this in your due diligence. This makes a company more expensive for another company to buy, because the buyer company will have to re-up the equity incentive of the workers. This re-upping may result in the buyer reducing the amount of consideration paid to the target company stockholders.

There are two types of change of control vesting:

- single trigger acceleration
- double trigger acceleration

Single trigger acceleration is 100% vesting upon one event—the change of control transaction. **Double trigger acceleration** is acceleration of vesting upon the occurrence of two events:

- a change of control, or
- the termination of the founder without "cause," and sometimes if the founder quits for "good reason" within a certain period of time (such as 12–18 months) after the change of control.

As an investor, you would prefer "double trigger" acceleration because this way the buyer of the company will not have to re-up the continuing employees on equity grants to the same degree it otherwise might if all of the continuing employees had their vesting equity fully vested on the sale.

The example above has both a single trigger and a double trigger provision. What should you do? You can try to negotiate aspects of that employee agreement as part of the investment. This is the "golden rule" at work. She who has the gold, rules.

12.3 *Legal Diligence on Other Founder, Board of Directors, and Employee Issues*

12.3.1 KEY CORPORATE FORMATION DOCUMENTS

✻ FOUNDER It is not uncommon for founders to form companies themselves, without any legal assistance. In almost all situations this means the founders have missed something. It is not uncommon for founders who try to do it themselves to not timely file 83(b) elections, fail to adopt bylaws, fail to execute stock purchase agreements at all, and other mishaps.

If you are reviewing the corporate documents for a startup, you should see at least the following documents:

- Certificate of Incorporation, or Articles of Incorporation
- Bylaws
- Organizational Consent of the Initial Directors of the Corporation
- Consent of Incorporator (if the Articles or Certificate of Incorporation was signed by the incorporator)
- Stock Purchase Agreements for each subscriber to the company's shares
- Intellectual Property assignments for each founder
- Equity Incentive Plan or Stock Option Plan (if the company has adopted one)
- copies of Section 83(b) elections[96] the founders filed with the IRS, if the founders' shares were subject to vesting

12.3.2 ISSUES WITH FOUNDERS

A few key items to add to your legal due diligence checklist:

- **Key person life insurance.** What if you invest in a company where one founder is key to the company's business, such that if the founder died or became disabled your investment would suffer a serious setback? What should you do to protect yourself? Consider requiring the company to buy key person life insurance. You could require the company not only to buy the insurance, but require it to expend the insurance proceeds redeeming the investors' shares if the founder died.

---

96. https://www.holloway.com/g/equity-compensation/sections/83b-elections

- **Conflicts of interest in founder compensation.** If you are going to invest in a company, it is a good idea to think about how the founders are going to be compensated. Before an outside investment, many founders are taking no salary. You should have a conversation with the founders about when they expect to take a salary and how much before you invest. This is part of the use of funds$^{\S11.6.4}$ review. In order to be able to insure that founder compensation stays within the expectations set between you and the founders, you may want to require in your investment documents that at least two independent directors or the majority of the independent shareholders review and approve conflicted party transactions.

- **Lack of ownership.** You want to make sure that the founder or founders are motivated to continue to be committed to the enterprise. If the founder gets too highly diluted (check the cap table) too early on, they may decide that there is not enough upside to keep grinding it out for little salary and long hours. This can happen if the company has to raise too much money early on before they can justify an increase in valuation.

12.3.3 ISSUES WITH BOARD OF DIRECTORS AND CONTROL PROVISIONS

We discuss boards of directors in detail in Boards and Advisory Roles.^{§26} For the purposes of creating a legal due diligence checklist, here are the key things to look out for:

- **Board of directors size.** The board of a very early startup should be small. A board of directors that is too big (anything greater than five members is unusual) means that the representative of the investors in a particular round may have less influence over important issues that come before the board; a large board also makes it hard to schedule meetings, which may be monthly rather than quarterly for early-stage companies.

- **Board of directors makeup.** Boards make extremely important decisions for the company, and if the board of directors is made up of the founders and their friends, that might make you nervous. Investors should be well-represented on the board, and ideally there would be one or more independent board members who both sides respect. Founders who control the company and show no ability to seek out and heed the advice of others are a warning sign.

- **Unusual control provision.** Google (now Alphabet) and Facebook are two examples of large companies in which the founders still have a very high degree of control, because they have engineered special classes of stock that give them outsized voting rights.[97] Many critical corporate transactions typically require stockholder approval (including approving the board of directors) so beware of any company that has an irregular voting, shareholder or proxy agreement that gives one individual near total authority over the affairs of a company.

12.3.4 **EMPLOYEE CATEGORIZATION AND AGREEMENTS**

Employee Categorization

◇ CAUTION   It can be tempting for early-stage companies to try to save money on payroll taxes by categorizing employees as independent contractors. This can result in problems. In general, if a person works only for one company and they work physically at that company every day and their boss is an employee and directs their work, then they will likely be considered an employee by the taxing authorities and not an independent contractor. Any improperly classified independent contractors can create a tax liability for the company. Make sure to ask the entrepreneur who is an employee and who is a contractor. While use of some contractors is normal, beware of companies where the majority of the team working at the office are classified as contractors.

Offer Letters, Employment Agreements

All employees should have signed an offer letter or employment agreement, and also an IP assignment agreement and a confidentiality or non-disclosure agreement.

The **intellectual property assignment agreement (or IP assignment agreement)** ensures that all the work produced by the employee belongs to the company, with customary exclusions that anything they do on their own time with their own equipment belongs to them, as long as it is not directly related to the business of the company. There is usually an addendum where the employee lists any of their own prior inventions or IP that they want excluded from the assignment.

---

97. https://www.vox.com/technology/2018/11/19/18099011/
mark-zuckerberg-facebook-stock-nyt-wsj

⚠ DANGER IP assignment is really important, because you don't want a key employee to leave and take their work, including all their code, to a competitor or their own startup. Founders should have similar agreements assigning their relevant work that was done before the startup was legally formed to the startup.

Employment agreements should also make it clear that employment is "at will," meaning that they can be terminated at any time.

A **confidentiality agreement (or non-disclosure agreement of NDA)** prevents employees from discussing information pertaining to their work at the company, including the status of the company or its customers. The confidentiality agreement is typically included as part of an employment agreement.

Contractors Agreements

It is very common for startups to use contractors for all kinds of services like website or app design or building, logo design, software development, and so on. Since they are scrappy and generally preserving cash, many of these arrangements may be informal. Check that the agreements have the following provisions:

- Work-for-hire, meaning that all rights to the work belong to the company once the contractor has been paid
- Confidentiality or Non-disclosure Agreement
- Intellectual Property Assignment or Proprietary Rights Agreement

If there are no written agreements or those agreements lack key provisions, you can ask the entrepreneur to get them in place or amended before closing the investment.

Former Employees

⬦ **CAUTION** Make sure to ask about any founders or employees who are no longer with the company. If the company is successful, there is a tremendous incentive for those involved early on to make a claim. Many expensive lawsuits have arisen from former early employees who might have been promised stock or who had not vested their stock before they were terminated or quit. Here are some questions to ask:

- Did the ex-employees sign IP assignment agreements and NDAs? Typically this would be a single agreement called a Proprietary Information Assignment Agreement or similar.
- Are any severance payments owed?
- Are there signed termination agreements? An important part of a severance or termination agreement is a release by the former employee of the company of any claims for any additional compensation. It is painful to see a portfolio company pay a severance to a former employee and still get sued for some bogus wrongful discharge claim. This is an unforced error.
- Were there other advisors or people who contributed to the early product or company's intellectual property who never signed on formally but might have a claim?

Deferred Salaries

Check that a company is not carrying accrued or deferred salaries on its balance sheet. It is a good idea to ask the founders if they have any unpaid compensation. Founders are not necessarily accounting experts, and they may not have hired an accounting or CFO equivalent service.

⬦ **CAUTION** Look out for founders who intend to use almost the entire proceeds of the offering to pay themselves back for foregone salaries or unreimbursed expenses or other accrued liabilities; as an investor, you usually want to fund growth, not pre-existing liabilities. This can also arise when a company has already accepted funds to provide a good or service at a later date. Many Kickstarter campaigns have turned into liabilities investors do not want to fund, for example.

12.4 *Legal Diligence on Company Tax Issues*

Most people procrastinate on their taxes. Entrepreneurs are busier than most of us, building a company and a product and hiring and selling and raising money. With a small team, there may be no one focused on finances and accounting and taxes. Entrepreneurs tend to focus on how much cash they have and how quickly they are burning through it.

◇ **CAUTION** That said, you don't want a big chunk of your investment going to pay taxes owed. Even if the company has no revenue, it may still need to file tax returns; and even if it is not making a profit, sales and payroll taxes still accrue.

☀ **FOUNDER** We discuss the various corporate forms (C-corp, S-corp, LLC) and the tax implications in detail[§24] (you can also visit Appendix B[§31] for further information on the differences between these entities, which will be helpful for founders). You can check in the public record whether a company has tax liens filed against it (or any other lawsuits). But here are the general tax issues to look into as part of your legal due diligence:

- **Section 83(b) elections.**[98] The founders should have given the company copies of their filed elections.
- **Federal tax returns.** If a company forms a state law corporation, they have a federal tax return filing obligation that first year, regardless of whether they have any income. This is the same with a multi-member LLC. There are penalties for failure to file. Make sure you know: What is the tax status of the company? C corporation? S corporation? Limited liability company taxed as a partnership? Limited liability company taxed as an S corporation?
- **State income taxes.** In what state(s) does the company pay income tax?
- **State sales taxes.** With respect to which states does the company collect and remit sales tax? (Failure to collect and remit sales taxes can add up to a large liability in a short period of time, and it is not uncommon for companies to fall out of compliance with sales tax collect and remit requirements.)
- **Payroll taxes.** Payroll taxes in general are worth digging into. Does the company use a payroll service so that you can feel assured that

---

98. https://www.holloway.com/g/equity-compensation/sections/83b-elections

employment tax withholding has been taken care of? Payroll taxes are especially scary because directors and officers can be personally responsible for them in certain circumstances. If they are not doing so already, insist that the company use ADP or a similar service for payroll.

> **❯ EXAMPLE**
>
> A company did not hire a payroll service provider that would have refused to process payroll unless the company gave them sufficient cash to pay the income and employment tax withholding to the IRS. Instead, the company was trying to process its own payroll. The CEO did not remit to the IRS the amounts of the income and employment tax withholding the company was required to remit by law. The board had to fire the CEO, and the company ultimately failed from this financial setback.

13 Retaining a Lawyer

Our goal with this book is *not* to make you a legal expert such that you don't ever need to hire a lawyer. Our goal is to give you enough background and context such that your time with a lawyer is efficient.

We will discuss for which parts of the investment process you or your lead investor would engage legal counsel, and additional considerations if you are investing alone. If you or your group of investors engage legal counsel for the investment, it is typical that the same lawyer would review the term sheet, any legal due diligence issues that you choose to pass on to them, and that they would create and/or review the definitive documents to make sure that they are consistent with the term sheet terms and are otherwise in proper legal form.

13.1 *When In the Process To Engage a Lawyer*

The lead investor typically makes the decision on when to bring in legal counsel and who to hire to represent the investors. They will also lead the negotiation over who pays for legal fees to document the deal. The sections below are useful for the scenario in which you are responsible for, or have influence in, deciding when to bring in an attorney.

13.1.1 FOR HIGH LEVEL DEAL TERMS

When you are first introduced to an angel investing opportunity via a pitch, you will likely get a very high-level summary of the proposed investing terms from the entrepreneur, such as:

- "We're raising $1M in a Series Seed on a pre-money valuation of $3M," or
- "We're raising $400K in convertible notes with a 20% discount and $3M cap."

Once you've read through Part III: Financings and Term Sheets, you will know what these terms mean and you can negotiate the pre-money valuation or the discount on a note without the help of a lawyer.

If instead you get a deal that does not look like one of the common forms that we describe in Part III, you might want to seek the advice of a lawyer to better understand what you are dealing with and determine whether it can be structured as something more familiar. As mentioned early on, you may save a lot of time and legal expense if you bring in a lawyer to help architect the deal.

13.1.2 FOR TERM SHEET NEGOTIATION

Typically, if you (alone or as a group) and the entrepreneur agree on the top-level terms like the amount and the form of financing, the real action starts with the term sheet. Because angel groups often have forms for the most common term sheet types[99] and experienced lead investors within the group, it is common to get to a final term sheet without needing to engage counsel.

That said, it is often worth having the attorney who is going to be engaged in drafting the definitive documents review the term sheet, since they need to be comfortable expressing the agreed terms across a number of legal documents. Because term sheets are short and concise, it should not cost a lot to have a competent attorney review one (typically less than

---

99. The Alliance of Angels provides a model term sheet for preferred stock[100] and convertible note[101] financings.

100. https://www.allianceofangels.com/wp-content/uploads/2015/11/pdf1.pdf

101. https://www.allianceofangels.com/wp-content/uploads/2015/11/pdf-2.pdf

$1K). One of the benefits of working with an experienced attorney who specializes in early-stage investment transactions is that they can give you a sense of what terms are typical or unusual or highly favorable to one party. They can also help you craft rights that can mitigate legal and financial risks that you might be particularly concerned about for a specific investment. As you can imagine, legal time (and money) spent in the term sheet negotiation is usually much more efficient than trying to change terms once the definitive documents are being negotiated.

13.1.3 FOR LEGAL DUE DILIGENCE

Whether you (as a group or individual) want to engage a lawyer for legal due diligence depends in large part on the history of the company you are considering investing in.

There are some scenarios in which you may *not* need to hire a lawyer for legal due diligence. If a company has just come out of an accelerator that takes an ownership stake as part of the program, or if the company has completed a prior financing round with competent investors who had skilled counsel, theoretically there is much less need to dig in deep on legal due diligence. Accelerators and incubators will typically clean up any pre-existing corporate legal issues as part of taking their own equity interest.

Similarly, if a company has worked with experienced legal counsel from the start, that should give you confidence that corporate matters are properly documented. In many cities there are law firms that will provide entrepreneurs with attractive packages of corporate formation documents, employee agreements, et cetera, and even act as secretary at board meetings. They provide this service at low cost as a loss leader, an investment in an ongoing relationship. They start to make their money when the entrepreneurs raise financing that has to be documented.

If neither of the above scenarios is true, remember that entrepreneurs are scrappy by nature, and legal counsel is typically expensive. So, if the startup has not worked with a competent law firm consistently, or if there are elements of a messy background you become aware of, you'll want to have legal counsel review the company's situation and standing.

> ⟩ EXAMPLE

A company has been around for years and started out as an LLC, before becoming a Delaware C Corp. Some initial founders have left, and at some point the company sold off some intellectual property to raise money. They have raised some money in the past in the form of convertible notes from friends and family, and while the notes have expired, the investors are "patient." They promised some equity to some former advisors and an early contract developer, but it was never properly papered because they were bootstrapping.

Any one of the details in this scenario is not as rare as you might think. Remember, good entrepreneurs are determined and will find a way to keep going despite obstacles. While it would be highly advisable to hire an attorney to review the company's history in the above situation, you have a practical difficulty. If the company has not spent money on legal services along the way, playing catch up and cleaning things up that weren't done right in the first place can be very time-consuming and expensive. This is one reason to look for companies that have hired able and competent counsel and have taken the time to do things correctly.

Another potentially messy scenario, which is also not uncommon, is when a startup spins out of an existing business, having leveraged the earlier business's employees and resources to develop the startup's idea and assets. Pete has personal experience with this scenario, and raising the first institutional round for the spun-out startup required extensive legal documentation of the separation of the assets from the parent company and agreements with many of the employees of the earlier business to document their respective contributions, assignments, and ownership of the new business.

13.1.4 FOR DEFINITIVE DOCUMENT NEGOTIATION AND REVIEW

With the exception of perhaps a simple individual convertible note, as mentioned above, the lead investor will almost always have a lawyer representing the investors when the definitive documents are being negotiated and drafted. Often the lead investor will prefer to have their attorney draft the definitive documents. If you are investing alone, we recommend that you have a lawyer review the documents to insure that they accurately represent the terms negotiated in the term sheet.

13.2 *Should You Retain Your Own Lawyer?*

Whether you should engage your own lawyer depends on a number of factors, including your level of experience, how much you are investing, and the context in which you are investing.

13.2.1 INVESTING AS PART OF A GROUP

If you are investing as part of a group of experienced angel investors, and someone else in the group is the "lead" in performing due diligence and negotiating deal terms, then it is likely that you do not need your own lawyer. The group of angels with whom you are investing should have a lawyer representing their interests collectively, including yours. Angel groups often work with the same law firm for many deals, and so they usually have high confidence in that firm's skills and experience.

In addition to managing deal terms, the lead investor in the group will play a role in assessing the need for and organizing any legal due diligence$^{\S 12}$ on the company. If you have any specific concerns regarding legal due diligence, whether that involves corporate formation,$^{\S 12.1}$ governance,$^{\S 12.3}$ or intellectual property rights, you can bring those concerns to the lead investor. If you do not feel your concerns are being adequately addressed, you can hire your own attorney to do a review.

That said, if you have a lot of money at stake or you do not have complete confidence in the law firm or individual lawyer representing you and your co-investors, then you can hire your own attorney (at your own expense) to review the documents for you. It would create an awkward dynamic, however, if your lawyer was also negotiating directly with the entrepreneur. You might instead hear the advice of your lawyer where it differs from the way the deal is being negotiated and documented, and bring it to the attention of your lead investor.

13.2.2 INVESTING SOLO

If you are investing on your own, especially if you are fairly new to angel investing, it is highly recommended that you use a qualified attorney with experience in early-stage investments to represent your interests.

◇ IMPORTANT   It's common when investing solo to do so through a convertible note. You may find an opportunity to invest in an exciting company via a convertible note with rewards for being an early investor. Convertible notes can be quite straightforward, but as we discuss in the section on the topic,[15] a properly drafted note which covers all of the potential scenarios of acquisition, default, non-qualified financing, and so on can become quite complex. If you have not made a similar convertible note investment before, we would recommend that you have a lawyer review the note. You can negotiate directly with the entrepreneur based on your knowledge of the general deal terms[18] while making it clear to the entrepreneur that you will still have your lawyer review it after you have come to general agreement on terms. A legal review of a convertible note should not be expensive.

> ⟩ EXAMPLE

Pete is a scrappy investor (having been a scrappy entrepreneur), and he came across an opportunity to invest early in a startup that had just come out of an accelerator. Pete did his business due diligence of this very early-stage company and relied on the reputation of the accelerator and the major law firm that it used for all of the companies in its class to give him confidence that no legal counsel was required for the legal due diligence. He also used a very standard two-page convertible note term sheet with an early investor preference and so was able to complete his $25K investment without incurring legal fees for himself.

- We do not suggest that you do this lightly or until you have had some experience investing. That company went on to do a priced round with an angel group and a local VC. As a warning, after that later investment round, Pete discovered that the CEO had hired a number of new employees with the money he raised, and they were all on the books as contractors to avoid employment taxes. The point is that when the company is young, just two or three founders, and it has been properly set up with reputable and competent counsel, there is much less legal concern. As the company grows, adds staff, and so on, the need for diligence grows.

13.2.3 INVESTING ALONGSIDE A LEAD INVESTOR

Another common scenario is that you are investing in a deal as a solo investor alongside an angel group or VC. The lead investor might be a VC or other institutional investor or another angel investor. You generally benefit from following their lead (figuratively and literally) in this scenario, with a couple of important caveats:

- **Major vs. non-major investors.** A "major investor" is usually defined as someone investing above a certain amount of money, depending on the amount the company is raising (in a $2M deal, major investors might be those investing $250K or $500K, for example). They may get certain rights that non-major investors do not get, such as information rights and pro rata participation rights. Review carefully any mention of rights that apply only to major investors.
- **Non-participation penalties (pay-to-play provisions).** Be aware of any terms that penalize investors who do not step up to the next round pro-rata (commonly referred to as pay-to-play provisions). You may not have the resources to participate in future investment rounds for a company. Follow-on rounds in companies that are succeeding is part of the institutional investment model, and so those institutional investors may be motivated to capture a bigger share of their winners at your expense.

You always have the right to have your own attorney review any documents at your own expense. Use your own judgment as to how sophisticated your co-investors are and whether or not your interests are aligned in all cases. If you do hire your own lawyer, be tactful as to how your lawyer interacts with the lead's attorney. In good times and bad, you are going to want a good relationship with your co-investors.

13.2.4 SIDE LETTER AGREEMENT

Some very active angel investors have terms and/or rights that they want to have in any deal. For example, they may feel that they don't want to make any investment in which they don't have the right to get quarterly financial statements from the company (information rights). Or they have been burned with other investors getting better terms, and they won't do deals in which someone else who is investing at the same time can get a better deal (most favored nation clause). Rather than arguing with the lead investor as to whether they should be considered a "major investor" and get information rights, for example, they have a side letter prepared to accompany almost all of their investments.

The **side letter (or side letter agreement)** is an agreement between an investor and the company in which the company agrees to provide the investor with certain rights that are not otherwise present in the investment documents. This side letter usually includes terms like information rights, pro rata rights, and a most favored nations clause.

Assuming that the company is willing to sign a side letter agreement, the investor now has assurance that they have the terms that they specifically care about, whether or not the lead investor worked to secure them those rights.

We have included in a robust investor side letter in the appendix.$^{\S30.8}$

13.3 *Managing Your Lawyer And Your Legal Bill*

13.3.1 SHOULD THE COMPANY REIMBURSE YOUR LEGAL FEES?

If investing in a group, it is not uncommon for the lead investor to ask the company to reimburse its reasonable attorneys' fees, subject to a cap. This gets more common the larger the size of the round. Venture capital funds almost always have companies reimburse their reasonable attorneys' fees. Series A rounds very often have a fee reimbursement provision for the investors. It is less common in Series Seed rounds or convertible debt or equity rounds. That said, the Series Seed Documents[102] is a commonly used set of fixed-price financing documents in early-stage investing; and it provides that the company will reimburse $10K in legal fees. The more you are investing, either individually or as a group, the more comfortable you should feel asking for this provision. If you are investing $500K, definitely ask.

13.3.2 MITIGATING RISK WHEN USING A LAWYER

Even if you don't ask the company to reimburse your reasonable attorneys' fees, or if you ask and the company declines, that doesn't mean you should not use a lawyer. The trick is to use a lawyer intelligently so that you do not unnecessarily run up legal fees or upset the deal.

---

102. https://www.seriesseed.com/

⚠ **DANGER** When you are using a lawyer, your risks include:

- You might incur much more in legal fees than you reasonably expect.
- Your lawyer might make unreasonable demands of the entrepreneurs, putting you at odds with the company, and jeopardizing your chance to make the investment.

How can you minimize these risks? With regard to fees, ask the lawyer to cap their fees. Get them to agree in writing that their fees for reviewing the legal documents will not exceed a set amount. With regard to the second risk, control the communications. Instead of having your lawyer communicate comments to the company, have your lawyer give you the comments. Then you can decide which comments to pass along to the company, or how to present them.

◇ **IMPORTANT** The best legal comments are the ones that your lawyer can easily explain the underlying rationale for. If you can't understand your lawyer's comments, and why he or she is asking for certain changes, ask for a clear explanation from them so that you can evaluate whether to press for the change in the legal documents or not.

13.3.3 HOW TO FIND A LAWYER

The best way to find a lawyer in your community who is very practiced in the early-stage company space is to ask fellow angel investors whom they like to work with. If you don't have a network of fellow angel investors yet, look up your local angel groups and reach out to them for recommendations. You could also ask company founders which lawyers they have heard are good in the community.[103] If there is a dearth of local legal talent working on startup deals, you might have to find someone to work with remotely in a bigger city in your state. Every state has angel groups, so you will always have a place to start your research on an experienced attorney.

⚠ **DANGER** Working with a lawyer who is not really practiced in early-stage investment is not a good idea. Your lawyer needs to know how these deals are typically structured, what risks to look for in a deal, and what is standard and market in the community for these types of transactions.

---

103. Many lawyers have experience working on both sides of an investment deal.

PART III: FINANCINGS AND TERM SHEETS

14 Term Sheets and Definitive Documents

14.1 *The Term Sheet*

A **term sheet** is a summary of the key business terms of the proposed transaction. It should be short, easy to understand, and it should be free of legalese—save perhaps a sentence about the non-binding nature of the proposal. Term sheets are helpful in reaching agreement on the principal business terms as they are very short (1—2 pages) and concise, and easily understandable by those at all familiar with the terms.

Each type of financing, (e.g., convertible notes, preferred stock) will have a fairly typical set of topics that are covered in the term sheet. For convertible notes, this will include interest rates, conversion conditions, and so on. For a preferred stock offering, the term sheet will cover price per share, liquidation preferences, et cetera. Part III will help you understand the common terms in typical angel financings such that you can quickly evaluate any term sheet you may come across. We'll also cover more unusual terms. Examples of the types of terms sheets you will encounter are collected in the appendix.§30

Often accelerators and angel groups have boilerplate term sheets that they like to use as starting points in negotiations. You can find an example at Alliance of Angels,[104] and take a look at the Techstars Series AA Term Sheet.[105]

To be clear, there are no "standard" terms for term sheets. There are typical terms and industry norms, but there is still quite a range out there. Some accelerators, like Y Combinator, put forth very entrepreneur-friendly term sheets§17.1 and encourage very little negotiation of them. Some angel groups put forth very investor-friendly term sheets. Once you

---

104. https://www.allianceofangels.com/wp-content/uploads/2015/11/pdf1.pdf
105. https://www.docracy.com/28/techstars-series-aa-term-sheet

have reviewed the types of investments here and seen a few in the field, you will start to get a sense for what is typical for different financings.

For term sheet terms that are most often associated with a single type of financing, we discuss them within that section. Some terms are applicable across a broad range of financing types, and these we will cover in General Investment Terms.§18

Sample term sheets of each type of financing can be found in Appendix A.§30

No matter what kind of deal you're negotiating, there are a couple of things to keep in mind:

⚠ DANGER **Avoid binding term sheets.** Binding term sheets are, in general, not advisable except in very unusual circumstances. A term sheet, by virtue of its brevity and lack of legalese, is not intended to capture every business term (remember, it is short, preferably a page or two in length). After reaching agreement on a term sheet, investors will continue refining their thinking about the prospective investment as due diligence reveals information about the company, the market, and other relevant considerations. That information may lead an investor to determine that the deal should not proceed or should proceed on different terms. If the term sheet is binding, however, the investor may not be able to get out of the deal or be stuck with the term sheet terms, even if unsatisfactory.

⚠ DANGER **Avoid ambiguous term sheets.** Although term sheets should be short, sometimes they fail to clearly define key terms or use imprecise language that later leads to confusion and conflict. Can you see how this language could lead to problems?

> *The "board" (which may be a board of directors or board of managers) shall be made up of both Founders and the Investors or their representatives. If more investors are added, the board shall become a representative board of five people, whose number and make up may be changed from time to time by vote all of the membership interests voting, but must always include at least one representative of the Investors as long as the Investors hold together more 5% of the Company on an as-converted basis.*

This paragraph introduces confusion on a number of fronts. How big is the board going to be, exactly? And whose representatives will make up the board? An ambiguous term can lead to mistrust and a broken deal.

Avoid these scenarios by taking care to use precise language. Frequently your best bang for the buck for lawyer fees can be had when you involve the lawyer[§13] at the earliest stages to help architect the transaction.

14.2 *Definitive Documents*

The term sheet outlines the details of a specific financing and is usually non-binding (save perhaps for exclusivity and confidentiality clauses). For the deal to be closed, legal contracts representing the details of the investment terms need to be drafted, negotiated, and signed. These contracts and potentially amendments to corporate documents are referred to as the definitive documents.

Definitive documents are the legal contracts between the buyers (investors) and seller (the company) that spell out in detail the terms of the transaction, and are drafted by a lawyer. The definitive documents will set forth the entire understanding of the parties. Definitive documents can include an amended corporate charter and/or articles of incorporation that need to be filed with the secretary of state in the state in which the company is incorporated and would be available for the investor to review. The documents must be signed by all parties in order for a closing to be reached.

Closing refers to the moment at which you sign the definitive documents requiring your signature, and send the company your money, typically either in the form of a check or a wire transfer. The company signs the required documents and delivers to you the security purchased.

What definitive documents are will depend on the specifics of the transaction, but they typically include:

- The note or the convertible equity instrument, in the event of a convertible note or convertible equity financing;
- In a preferred stock financing, in addition to the purchase agreement, you might have an Investor Rights Agreement, a Voting Agreement, and a right of first refusal and co-sale rights.
- The security you purchased could take the form of an original copy of the convertible note you bought, or common or preferred stock certificates accompanied by the stock purchase agreements executed by all

parties. Increasingly, the stock certificates are represented electronically through systems such as Carta.[106]

There are often multiple ways to express a desired outcome within the definitive documents, and different lawyers will have their own language they prefer. However, any aspect of the deal that will materially impact the cost per share or the rights of the investor should be worked out as part of negotiating the term sheet. It's cheaper to figure things out during the term sheet stage, where you might have just two pages to get through, than during the definitive documents stage, where the documentation can be hundreds of pages and cost a lot of money in legal fees to develop. Every major term that you care about should be represented in the term sheet, and then it's the lawyer's job to organize them and add a bunch of agreements, charter amendments, and so on in the definitive documents. The point is, the definitive documents are typically several sets of documents that will express in detail and make binding all the things you worked out in the term sheet. They are two different things, two different parts of the process, and two different sets of paper. But the definitive documents should reflect the understandings reached in the term sheet.

15 Convertible Debt

Convertible debt is the most popular financing structure startups choose when they are raising less than $500K. Companies typically issue convertible debt when they are not raising enough money to justify a preferred stock round. This is because a company raising $200K, for example, can't really justify the legal fee cost or time needed for a preferred stock financing. Convertible debt is relatively straightforward.

Convertible debt (or convertible note or convertible loan or convertible promissory note) is a short-term loan issued to a company by an investor or group of investors. The principal and interest (if applicable) from the note is designed to be converted into equity in the company. A subsequent qualified financing round or liquidity event triggers conversion, typically into preferred stock. Convertible notes may convert at the same price investors pay in the next financing, or they may convert at

---

106. https://carta.com/

either a discount or a conversion price based on a valuation cap. Discounts and valuation caps incentivize investors for investing early and not setting a price on the equity when it would typically be lower. If a convertible note is not repaid with equity by the time the loan is due, investors may have the right to be repaid in cash like a normal loan.[107]

Convertible note rounds can be as small as $50K–$100K in size, but more typically they are on the order of several hundred thousand dollars (but below $500K). Rounds in this size can also be raised by selling convertible equity or common stock (which we'll cover), but neither method is as popular as convertible debt.

Frequently a company will start a convertible note offering by showing potential investors a term sheet, rather than the note itself. This is also true in fixed price financings. You can see an example convertible note term sheet[§30.1] and an annotated convertible note[§30.10] in the appendix.

If you are doing a convertible note deal, the definitive documents might be:

- the convertible promissory note (in which case the investor as well as the company will sign the note) *or*
- a convertible note (signed by the company and delivered to the investor), and a note purchase agreement (signed by both the company and the investor) *or*
- a convertible note (signed by the company and delivered to the investor), a warrant (signed by the company and delivered to the investor), and a note and warrant purchase agreement (signed by both the company and the investor).

15.1 *Entrepreneur Perspective on Convertible Debt*

⚑ FOUNDER Convertible debt can be beneficial for startups in the following ways:

- **Immediate access to funds.** Unlike a fixed price equity round where there is typically a formal closing date on which a substantial portion of the money comes in, notes can be signed in small amounts ($25K)

---

107. This definition has been adapted from the *Holloway Guide to Raising Venture Capital.*[108]

108. https://www.holloway.com/g/venture-capital/sections/exits-and-returns

which individual investors and the company can start using right away. An exception to this is if the convertible note document itself requires a minimum amount of funds to be raised, but this is unusual. If a company is short on cash or needs additional funds to hire engineers or kick off patent work, this quick access to cash as individual investors come on board can be very useful.

- **Lightweight deal documentation.** A convertible note may be only a few pages long, whereas the documentation for a fixed price equity round typically spans multiple long documents. As a result, notes can be executed quickly and legal costs are usually significantly less. If a company is raising $250K or less it does not make sense to spend $10K–$15K or more on legal fees for a fixed price round. Legal fees for a convertible note round are typically on the order of $5K.

- **Ability to reward early investors.** There are several mechanisms for rewarding investors who come into the deal early, in addition to the general accumulation of interest over time. These can include a discount rate on conversion, a valuation cap, or some combination of those factors (each of which will be discussed in detail). It is also possible for the earliest note investors to get higher discounts and lower caps than subsequent convertible note investors.

  - For example, the first investor in a startup might get a 25% discount and a $1M conversion cap on their note, while an investor who comes in two months later could get a 15% discount and a $2M cap.

  - When a startup is trying to get its fundraising going it can be helpful to create inducements for the early investors. And as an investor, if you have faith in the company early on you can reap rewards for taking on the extra risk of being first in.

- **Delay in valuing the company.** Generally speaking, convertible notes allow the company to delay setting a pre-money valuation on the company. For a very early-stage company it can be challenging to convince investors that the company is worth $5M, for example. By issuing convertible notes, setting the valuation can be delayed until the first priced equity investment, by which time hopefully the company has made more progress. The valuation cap, discussed below, effectively puts an upper limit on the value if it is included in the note.

While there are many benefits for founders, some founders and investors believe that convertible debt creates a misalignment of incentives.[109]

15.2 *Investor Perspective on Convertible Debt*

Angel investors used to complain that convertible notes prevented them from getting fairly compensated for taking on the added risk of investing in a very early-stage company. A priced round by contrast would allow them to lock in a low cost for their shares. With the popularity of the valuation cap[110] as a feature of the convertible note, that argument has largely been addressed; but some investors still do not like notes.

From an investor's point of view, sometimes convertible debt can be better than a fixed price equity round, because:

- Debt sits on top of equity; meaning, if the company goes defunct, debt holders are entitled to be paid first, before equity holders.
- Noteholders can have favorable conversion provisions, such as discounts and caps.
- Noteholders can charge interest.
- Noteholders can have warrants appended to their notes as an additional benefit of investing, if that is part of the deal.
- Debt documents can contain "event of default" provisions, entitling the holder to declare the note in default and demand payment in cash in full. (In contrast, it is rare to be able to demand the repurchase by the company of your stock, and even if you have that right, state insolvency laws might prohibit the redemption of your shares.)
- Noteholders can charge higher rates of interest when the note is past due or the company is otherwise in default on the terms of the loan.
- Noteholders can take a security interest in the company's assets.
- Noteholders can have the right to optionally convert if the company raises money in a non-qualified financing at a lower than expected valuation.

---

109. https://trueventures.com/blog/why-we-still-dont-invest-in-convertible-debt
110. While caps are now built in, there was a time when notes didn't have caps!

- Noteholders can still obtain standard contractual rights, such as a board seat, observer rights, participation or pro rata rights, information rights, and so forth.

In other words, with notes, you can do just about everything you could imagine, all in a relatively short document.

15.2.1 TAX ISSUES WITH INTEREST FROM CONVERTIBLE DEBT

If you invest in a convertible note that bears interest, depending on the circumstances you might be forced to take this interest into income on an accrual basis even though you don't receive any cash payments of interest. How could this be, you ask? Well, because the IRS has rules in place that force note holders in certain situations onto the accrual method of accounting when it comes to interest on private company convertible notes. What happens if the interest is converted into stock? Well, the IRS will still tax you on the interest, even though it is paid in stock.

For most angel investments in convertible notes, this interest income problem is not that big of a deal, because the total interest amount that you might be forced to take into income doesn't add up to much.

⚠ DANGER But beware if you are investing a considerable amount of money. The tax on the interest income might turn out to be more than you wanted to bear. In these cases, you might want to ask the company to pay the interest in cash so that you can pay the tax on this interest income.

Notes are not required to bear interest if the lender is not related to the company. Thus, another possibility is—just don't include an interest rate in the note.

15.3 *Terms of Convertible Debt*

Common provisions of a convertible debt financing include:

- **The interest rate.** Usually somewhere between 4% and 8%.
- **The maturity date.** Usually 12–24 months.
- **A mandatory conversion paragraph.** Specifies the minimum size of the round that the company must close in the future (a qualified financing) to cause the debt to automatically convert into equity of the company.

- **An optional conversion paragraph.** Gives the investors the option to convert into whatever equity securities are sold by the company in its next financing, even if the financing does not meet the definition of a qualified financing (a non-qualified financing). This term is both common and recommended.
- **A change of control provision.** Addressing what happens if the company is sold before the note converts (highly recommended).
- **A conversion discount.** Specifies a discount note holders receive relative to the equity price in the qualified financing (common but optional).
- **A valuation cap.** Specifies the maximum pre-investment value that will be used to convert the note into equity in the qualified financing (common but optional).
- **An amendment provision.** Entitles the company, typically with only the consent of holders of the majority in principal amount of the notes, to amend the terms of the notes.
- **No prepayment.** Notes typically say that the note cannot be prepaid without the consent of either the holders or holders of a majority in principal amount of the outstanding notes.
- **An attorneys' fees clause.** Entitles the holder to repayment of its fees if it sues to enforce the terms of the note.

🔍 CONFUSION Note that while the interest and maturity date only apply to convertible debt, the rest of the terms here can be found in a convertible equity financing, which we'll cover next.

15.3.1 **INTEREST**

Interest on a convertible note is not typically paid in cash while the note is outstanding. Most typically, it accumulates and is paid in stock on conversion. However, sometimes note holders negotiate for the right on conversion to have the interest paid in cash. Interest rates on convertible notes typically range from 4%-8%. Startups are very high risk, and the rate of interest typically would not adequately compensate an investor for that risk relative to alternatives; so it is best to think of the interest as a sweetener to the deal, since the main reason for buying the note is to end up with the equity when it converts.

⚠ CAUTION You should know that even if the interest on the note is paid in stock, it is taxable to you as if paid in cash. In fact, you might be taxed on interest before it is paid in stock—in other words, you may be put on the accrual method of accounting for income taxes when it comes to the interest component of your note (and be taxed even if you haven't received anything yet). We address tax issues in detail in Part V.

15.3.2 MATURITY

The **maturity** of the note—the length of time before it is due—typically ranges from 12–24 months. It is common that startups take longer to achieve their milestones then they or you expect. A shorter maturity date (12 months) is a ticking clock that might pressure an entrepreneur to raise money on unfavorable terms.

If progress is slow, startups may extend the note. This is quite common—in fact, this is one of the common uses of an amendment provision. In this case, the maturity of the note would be extended with the consent of a majority of the existing note holders.

Sometimes a company will try to negotiate for the note to not come due until after the stated maturity date holders of a majority of the principal amount of the notes demand payment. This is a helpful provision for companies, because they do not have to worry about one small note holder demanding payment in cash at the maturity date. It is also a helpful provision if you are in the majority, because you can control the demands of minor note holders as well.

15.3.3 CONVERSION

Mandatory Conversion In A Qualified Financing

Convertible notes usually automatically convert to stock when the company raises money in what is typically defined as a qualified financing.

A **qualified financing** in a convertible note is usually defined as a fundraising of at least a fixed amount of money (for example, $1M), either including or excluding amounts raised under the note. These criteria cause the note to automatically convert into the type and number of shares being sold in the qualified financing. There are subtleties to how a qualified financing is defined.

A **non-qualified financing** is a financing that does not meet the definition of a qualified financing in your note, and thus does not cause your note to be automatically converted into shares of stock sold in the financing.

Here is an example of a definition of a qualified financing:[111]

> In the event that the Company issues and sells shares of its Equity Securities to investors (the "**Investors**") on or before the date of the repayment in full of this Note in an equity financing resulting in gross proceeds to the Company of at least $ _____ (including the conversion of the Notes and other debt) (a "**Qualified Financing**"), then...

You want to be sure the financing is a "real" financing and not a financing of some small amount by the founders to simply convert your debt to equity. You also want to make sure that there is going to be enough new money coming in to give the company the runway it needs. This is why the amount is usually on the order of *at least* $500K or more. The definition can be written to include the money previously raised on the convertible notes or not, but usually excludes amounts raised in convertible debt.

You may also negotiate whether the qualified financing is only triggered on the sale of preferred stock or whether the common stock financing could trigger the auto-conversion on a qualified financing as well. Many investors prefer that their notes expressly say that a qualified financing has to be a preferred stock financing.

Optional Conversion

Optional conversion clauses address the ability for the investors to convert their notes under scenarios that do not meet the qualified financing definition. For example, an optional conversion clause can be written to allow the investor to convert if the company raises money in a fixed-price financing at attractive terms, but not enough to trigger automatic conversion under the qualified financing definition.

Another optional conversion scenario is the company does not raise any money before the notes mature. In that situation, if you do not want to extend the note, you might want the right to convert into common stock or a predetermined series of preferred stock at a pre-agreed valuation.

To break it down, there are three different moving parts that can be specified in optional conversion paragraphs:

- **At whose option does the conversion happen?** Typically the investors have the right to invoke the optional conversion, and it is

---

111. From the Techstars Term Sheet (no longer available online).

what you want as an investor. The founders will not want conversion at the option of the investor in the absence of a qualified financing until the company passes the maturity date. They might also want a clause giving them the right to invoke the optional conversion, but this is not a typical formulation.

- **At what value?** If the company consummates an equity financing that does not constitute a qualified financing, an optional conversion clause can stipulate that the note holders have the option to convert at the price per share or at a discount to the price at which shares are sold in that financing (this is fairly common). Another possibility is that the clause includes the valuation cap and stipulates that the conversion price is the better of a predetermined discount to a non-qualified financing or the price determined by the valuation cap.
- **Into what type of security do the notes convert?** Some optional conversion clauses say that in the absence of a qualified financing the note will convert into a series of default preferred stock. Alternatively, the note could convert into common stock.

What if the note does not specify an optional conversion? If the convertible note does not specify an optional conversion in the event the company does not achieve a qualified financing, there is a risk to the company that the investors may make a demand that their notes be repaid in full. It also means that the parties may just have to meet and hash out a negotiated compromise. Negotiating changes to the note when things are not going well and the company is trying to secure additional funds can take up a lot of the CEO's time, and it may jeopardize or delay the future funding due to the uncertainty. At a minimum, it is important that the notes contain a provision that they can be amended with the consent of a majority of the note holders, as we discuss below.[§15.3.7]

Sale of the Company Before Conversion

A convertible note should address what happens if the company is sold before the note converts to equity. Typically, this is addressed through a provision that states that if the company is sold before the debt converts into equity, the note holders get something more than just their principal and interest back (that would be a bad deal). Typically, they are entitled to the greater of some multiple on their principal and interest (for example,

2X or 3X), or a greater amount as if they had converted at the valuation cap or another value specified in the note.

15.3.4 VALUATION CAP

A **valuation cap** is a term included in a convertible note that sets the maximum valuation of a company at which an investor's note can be converted into stock of the company. An angel investor will typically want a valuation cap in a convertible note so that they are not converted at an unexpectedly high valuation.

> ❯ EXAMPLE
>
> An investor makes an investment of $50K in a convertible note with no valuation cap. The terms of the note state that the note will be automatically converted into equity of the company once the company raises $1M in equity in a fixed price financing (a qualified financing). The company raises $1M in a qualified financing at a $100M valuation. Without a valuation cap, the investor's stock would convert at the $100M valuation. The investor believes that the increased valuation was attributable in part to their investment. However, the investor does not share in the valuation increase between the time of her investment and the subsequent round at the $100M valuation because there was no valuation cap when the investment was made.

- But assume there had been a valuation cap of $5M. In that case, the investor's note would have converted at a much better price per share and the investor would have gotten more shares and not been so heavily diluted.
- Let's do the math. Assume there had been 3M shares outstanding, and no warrants, options, or any other convertible securities outstanding except the notes. The price per share at the cap would have been $5M divided by 3M shares, or $1.66 a share, and the investor would have received $50K divided by $1.66 a share, or 30,120 shares, excluding interest. At a $100M valuation the price per share would have been $33.33 a share, and the investor would have received $50K divided by $33.33 a share, or 1,500 shares, a stark and dramatic difference.

While this is an extreme example, you can see that valuation caps can be very important.

⚑ FOUNDER There are two schools of thought on what an ideal valuation cap should be:

- The first—let's call it the "Investor's School of Thought"—says that the cap should be the current fair market value of the company. In other words, the cap should be the valuation that you would place on the company at the time of the investment, as if you were doing a priced round.
- The second school of thought—let's call it the "Founder's School of Thought"—says the cap should be the outside range of potential values for the company. Ultimately, this is a philosophical question for which there is no precise answer.

15.3.5 **CONVERSION DISCOUNT**

A **conversion discount** provides that the holder of the note gets a purchase price discount when the note is converted into stock. Typically, the discount is 10%-20%, but discounts higher than that are not out of the question.

> ❭ EXAMPLE
>
> The note might say that upon conversion in a qualified financing, the note will convert at a price per share equal to 75% of the price per share at which shares are sold in the offering (meaning, a 25% discount). If in the qualified financing round, shares were priced at $1, you would be getting them at $0.75; so your $25K investment in the note would result in your owning 33,333 shares rather than 25K shares.

Conversion discounts are very common in convertible notes. It is a term that you should always look for when you are reviewing a convertible note offering. However, not all convertible notes provide discounts. For example, at one time companies graduating from Y Combinator were issuing notes with no cap, no discount, and no interest rate. Of course, these are exceptional circumstances and very founder-friendly.

15.3.6 **INTERACTION OF CAPS AND DISCOUNTS**

◇ IMPORTANT If a note has both a cap and a discount, the note should read that you get the better of the two conversion possibilities. If you would get more shares at the discounted price, then you would get the discounted price. If you would get more shares at the valuation cap price, then you will convert at the valuation cap price.

15.3.7 AMENDMENT PROVISIONS

Amendment provisions exist so that the investors and the startup can adjust the terms of their relationship as conditions change. It may be that a non-qualified financing opportunity comes along and the note holders want to convert. If this is not specifically addressed in other clauses within the note, the note could be amended to allow the investors to take that action. It is also possible that the lead investor in the upcoming priced round does not like some term in the note and wants to negotiate that with the note holders. The note investors may be willing to do that to get a deal to close on otherwise favorable terms.

Generally, notes are amendable with the consent of the company and holders of a majority in interest of the notes. This prevents any single investor from holding up progress of the company. Most of the time, these amendment provisions do not specify a supermajority requirement to amend. Similarly, most of the time the amendment provisions do not say anything special about minority rights—such as a provision that an amendment cannot treat a single note holder differently from other holders of the same note (although if you can ask for this you should). The only scenario in which this could be problematic is if a majority of the convertible notes are owned by someone or some entity, such as a strategic investor, with a different set of goals than yours.

15.3.8 ATTORNEYS' FEES

Your note should contain an attorneys' fees clause, entitling you to an award of attorneys' fees if you have to sue to enforce the terms of the note. (There is sometimes a separate provision in which the company agrees to reimburse the investor their attorneys' fees, usually capped.)

15.4 *Advanced Topics on Convertible Debt*

15.4.1 DEFAULT PROVISIONS

Sometimes notes will specify what happens in the event the company defaults on the note. Most of the time the primary default is the non-payment of the note on the maturity date. Higher interest rates in the event of default are not common.

It is not uncommon for a note to require that before an action is taken against a company to enforce the terms of the note, the holders of a majority in principal amount of the notes approve the action, rather than just one note holder. Sometimes the majority required is a supermajority, set at something like 70%, to ensure that a large minority investor has a veto right on any amendments.

> ❭ EXAMPLE
>
> If there are eight investors, three who put in $100K and five who put in $50K, there are $550K of notes outstanding. Holders of notes with principal amounts aggregating more than $275K can, with the company's consent, amend the note.

15.4.2 SHOULD YOUR NOTE BE SECURED?

When you say that a loan is **secured** by the company's assets, what you mean is that the company will grant the lender a security interest in its assets, which the lender may perfect.[112] A **security interest** is a direct interest in the assets of a company that the borrower grants to the lender. If the lender has a security interest in the company's assets, the lender can **perfect** its security interest by filing a financing statement (typically, a UCC-1) to ensure that subsequent creditors are behind it in line with respect to payment from proceeds of a sale of the assets. Once the lender does this, they have priority over subsequent creditors. A secured party can take action to seize the collateral and dispose of it in the event of a default on the loan.

Secured notes are not typical in angel financings. There are a few reasons why angels rounds are rarely secured:

- First, many angel rounds are pretty small financings and people do not want to take the additional time and hassle to put a security agreement in place.
- Many early-stage companies do not have a lot in the way of assets to secure.

---

112. Perfection[113] is a legal concept meaning you have done what you have to do to prevent someone who comes in later from getting ahead of you.
113. https://en.wikipedia.org/wiki/Perfection_(law)

- The investors frequently feel more like equity investors than debt investors in these transactions.
- All parties involved in the early stages typically want to make sure that the company does not have any legal impediments to raising its next round of financing (such as having to subordinate the angel debt to a bank loan).
- Secured debt adds a layer of complexity. Not having secured debt removes a layer of complexity.

But that does not mean that your note should necessarily *not* be secured, just that it is not a very common practice and might be viewed as aggressive by founders. If you decide you do want a secured note, make sure you consult with legal counsel to ensure that the "grant" of the security interest is adequate under the law of the jurisdiction governing the note, and that you file a Uniform Commercial Code financing statement[114] perfecting your security interest.

15.4.3 LIQUIDATION PREFERENCE OVERHANG

FOUNDER One issue that comes up with convertible notes is that it is possible, depending on how a note is drafted, for note holders to receive shares with a liquidation preference per share greater than the amount of their actual cash investment per share. This happens when the note converts at a discount or valuation cap and no special allowance in the note is made to address this issue.

Liquidation preference overhang refers to how you might, if you invest in a convertible note or convertible equity instrument with a valuation cap or a discount (or both), ultimately might receive shares of preferred stock with a liquidation preference in excess of what you paid.

For example, if you invested $100K in a convertible note with a 20% discount on conversion. If the company ultimately sold preferred stock for $1 a share, you would buy your shares for $0.80, but you might receive shares with a liquidation preference per share of $1. Sometimes notes and convertible equity instruments are set up so that you don't receive shares with a liquidation preference in excess of what you paid, or you receive common stock to make up the difference in the number of shares you are supposed to receive. So, instead of receiving that number of shares of

---

114. https://en.wikipedia.org/wiki/UCC-1_financing_statement

preferred stock equal to $100K/$0.80 per share, in this example, or 125K shares of preferred stock, you would receive 100K shares of preferred (so that your liquidation preference matches the amount you invested, ignoring interest for the sake of this example), and you would receive 25K shares of common stock.

Another way to handle this is for the company to create two classes of preferred stock, one with a liquidation preference per share equal to $0.80 and one for $1 per share, and then issue you the $0.80 liquidation preference per share shares (and all the other terms of the preferred stock would be the same).

This problem can become especially acute when there is a valuation cap, and the cap comes into play. A note investor may receive a significant amount of liquidation preferences beyond what they invested in the convertible notes.

⚹ FOUNDER Founders may think this is problematic. Some investors think it is unfair to founders. It is not really a problem for the investors, except to the extent that the founders and other investors think it is unfair.

One solution is to have the discount shares convert into common stock. Another possibility is to have the debt convert to a series of preferred stock whose liquidation preference matches the amount of capital actually invested, but otherwise has the same rights, preferences, and privileges sold in the round. This is becoming more common and is the standard set by Y Combinator in the SAFE.[115]

15.4.4 CALCULATING NUMBER OF SHARES TO BE ISSUED AT THE CAP

If a company is going to issue shares to you at the valuation cap, you will want to know how the number of shares will be determined. Will the number of shares be determined on a fully diluted basis or on some different measure? It is typical to exclude the debt being converted.

Some convertible notes are written this way:

> The price equal to the quotient of [the Valuation Cap] divided by the aggregate number of outstanding shares of the Company's Common Stock as of immediately prior to the initial closing of the Qualified Financing (assuming full conversion or exercise of all con-

---

115. https://www.ycombinator.com/documents/

vertible and exercisable securities then outstanding other than the
Notes)...

Note that the "then outstanding" language implies that you are not
going to count the entire stock option pool—you are only going to count
options that have been issued to workers and that are still in the hands
of workers at the time of conversion. Other notes might say "including
the Company's shares reserved for future issuance under the Company's
equity incentive plans," meaning the issued options and the available
option pool.

◇ IMPORTANT From an investor's perspective, you want clarity on what is
going to be counted in determining your price per share—you don't want
the note to be silent on this point. You would prefer the entire available
option pool plus all outstanding options be counted in the denominator.
The text below provides an example of including the option pool under
the definition of "Fully Diluted Capitalization."

> In the event the Company consummates, prior to the Maturity
> Date, a Qualified Equity Financing, then the Principal Balance will
> automatically convert into shares of capital stock of the Company
> at a price per share equal to either: (i) the "**Preferred Purchase
> Price**": the price per share of preferred stock sold in the Qualified
> Equity Financing (notice no discount here) or (ii) the "**Target
> Price**": the price obtained by dividing the Target Valuation (where
> the "Target Price" is the Valuation Cap) by the Fully Diluted Cap-
> italization (defined below). The lower of the Preferred Purchase
> Price and the Target Price is the "**Conversion Price**."
> "Fully Diluted Capitalization" means the sum of (i) all shares of
> the Company's capital stock (on an as-converted basis) issued and
> outstanding, assuming exercise or conversion of all options, war-
> rants and other convertible securities (other than this Note and
> Other Debt) and (ii) except with respect to conversions of this Note
> in connection with a Change of Control, all shares of the Company's
> common stock reserved and available for future grant under any
> equity incentive or similar plan of the Company.

It is better for the note holder to count the whole stock option plan
share reserve. Notice this is done in the above example but not in the
event of sale of the company where it wouldn't make sense in any event

(because unused pool shares are disregarded in a company sale, just like authorized but unissued shares).

The details of dilution and ownership calculation, as well as valuations, are discussed in Part IV.

15.4.5 MOST-FAVORED NATIONS CLAUSE

A **most-favored nations clause (or MFN clause or MFN)** is a clause in a convertible note or convertible equity purchase agreement (or side letter agreement) that provides that the holder of the security is entitled to the benefit of any more favorable provisions the company offers to later investors. If you are an early investor in a convertible note round, an MFN clause can be a very good idea.

The reason MFNs exist in convertible debt and convertible equity is that these investment instruments are often sold to individual investors over a period of time. If you make an early investment via a convertible note, you are taking more risk than someone who comes in later, and you want to make sure they don't get better terms. A most-favored nations clause in a note or side letter agreement might look like this:

> The company hereby agrees that if it offers any subsequent investors convertible-note terms that are more favorable to the subsequent investor than the terms included herein, the company will provide the holder of this instrument with those more favorable terms.

Here's the most-favored nations clause included in Y Combinator's SAFE documents,[116] which more clearly addresses the mechanics:

> **MFN Amendment Provision.** If the Company issues any Subsequent Convertible Securities prior to the termination of this instrument, the Company will promptly provide the Investor with written notice thereof, together with a copy of all documentation relating to such Subsequent Convertible Securities and, upon written request of the Investor, any additional information related to such Subsequent Convertible Securities as may be reasonably requested by the Investor. In the event the Investor determines that the terms of the Subsequent Convertible Securities are preferable to the terms of this instrument, the Investor will notify the

---

116. https://www.ycombinator.com/documents/

Company in writing. Promptly after receipt of such written notice from the Investor, the Company agrees to amend and restate this SAFE to be identical to the instruments evidencing the Subsequent Convertible Securities.

> ❯ EXAMPLE

You want a 20% discount on a convertible note because you are the first investor. The entrepreneur resists going past 15%. To get the deal done, you agree to 15% but you add an MFN, so that if the entrepreneur grants a higher discount to any later convertible note investors you also get that higher rate.

15.4.6 PRO RATA RIGHTS AND CONVERTIBLE NOTES

Although convertible notes don't typically contain pro rata rights (which are typically handled on the company's first fixed-price financing), this is definitely something you can ask for. For an example of pro rata rights language, see Y Combinator's pro rata side letter.[117]

15.5 *Convertible Note Cheat Sheet*

◇ IMPORTANT When negotiating a convertible note financing, focus on the following elements of the term sheet:

- What is the valuation cap?
- What is the conversion discount? (10% to 20% typically.)
- What is the repayment premium in the event of a sale before conversion?
- What defines the qualified financing?
- What happens if the company does not achieve a qualified financing?
- Do you have the right to participate in any financings which are not qualified financings?
- Is there an optional conversion provision that is at your option, or the company's option?
- Do you have or want a most-favored nations clause?
- Will interest be paid in cash or stock or a combination of cash and stock? (Although this is less common, if you are being paid a consider-

---

117. https://www.ycombinator.com/documents/

able amount in interest because you are making a sizable investment, this is something you could ask for.)

⚠ **DANGER** Provisions to watch out for in a convertible note financing:

- Make sure that in the event of the sale of the company the company can't just return your principal and interest. You are investing in a note for the potential equity upside, *not* interest.
- You will usually want a valuation cap that is acceptable to you (not too high).
- A mandatory conversion paragraph that doesn't convert you at the lower of the discounted price or cap.
- The lack of a change of control payment provision.
- A mandatory conversion paragraph that does not contain a sufficiently sized round to justify your forced conversion.
- The lack of an optional conversation paragraph, giving you the option to convert into equity either (i) when the company closes a financing round that does not meet the definition of a qualified financing, or (ii) after the maturity date, at a specified valuation (for example, the cap).

16 Preferred Stock

Preferred stock rounds are the most common type of fixed price round for angel investments—in fact, when investors and founders refer to a *fixed price round* or a *priced round*, they usually mean a preferred stock financing, although common stock fixed price rounds are possible. **Preferred stock** is equity that has specified preferences relative to common stock and potentially to other classes of preferred stock. Those preferences are negotiated as part of the term sheet and documented in the definitive documents of the stock sale.

The most common preferences conferred to preferred stockholders are:

- a liquidation preference
- a dividend preference
- purchase price anti-dilution protection
- protective provisions (these are provisions that require the separate vote or approval of the preferred stockholders to do certain

things—such as sell the company, sell all or substantially all of the assets of the company, any amendment to the terms of the preferred stock, issue preferred that is on a parity with or senior to the preferred stock, et cetera).

The above rights, if they are part of the deal, will have to be reflected in the company's charter document filed with the Secretary of State of the state in which the company is incorporated. The company's articles of incorporation or certificate of incorporation are typically amended to include these negotiated provisions immediately prior to the closing of the financing.

Preferred stock is convertible into common stock. Usually, preferred stock starts out as convertible to common stock on a 1:1 basis. This means that each share of preferred stock is convertible into one share of common stock. The preferred stock term sheet may contain additional details on conversion.[§16.5.1]

Preferred stock rounds are usually larger than convertible debt or convertible equity rounds; $500K at the low end, and up to tens of millions. Over the life of a startup, it may raise multiple rounds of preferred stock. The first round of preferred stock may be referred to as a Series Seed Preferred Stock if it is a relatively small round (less than $2M). If it is a larger round, it will typically be labeled Series A Preferred Stock. Subsequent rounds are referred to as Series B, Series C, and so on. Each round usually contains preferences that are senior to those of the prior rounds; in some cases, the lead investor may insist on revisions to the rights of prior rounds. It is a classic example of the Golden Rule—the holder of the gold makes the rules.

16.1 *Fixed Price vs. Convertible Rounds*

A **fixed price financing (or fixed price round or priced round)** is a type of financing where the investors buy a fixed number of shares at a set price (in a common stock or preferred stock round), as opposed to rounds in which the number of shares and the price of those shares will be determined later (such as convertible note or convertible equity rounds). The most common type of fixed price round are preferred stock deals, which often represent rounds larger than convertible rounds, greater than $500K for example, which justifies the legal cost of documenting the round.

By definition, in a fixed price financing *a price must be set* or *fixed* for the security being sold (preferred stock, or less frequently, common stock) by the company. There are a number of factors that come into play when determining the price, and some of those factors are a function of negotiation. In order to provide a full understanding of how this works, in Part IV we'll dig into pre-money valuation, post-money valuation, stock option pools, and dilution generally.

We talked about some of the advantages of convertible notes in the prior section. Convertible rounds are built on the assumption that the company will raise another round in the future that will fix the price of the non-priced round. But if no subsequent round is planned, then a non-priced round is not a good fit, and a fixed price financing is called for.

Investors may prefer fixed price financing over convertible debt so they can lock in the valuation of the company earlier (while it is presumably lower) and receive the rights and preferences associated with preferred stock. Some investors are also wary of convertible debt or convertible equity rounds because they don't want to have to wait to become a shareholder, or because they believe (or they believe founders believe) that convertible debt creates a conflict of interest between the founders and the investors.

If a company raises capital through one or more convertible debt or convertible equity rounds, eventually they will want to do a preferred stock financing to convert that debt to shares (equity). Convertible securities typically need a qualifying (minimum size) priced round to convert into stock. Angels really like preferred stock financings because, as you will see below, they are able to attach a wide variety of preferences to the stock—that is, privileges and control provisions for the preferred stockholder.

16.2 *Entrepreneur Perspective on Preferred Stock*

⚑ FOUNDER Entrepreneurs have a mixed perspective on preferred stock, depending on the particulars of the preferences. On the plus side, raising a preferred stock round means they are raising a significant amount of money, and that is likely what they need to keep going and growing.

The downsides for the entrepreneur are:

- The benefits of the preferences that accrue to investors in a preferred stock round come generally at the expense of the entrepreneur and the pre-existing stockholders. Convertible note and convertible equity holders usually convert into the same class of stock (the preferred) that is creating the qualified financing and triggering the conversion. (The most common exception to this is when the convertible debt or equity is converted into a subclass of the preferred stock to avoid the problem of the liquidation overhang.)
- Negotiating the preferences and pricing can consume a lot of legal resources, especially if they are unfamiliar with the terms. (If you're a founder raising your first angel round, we suggest reading the *Holloway Guide to Raising Venture Capital*,[118] which dives deep on term sheets from the entrepreneur's perspective.)
- In addition, one of the typical terms of a preferred stock round is a requirement that the company pay the reasonable attorneys' fees of the investors.

What can often feel the most onerous to entrepreneurs are the liquidation preferences, especially if these stack up across multiple rounds. As we will explain below, it can mean that in an acquisition scenario that is not a home run, the investors might double their money, while the entrepreneur is left with little.

16.3 *Investor Perspective on Preferred Stock*

Investors like preferred stock rounds for a number of reasons:

- The price is set and the investor knows what percentage of the company they own.
- If an investor has participated in non-priced rounds like convertible debt or convertible equity, they will finally know what they have bought for their money. This is the case as long as the preferred stock round is a qualified financing that converts the convertible notes into stock shares and any convertible equity into actual stock shares on the cap table.

---

118. https://www.holloway.com/g/venture-capital/about

- The investors get specific preferences reflected in the definitive documents that can improve their outcomes in both good and bad scenarios, and sometimes give them a measure of control beyond what their specific share count would provide.

VCs almost universally insist on preferred stock, because they want to price the stock and have as much upside in good times and as much control in bad times as they can. You will start to get a feel for how this works as you read through the specific types of preferences below.

16.4 *Terms of Preferred Stock*

The term sheet for a preferred stock offering will contain the following key elements:

- The type of security (for example, series A convertible preferred stock). (Note that the word "convertible" here refers to the fact that the preferred *converts* to common.)
- The amount of money being raised in the round (referred to as an "offering").
- The number of shares authorized to be sold in the round.
- The price per share.
- A summary of the cap table post investment. Because the cap table represents the ownership of the company, it is really useful to have a summary cap table in the term sheet, so that there are no surprises on either side as the deal comes together. Everyone has a clear picture of what they are going to end up with.

The preferred stock term sheet will also contain a list of preferences for the preferred stockholders, discussed in this section.

16.4.1 LIQUIDATION PREFERENCES

A **liquidation preference** entitles the holder of the security with the liquidation preference to be paid before other stockholders on a sale of the company or all of its assets.

> ⟩ EXAMPLE
>
> For example, suppose you invest in Series A Preferred Stock at $1 per share, and the Series A Preferred Stock has a 1X liquidation

preference. On the sale of the company, after the payment of creditors (lenders), the Series A Preferred stockholders would get paid back their $1 per share liquidation preference before the common stockholders received anything.

Liquidation preferences come in a variety of different flavors. A preferred stock might have a liquidation multiple. In this case, the Series A Preferred might have the right to receive twice its purchase price per share (a 2X liquidation preference) before any other stockholder is entitled to receive any liquidation proceeds.

Another critical characteristic of each liquidation preference is whether the preferred is "participating" or "nonparticipating" preferred.

Non-participating preferred stock is preferred stock that entitles the holder on a liquidation to receive the *greater* of either (i) its liquidation preference, or (ii) what the preferred stock would receive if it converted to common stock.

Participating preferred stock is preferred stock that entitles the holder to a return of its liquidation preference, and then to participate with the common stock on an as-converted to common stock basis.

> ❯ EXAMPLE

For example, suppose you invest $1M in *non-participating* Series A Preferred Stock with a 1X liquidation preference, for a post-closing ownership of 10% of the company and a post-money valuation of $10M (the company has 9M shares of common outstanding in this example). If the company is sold for:

- $1M, you would be entitled to all of the liquidation proceeds. There would be nothing left for the founders and earlier investors.
- $3M, you would receive the first $1M, and the common would get the remaining $2M; you would only get your money back.
- $100M, you would forgo your $1M liquidation preference, and either convert to 10% of the issued and outstanding common stock or be treated as if you had converted, and receive $10M on the sale.

❯ EXAMPLE

Now let's look at the same example above, with a *participating* preferred stock, with a 1X liquidation preference. If the company is sold for:

- $1M, you would be entitled to all of the liquidation proceeds.
- $3M, you would get the first $1M, and then 10% of the remaining proceeds (10% x $2M = $200K) for a total of $1.2M.
- $100M, you would get your $1M liquidation preference, and then your 10% share of $99M, for a total of $10.9M.

❯ EXAMPLE

Using the same example, if there were no liquidation preference, the outcomes are very different.

If the company is sold for:

- $1M, you would get only $100K back, a 90% *loss* on your investment.
- $3M, you would get $300K, a 70% loss on your investment.
- $100M, you would get $10M.

As you can see, the liquidation preference—and especially the participating preference—is very important to achieving a positive ROI if the company is not acquired for a very large multiple of its post-money valuation.

16.4.2 ANTI-DILUTION PROTECTION

Anti-dilution protection, or, more precisely, **purchase price anti-dilution adjustment protection**, refers to provisions of stock, most typically preferred stock, that automatically adjust the conversion ratio of the stock to greater than 1:1 if the company sells shares in the future at a price less than what the investor paid.

⚠ CONFUSION Anti-dilution adjustment protection typically only comes with preferred stock, but it is possible (though very rare) under corporate law to make it part of any type of stock, including a subclass of common stock, for example.

Preferred stock starts out as convertible into common stock on a 1:1 basis. However, if the company issues shares of stock in a financing at a lower price than you paid, the anti-dilution conversion adjustment protection may be triggered. If it is triggered, you become entitled to more than one share of common stock on conversion of each share of your preferred stock.

> ❯ EXAMPLE
>
> You buy Series A Preferred Stock at $1 per share with anti-dilution protection. The company later sells Series B Preferred Stock at $0.50 per share. Your shares of preferred stock would become convertible into more than one share of common stock. The exact ratio at which your preferred would convert into common depends on what type of anti-dilution protection you have.

⚡ CONFUSION Anti-dilution protection is a typical preferred stock preference but it is not included in all preferred stock. For example, Series Seed Preferred Stock typically does not have it. Instead, the Series Seed Preferred Stock terms say that on the company's next round of preferred stock, if that round has anti-dilution adjustment protection, at that time the Series Seed will be conferred those rights as well.

◇ IMPORTANT If the valuation of the company and its stock is increasing with each successive round of funding, anti-dilution adjustment provisions are not triggered. If, however, the company needs to raise money at a *lower* valuation for whatever reason (called a *down round*), the anti-dilution protection could be valuable. The anti-dilution clause is intended to prevent the prior investors from getting too badly diluted by the new money coming in at a lower valuation. However, if the company is really struggling to raise new money, a new investor coming in can essentially dictate terms, which may mean that you have to negotiate away some or all of this protection to close the deal (the golden rule again)—but at least you have some say in the matter.

There are a few different types of anti-dilution adjustment protection:

- Broad-based, weighted average anti-dilution adjustment
- Full ratchet anti-dilution adjustment protection
- Narrow-based, weighted average anti-dilution adjustment protection.

Broad-Based, Weighted Average Anti-Dilution Adjustment Protection

Broad-based weighted average anti-dilution protection is the friendliest anti-dilution protection for founders

Broad-based weighted average anti-dilution protection is a type of purchase price anti-dilution protection that has the effect of adjusting the conversion price of a class or series of preferred stock entitled to the protection if the company subsequently raises money by selling shares at a lower price per share than the price per share paid. This type of repricing takes into account the amount of shares the company sold at the lower price. The more the company raises at the lower your conversion price becomes.

The formula for broad-based weighted average anti-dilution, from NVCA,[119] is:

$$CP2 = CP1 \times \frac{A + B}{A + C}$$

For purposes of the foregoing formula, the following definitions shall apply:

(a) "CP2" shall mean the Series A Conversion Price in effect immediately after such issue of Additional Shares of Common Stock

(b) "CP1" shall mean the Series A Conversion Price in effect immediately prior to such issue of Additional Shares of Common Stock;

(c) "A" shall mean the number of shares of Common Stock outstanding immediately prior to such issue of Additional Shares of Common Stock (treating for this purpose as outstanding all shares of Common Stock issuable upon exercise of Options outstanding immediately prior to such issue or upon conversion or exchange of Convertible Securities (including the Series A Preferred Stock) outstanding (assuming exercise of any outstanding Options therefor) immediately prior to such issue);

(d) "B" shall mean the number of shares of Common Stock that would have been issued if such Additional Shares of Common Stock had been issued at a price per share equal to CP1 (determined by dividing the aggregate consideration received by the Corporation in respect of such issue by CP1); and

(e) "C" shall mean the number of such Additional Shares of Common Stock issued in such transaction.

How broad an anti-dilution adjustment is depends on what is included in the "A." Typically you include issued and outstanding options in the

"A." We have included an §interactive spreadsheet for you to play with these formulas.

Full Ratchet Anti-Dilution Adjustment Protection

Full ratchet anti-dilution adjustment protection (or **full ratchet**) refers to a method of purchase price anti-dilution protection in which an adjustment is triggered upon the sale of stock at a lower price. Full ratchet rights entitle the holder to have their conversion adjustment formula reset in order to give them the number of common shares that they would have received had they purchased their shares at the lower price.

With full ratchet protection, if the company sells shares at a price per share that is lower than you paid, your purchase price gets adjusted to the new, lower price, regardless of how many shares are sold at the lower price. Even one share sold at a lower price triggers the adjustment in the price you paid for all of your shares.

Narrow-Based Anti-Dilution Adjustment Protection

In a **narrow-based purchase price anti-dilution** formula, the investors receive more shares on an as converted to common stock basis than with broad-based protection because in narrow-based you do not count the issued and outstanding options in "A" in the formula above, only the issued and outstanding stock. This results in a lower conversion price, making it less friendly to founders than broad-based. Narrow-based anti-dilution results in a greater adjustment than broad-based, weighted average anti-dilution adjustment provisions, but less than full ratchet adjustment provisions.

16.4.3 **DIVIDEND PREFERENCES**

Preferred stock usually has a **dividend preference**, which means that dividends cannot be paid on the common stock unless a dividend is first paid on the preferred stock. A dividend preference might say that the preferred stock is entitled to a certain percentage dividend—say, 8% of the purchase price of the stock, per year, noncumulative, "as, if and when" declared by the board. The preference would go on to say that no dividends may be declared on the common unless and until the preferred dividend is paid.

If the preferred stock is participating preferred, the dividend preference would also dictate that after payment of the preferred dividend, the preferred would participate with the common on any dividend paid on the common stock on an as-converted to common stock basis. For example:

> Holders of the Series A Preferred shall also participate pro rata on an as-converted basis with respect to dividends, if any, declared with respect to the Common Stock.

If the preferred stock is not participating (meaning, it is not entitled to its liquidation preference *and* to participate alongside the common, it is only entitled to either its liquidation preference or to participate alongside the common), there is no need for the language immediately above, and in fact its presence would not be appropriate.

Dividends can also be "cumulative."

A **cumulative dividend** would accumulate every year, year over year, but be paid only "as and when" declared by the board. Cumulative dividends would be paid on liquidation, if not paid before. Cumulative dividends can be economically harsh on founders and junior investors and are not common in competitive deals.

For most startup and early-stage companies, dividends are not paid. However, the language remains in investment documents to protect the preference of the preferred stock over the common. One scenario preferred stock investors are protecting themselves from is the following: The company grows slowly but is cash flow positive. The founders treat it as a lifestyle business and pay themselves out a dividend to the common stock without paying a dividend to the preferred stock.

16.4.4 PROTECTIVE PROVISIONS

The **voting rights** of stockholders come into play whenever the company is taking an action that requires stockholder approval. The typical items that require stockholder approval include, among other things: the election of directors; an increase in the company's equity incentive or stock option plan share reserve; an amendment to the company's charter (other than purely a change of the company's name).

Preferred stock usually votes on an as-converted to common stock basis. Meaning, it votes just like common stockholders. It also usually, but not always, has additional, special voting rights known as protective provisions.

Voting rights are part of the company charter.

Protective provisions are provisions in a set of investment documents which require the separate approval of a particular class of investor before the company can take certain actions. For example, the separate approval of holders of a majority of the Series A Preferred Stock might be required before the company can undergo a sale transaction.

It is not a requirement that protective provisions appear in a charter filed with the Secretary of State. It is the most common place for them to appear, but they can also appear in an agreement signed by the company. For example, suppose you were investing in common stock, but wanted protective provisions. In that instance, you could put the protective provisions in a side letter agreement with the company, or in an Investor Rights Agreement.§18.6.2

The Series Seed term sheet[120] includes the following pretty typical protective provisions:

> Votes together with the Common Stock on all matters on an as-converted basis. Approval of a majority of the Preferred Stock required to (i) adversely change rights of the Preferred Stock; (ii) change the authorized number of shares; (iii) authorize a new series of Preferred Stock having rights senior to or on parity with the Preferred Stock; (iv) redeem or repurchase any shares (other than pursuant to the Company's right of repurchase at original cost); (v) declare or pay any dividend; (vi) change the number of directors; or (vii) liquidate or dissolve, including any change of control.

Below is a list of the types of items that may be listed in the protective provisions:

- amendments to the charter or bylaws
- changes to the terms of the preferred stock
- the issuance of a series of preferred stock that is on a parity to or senior to the preferred stock

---

120. https://www.seriesseed.com/

- a merger or share exchange
- a sale of all or substantially all of the assets of the company
- the entry into an exclusive license for the company's intellectual property
- a change to the size of the company's board of directors
- the authorization or payment of a dividend
- the repurchase of any shares of capital stock (other than pursuant to an at-cost repurchase right with service providers)
- the incurrence of debt above a certain amount.

Other open source documents that include protective provisions include:

- NVCA[121]
- Alliance of Angels[122]

16.4.5 **REDEMPTION RIGHTS**

Redemption rights (or put right) are the rights to have your shares redeemed or repurchased by the company, usually after a period of time has passed (3-7 years). It is also possible to prepare these provisions to allow redemption in the event the company fails to reach a milestone, or breaches a covenant.

◇ CAUTION Be aware, however, that even if you have redemption rights, if a company is insolvent it will not be able to legally satisfy a redemption demand. Under most states' corporate laws, corporations are disallowed from redeeming shares when the corporation is insolvent either on a balance sheet or ability to pay its debts as they come due, and directors are personally liable if they authorize a redemption when the corporation is insolvent.

Redemption rights are not common in angel deals.[123] However, they can be appropriate and a good mechanism to employ if a business has the danger of becoming a lifestyle business for the entrepreneur. If you want to put redemption rights in place, in order to avoid a lifestyle business outcome, you will probably also want to put in place covenants, such as

121. https://nvca.org/

122. https://www.allianceofangels.com/wp-content/uploads/2015/11/pdf1.pdf

123. Redemption rights can be negotiated in other financings, but are most likely to occur in preferred stock deals, if at all.

restrictions on founder salaries—perhaps subject to the approval of a compensation committee composed entirely of independent directors—to ensure that the redemption rights will have value and are enforceable when they come due.

16.4.6 PRO RATA RIGHTS

Pro rata rights (or pro rata) in a term sheet or side letter guarantee an investor the opportunity to invest an amount in subsequent funding rounds that maintains their ownership percentage.

You will want to try to negotiate for pro rata rights. If a company is doing well, you will want to own as much of it as possible. Some founders include a major investor clause in the term sheet, which reserves certain rights and privileges to those they deem "major investors." Whether to grant pro rata rights to all investors or only those above a major investor threshold is a tricky decision.

When companies use a major investor threshold to determine who gets pro rata rights and who does not, angel investors usually don't make the cut. Angels hate this because it limits their ability to gain more ownership in a company they see themselves as having spotted and supported early on. VCs want the threshold because they don't want to share pro rata rights with a larger group of investors. This is a major source of conflict between angel investors and VCs.[124]

Pro rata rights, when they appear in an angel round, typically show up in a preferred stock financing. But they can appear elsewhere.

16.5 *Preferred Stock Mechanics and Definitive Documents*

The topics below are important elements of a preferred stock financing. These issues may or may not be represented in the term sheet.

16.5.1 PREFERRED STOCK CONVERSION

In early-stage company financings, preferred stock is almost always convertible into common stock at the option of the holder. It is also typically converted automatically upon an event such as an initial public offering that meets a certain size, or upon the election of a majority (sometimes

---

124. This section has been adapted from the *Holloway Guide to Raising Venture Capital.*[125]

125. https://www.holloway.com/g/venture-capital/about

supermajority) of the preferred stock to convert to common. This clause in the term sheet will typically specify the conversion ratio of preferred stock into common stock (always at a 1:1 ratio) and any events or other provisions that would impact that conversion ratio. For example, take a look at the Series Seed Term Sheet, which says:

> Convertible into one share of common (subject to proportional adjustments for stock splits, stock dividends and the like) at any time at the option of the holder.

16.5.2 SUBSCRIPTION PROCEDURE

Subscription procedure refers to the documents you as an investor will be asked to sign. In a preferred stock financing, the documents you will be asked to sign will depend on what type of preferred stock is being sold. If it is a Series Seed Preferred round, you might just be asked to sign the Stock Investment Agreement. If the round is a Series A or beyond, you will probably be asked to sign a number of documents, including:

- a Stock Purchase Agreement,
- an Investors' Rights Agreement;
- a Voting Agreement, and
- a right of first refusal and co-sale rights.

16.5.3 CAPITALIZATION REPRESENTATION AND WARRANTY

In a fixed-price financing it is critical that the company and the investors have clarity on the ownership of the company's capital stock. Without clarity it is impossible to determine the price per share. There is usually a representation and warranty in the stock purchase agreement in which the company represents and warrants to the investors the current capitalization of the company.

16.5.4 FIXED PRICE ROUND FOLLOWING CONVERTIBLE ROUND

If you are investing in a fixed price round in a company that has convertible debt outstanding, you will want to make sure the convertible debt converts when you invest. This is accomplished by adding a condition to the closing that all convertible securities must convert. Otherwise, your interest will be subordinate to the outstanding debt of the company.

16.5.5 PREFERRED STOCK DEFINITIVE DOCUMENTS

For a preferred stock deal, the definitive documents will include, at a minimum:

1. A preferred stock purchase agreement, including any disclosure schedules which may be attached to the stock purchase agreement.
2. An amended charter, or amendments to the company's charter (a preferred stock financing requires that the company's charter be amended to include such things as the liquidation preference per share, the anti-dilution adjustments, protective provisions).
3. If there are ongoing investment rights such as the right to a board seat, information rights, et cetera, then there will be a shareholder agreement of some kind, such as an Investor Rights Agreement, a Voting Agreement, and so on.

Disclosure schedules are attachments to a stock purchase agreement in which the company discloses any items required to be disclosed on the schedule. If you are not familiar with stock purchase agreements, the representations and warranties are written in absolutes. The disclosure schedules are there to provide the details. Disclosure schedules are important to review as part of your diligence before signing the definitive documents.

> ⟩ EXAMPLE
>
> The representation and warranty might say that the company has never had its tax returns audited. But the company might be under an audit, or might have been audited in the past. In such a case, the company would typically disclose this on the schedules rather than re-negotiating the phrasing of the representation and warranty.

16.6 *Example Preferred Stock Term Sheets*

Preferred stock term sheets come in a variety of different shapes and sizes. You can find example preferred stock term sheets at the following sites:

- Series Seed[126] (a simple term sheet that's appropriate for smaller preferred stock rounds)

---

126. https://www.seriesseed.com/

- Techstars[127] (intermediate-length term sheet)
- NVCA[128] (full-blown, full-length VC-style term sheet for large rounds)
- Alliance of Angels Model Term Sheet[129] (a middle ground approach, more detailed than Series Seed, but less complex and lengthy than the full-blown, full-length VC-style term sheet found at NVCA)

In the appendix, you'll find an example[§30.2] of what you would call a light-weight Series A Term Sheet.

17 Other Investment Vehicles

While purchasing convertible debt and preferred stock are the most common types of investments angels make, there are other financings out there that you or a company you're investing in may prefer. Some of these are newer to the angel investment world.

17.1 *Convertible Equity*

Convertible equity is an entrepreneur-friendly investment vehicle that attempts to bring to the entrepreneur the advantages of convertible debt without the downsides for the entrepreneur, specifically interest and maturity dates. The convertible equity instrument the investor is buying will convert to actual equity (stock ownership) at the subsequent financing round, with some potential rewards for the investor for investing early. Those rewards are similar to the rewards for convertible debt, such as a valuation cap and/or a discount.

The amount of the equity the investor is entitled to receive is determined in the same way as a convertible note. The investor usually (but not always) converts at a discount to the next round's price or at the valuation cap if that would result in a better price. As with convertible notes, the company avoids pricing its equity, which can be helpful when hiring employees.

---

127. https://www.docracy.com/28/techstars-series-aa-term-sheet
128. https://nvca.org/
129. https://www.allianceofangels.com/wp-content/uploads/2015/11/pdf1.pdf

Convertible equity is expressly defined as *not* being debt, so it does not bear interest. Nor does it have a maturity date.

Convertible equity is similar to convertible debt in that the documentation is simple—and therefore much cheaper—compared to a priced round, and so it is appropriate for earlier, smaller investment rounds, which can be anywhere from $50K to several hundred thousand dollars in size.

⚘ FOUNDER Convertible equity is an attempt to address the problems with convertible debt from the company's perspective. Convertible notes bear interest, which is often small in amount but creates additional complexity; and convertible notes come due (that is, they have a maturity date). Companies would rather not have to confront interest rates and maturity dates if such issues could be avoided.

Convertible equity is a relatively new investment instrument in the angel investment world. You can access several different types of convertible equity term sheets on the web, including Y Combinator's SAFE[130] (Simple Agreement for Future Equity), and 500 Startups' KISS[131] (Keep It Simple Security). The Founder Institute has also published a form[132] of convertible equity instrument.[133]

17.1.1 ENTREPRENEUR PERSPECTIVE ON CONVERTIBLE EQUITY

⚘ FOUNDER The convertible equity deal structure is intended to give the startup the benefits of the simplicity and low legal costs of the convertible note format, without the downsides of debt.

For one thing, having large amounts of debt on the balance sheet can be a turnoff for suppliers and potential partners the company may seek as they grow; convertible equity helps companies avoid this red flag.

Additionally, the maturity date attached to convertible debt can cause stress and distraction for a startup because it puts a deadline on when the

130. https://www.ycombinator.com/documents/

131. https://www.cooleygo.com/documents/kiss-convertible-debt-equity-agreements/

132. https://fi.co/insight/
   founder-institute-s-convertible-equity-featured-in-the-wall-street-journal

133. You can read more about SAFE and KISS documents, as well as the differences between convertible equity and convertible debt, in the *Holloway Guide to Raising Venture Capital.*[134]

134. https://www.holloway.com/g/venture-capital/sections/choosing-a-financing-structure

company has to raise a qualified financing. There are a host of other provisions that may kick in if there is no qualified financing before the note matures; and at a minimum the company will have to do the legal work to extend the note.

This ticking clock problem is exacerbated if the company has issued a series of convertible notes over the course of months, each with a different maturity date. Calculating the conversion of the accumulated interest into stock at the time of financing can also be complicated, and the interest itself is dilutive to the founders, so there are benefits to eliminating the interest associated with convertible notes. (Like convertible debt, convertible equity can still contain a discount and valuation cap.)

17.1.2 **INVESTOR PERSPECTIVE ON CONVERTIBLE EQUITY**

The convertible equity financing structure is currently being promoted by several incubators and accelerators, including Y Combinator—if you want to invest in one of those companies, you will likely have to accept a convertible equity deal structure.

From an investor's point of view, you might prefer convertible debt rather than convertible equity, because:

- Convertible debt sits on top of equity; if the business fails, debt gets paid first.
- Convertible debt is debt; it exists within a known and well understood legal category. Convertible equity is nebulous, where investors must accept equity of an unknown amount.
- Convertible debt can bear interest, yielding a bigger payday for investors.
- Convertible debt has a maturity date, meaning investors know when the loan is expected to be paid back.
- If the company doesn't achieve a qualified financing, you can probably demand a loan's repayment and not be forced to accept stock in the company.

◇ IMPORTANT Convertible equity is entrepreneur-friendly, but with discounts and valuation caps, you can still be rewarded for your early participation. As an angel investor who comes in early when there is significantly more risk, you have the right to demand a benefit relative to investors who come in later when the company has made more progress. Those benefits are the discount on the price per share relative to later investors, and the valuation cap. You should negotiate hard for those, because if the company's value increased dramatically from the time you invested to the time they raise a priced round, you deserve to benefit from that increase because you took the early risk.

17.1.3 TERMS OF CONVERTIBLE EQUITY

Convertible equity deals do not have interest or maturity dates, but may contain any of the following terms described in the section on convertible debt:$^{\S15.3}$

- mandatory conversion
- optional conversion
- change of control provision
- conversion discount
- valuation cap
- amendment provision

The following topics discussed in Advanced Topics on Convertible Debt$^{\S15.4}$ may also apply to convertible equity deals:

- liquidation preference overhang
- calculating the number of shares to be issued at the cap
- most favored nations clause
- pro rata rights

17.2 *Common Stock*

As an angel investor, from time to time you might be asked to invest in common stock.

Common stock is stock that entitles the holder to receive whatever remains of the assets of a company after payment of all debt and all preferred stock priority liquidation preferences. Common stock does not usually have any of the special rights, preferences, and privileges of preferred stock (although it is possible to create a class of common that does, such as a class of common stock that has multiple votes per share, or is non-voting, or that has protective provisions).

When a corporation is initially organized, typically only common stock is issued to the founders and set aside for issuance under the company's stock option or equity incentive plan for service providers. (However, sometimes founders will issue themselves a special class of common stock with 10 or 100 votes per share and protective provisions.)

◇ **IMPORTANT** Though common stock can be raised in a priced round, it is not usual for angels to purchase common stock. Common stock usually has one vote per share, no liquidation preference, no anti-dilution adjustment protection, and no protective provisions. As we have previously discussed, preferred stock is "preferred" because it has these types of special preferences. However—and though many angels will refuse to buy common stock—common stock deals are not necessarily bad deals. In fact, one of the best investment returns Joe has ever seen was a $100K angel investment in common stock that turned into $20M in cash.

If you are doing a common stock deal, the definitive documents will include a common stock purchase agreement, and may include other agreements such as a Voting Agreement.

17.2.1 STARTUPS' PERSPECTIVE ON COMMON STOCK

🌱 **FOUNDER** The benefits to the entrepreneurs of a common stock round relative to a preferred stock round include:

- A lack of liquidation preference for the common stock investors.
- A lack of dividend preferences typically associated with preferred stock.
- A general lack of other voting and control provisions typically associated with preferred stock. (That said, it is possible to put many provisions favorable to the investors$^{\S16.4}$ in side letter agreements and other definitive documents associated with the financing.)
- Significantly lower legal fees for documenting the deal.

From the company's perspective, there are drawbacks to selling common stock to investors:

- Once the company sells common stock, it will have fixed the value of its common shares for the purposes of granting stock options. If the company sells common stock at $1 a share, it cannot grant stock options at $0.25 a share without causing any optionees to have negative tax consequences.
- In contrast, if the company sells preferred stock, it can typically continue to grant stock options, which will be options for common stock,

at a price per share less than the price per share at which it sold preferred stock.

17.2.2 INVESTORS' PERSPECTIVE ON COMMON STOCK

The reason angels do not normally invest in common stock is because common stock does not have the privileges of preferred stock (specifically, a liquidation preference). However, in some instances founders will not want to issue preferred stock because they will not want a liquidation preference ahead of their founder shares, and sometimes investors are willing to do this to get into the deal. The other situation where common stock might be sold is when the amount of money being raised is not large enough to justify the costs of a preferred stock round and the investors are willing to take common stock in a fixed price round rather than convertible debt or convertible equity. In general, as a rule of thumb, if a company is raising less than $500K, a preferred stock round does not make sense from a legal fees perspective, and a convertible note or equity round or common stock round makes more sense.

As the example common-stock term sheet[§30.3] suggests, investing in common stock can be relatively straightforward. However, as described above, there are drawbacks and potential pitfalls to consider:

⚠ DANGER If the company raises money at a lower valuation shortly after an investor's common stock investment, the investor will not be entitled to the lower valuation (unless the investor negotiated a most favored nations or purchase price anti-dilution adjustment in a side letter or elsewhere in the definitive documents).

> ❯ EXAMPLE

> You buy common stock at $1 per share. Six months later the company sells preferred stock at $0.60 per share. Because you did not negotiate for an MFN or anti-dilution adjustment protection, or the right to convert your common stock into the next round of preferred, there is nothing you can do. You have your common stock, but you are probably not too happy that the preferred stock investors made a much better deal and at a 40% discount to your price.

⚠ **DANGER**   If the company issues preferred stock with a liquidation prefer-ence, and the company is liquidated for less than the liquidation prefer-ence, you won't receive anything.

> ⟩ **EXAMPLE**
>
> You buy common stock at $1 per share. Preferred stock investors subsequently invest $1M at $1.25 per share, with a 1X liquidation preference. The company does not succeed and ultimately sells all of its assets for $500K. The preferred stockholders are entitled to receive all of the proceeds. You are not entitled to receive anything on liquidation in this scenario.

◇ **IMPORTANT**   Generally, common stock investments do not have any con-trol mechanisms built into the deal. If you are a small investor (for instance, in the amount of $25K), it would not be reasonable for you to assert any control rights. But if your investment is larger, something on the order of $200K or more, you may want to request control mechanisms including a board seat and/or approval for certain company actions, such as the sale of the company. These controls can be built into the definitive documents or appear in a side letter.

How to Protect Yourself in a Common Stock Round

There are a number of ways you can try to protect yourself if you are investing in common stock. For example, you could have the company agree (perhaps in a side letter) that if it sold preferred stock in the future, it would convert your common stock to preferred. That would be unusual, but it is possible to do this.

Another possibility is that you negotiate for purchase price anti-dilu-tion protection (perhaps to be embodied in a side letter agreement with the company).

Another idea is to set a pro rata right, so you can apply your pro rata right in subsequent rounds of financing by the company.

You can find an example of a side letter agreement from a common stock investment that gives the investor full ratchet anti-dilution protec-tion in the appendix$^{\S30.6}$ (though this is rare).

17.3 *Revenue Loans*

Revenue loans are another relatively new financial innovation in the early-stage company space.

A **revenue loan** is a loan that has a monthly or periodic repayment amount that is a percentage of the company's gross or net revenue in the period with respect to which the payment is going to be made (for example, the preceding month or quarter). The payment amount is typically somewhere between 5-10% of the preceding period's gross or net revenue. In other words, the payment amount is not set and fixed like in a traditional loan. It goes up and down based on the performance of the business. A revenue loan may have a four-, five-, seven-, or ten-year term, and is considered repaid when the lender has received the negotiated multiple of the loan amount (anywhere from 1.5X-3X) and any other costs of the loan.

Revenue loans may or may not be secured by the company's assets and may or may not be guaranteed by the company's founders. They may or may not have any financial operating covenants. They may or may not have any equity component (for example, they could come with warrant coverage.[§17.4] They may also come with a "success fee," meaning a payment of some additional amount to the lender on the sale of the company.

Revenue loans fill a gap between typical commercial loans and traditional equity-based financing instruments. They are often used by companies that have cash flow and are looking for expansion capital but do not want to give up any equity in the business. For example, if a new coffee shop is doing really well and the owners want to open three more locations, they may not have the working capital required for that expansion. A traditional bank may not see enough operating history or might want personal guarantees from the owners along with constraining financial covenants. With a revenue loan, once those new venues start generating cash the owners can use margin on that new revenue to pay off the loan over time. The other advantage of the revenue loan structure is that if it took several months for those new locations to ramp up sales, the company would not be burdened with a high fixed monthly loan payment from a traditional loan. The revenue loan payments would start low and ramp directly with the sales.

For a revenue loan to work, it is important that the company have a high-margin product since they will be using a percentage of revenue to pay off the loan. For example, a company sells a product for $100 and the direct costs of producing and delivering that product are $50. They have a 50% product margin, (revenue-cost)/revenue. They will also have operating costs. Let's say the cost of product support and the sales team and marketing average 30% of the revenue. The company now has $100 - $50 - $30 = $20 from each product, which they can use to cover their overhead and provide a profit. For our purposes, let's call that the operating margin: 20%. It would be very risky for this company to take a revenue loan that takes 15% or even 10% of revenue, as it would leave them almost no cash (5% or 10% of revenue) to cover overhead and other needs. Software and SaaS (software as a service) companies are the canonical example of the high-margin products, with typically 80% or higher margins. For that reason, revenue loans have come to tech companies as well. Lighter Capital, for example, a revenue loan business based in Seattle, is an active lender to SaaS and technology services companies.

⚠ DANGER   One legal issue you will need to watch out for in the revenue loan context is usury. Some state usury laws specifically exclude from the definition of interest a share of the revenue of the business. Other states do not have usury laws at all in the context of commercial loans. But some state usury laws apply to revenue loans and prohibit effective interest rates above a certain amount. This is an issue that needs to be thought through when making revenue loans.

17.3.1 STARTUPS' PERSPECTIVE ON REVENUE LOANS

Assuming that the company has a high-margin product or service, a revenue loan has advantages over a bank loan, including:

- Flexible payments, which go up only when the revenue is flowing, as opposed to the fixed payments of a bank loan, which can be especially helpful if there is a lead time to develop revenue from the investment.
- Typically fewer financial covenants, so more flexibility to run the business.
- Potentially no personal guarantees for the founders.
- Potentially no equity in the business has to be given up.

The cost of a revenue loan in terms of the effective interest rate paid by the company is typically significantly higher than for a bank loan. That can still be very attractive to founders compared with equity financing due to the following factors:

- Potentially no ownership dilution.
- Potentially not much in the way of lender control provisions or operating covenants (no investors on board seats, for example).
- Usually much faster and cheaper access to capital than traditional equity financings.
- No need for an exit strategy, meaning it's fine if the business turns out to be a lifestyle business for the founders.

The downside of a revenue loan to the company of course is that loans can drain cash from the company. If a company wants to continue to expand beyond where its initial revenue loan took it, then they have to find the cash within existing operations for the next product development effort or business initiative. If a business suffers pricing pressure, cost increases, or other margin erosion, a revenue loan can be challenging.

17.3.2 **INVESTORS' PERSPECTIVE ON REVENUE LOANS**

Revenue loans can be great for investors because they allow investors to get a return on their investment without having to wait years for a company to be sold or go public. In equity financings, many angel investors run into the following problem: They are investing in stock and convertible debt in startups and early-stage companies. They are making a number of investments per year. Years roll by. They keep making investments. But none of the companies are getting sold or going public. "I've got plenty of deals *on* the conveyor belt," Joe heard an angel investor once cry. "But I've got nothing coming *off* the conveyor belt."

◇ IMPORTANT When you invest in a private company, you are signing up for the long haul. The lack of liquidity in angel investing can be challenging. For this reason, revenue loans can be a complementary part of your startup investing portfolio. You are not going to get the big win, but you are much more likely to get the 2X-3X return on your investment; and as the loan is paid off, you will have additional capital to deploy.

The other advantage of revenue loans to the investor is that the loan is debt and it can be secured. Debt is senior to equity—meaning that if the company fails, debt gets paid back first, before equity.

17.4 *Warrants*

A **warrant** is a contract entitling the warrant holder to buy shares of stock of a company. It is not stock itself. It is merely a contractual right to buy stock.

A warrant will set out:

- the price per share at which you can buy the shares (for example, $0.01 per share)
- the type of shares you have the right to buy (common or preferred)
- the period of time during which you can exercise the purchase right (for example, two, five, or ten years).

Warrants are fundamentally the same as stock options (both are rights to purchase stock), but warrants and stock options differ in their format, complexity, and the contexts in which they are used. Warrants are usually issued in investment transactions, such as convertible debt financings that include warrant coverage, and stock options are used for compensatory purposes (a stock option for employees and advisors, for example).

Warrant coverage most frequently arises in the context of a convertible debt financing, but it can also arise in the context of a preferred stock financing.

Warrant coverage has fallen out of favor in convertible debt financings because of the tax issues[§17.4.3] (forced inclusion in income on an accrual method basis of phantom interest income) and the ability to mirror (at least in part) some of the economics of a warrant through discounts and caps in convertible notes while avoiding the tax issues associated with warrants.

Very rarely,[§17.4.4] warrants are issued as stand-alone instruments—meaning, by themselves, with no accompanying purchase of a note or stock.

A warrant can be very valuable. Suppose you had acquired a ten-year warrant to buy 100K shares of an early stage company's stock for $0.40 a share. Five years later the company goes public and the shares are worth $40 a share. You can now exercise your warrant for $0.40 a share, and sell the shares on the open market for $40 a share.

17.4.1 WARRANT TERMS

In addition to the exercise price, the type of shares for which the warrant is exercisable, and the duration (term) of the warrant, warrants typically also have the following terms:

- A **net exercise** provision ("net exercise" means that if the shares underlying the warrant have a value greater than the exercise price per share at the time of exercise, rather than paying cash to exercise the warrant, you can pay the exercise price with shares that would otherwise be deliverable on exercise).
- An **automatic exercise** on a "net exercise" basis prior to termination (you would hate to have an in-the-money warrant suddenly terminate; an auto-exercise provision prevents that from happening).
- Notification of a pending sale of the company and other material events.
- Adjustments to the purchase price and number of shares covered for capital restructures, such as a stock split or stock dividend.

17.4.2 CALCULATING THE NUMBER OF SHARES REPRESENTED BY WARRANT COVERAGE

When negotiating a financing, you might hear a founder say, "We are offering 50% warrant coverage." Calculating the number of shares you are entitled to purchase based on a warrant coverage percentage requires the following inputs:

- the amount of your investment
- the exercise price per share of the warrant
- the warrant coverage percentage.

> ⟫ EXAMPLE
>
> Suppose you are investing $200K in a convertible debt investment, and the deal carries 50% warrant coverage. The price per share of the company's shares is not yet set because the company is offering this warrant coverage to you in a convertible debt round and your warrant is going to be exercisable into the preferred stock sold in the next round at that round's price. How do you calculate the number of shares covered by your warrant?

- In this example, the number of shares represented by the warrant coverage will depend on the price per share in the fixed-price round, once that is set. Suppose you invest $200K in the note round and the company ultimately consummates a "qualified financing" at $2.50 per share. In that case, you would be entitled to purchase 40K shares under the warrant. How?

- Start by calculating the number of shares from the conversion of your investment, excluding the warrant—$200K, divided by the price per share in the offering, $2.50, equals 80K shares. Now multiply the 80K shares you get from the conversion by the warrant coverage percentage, 50%, to get 40K additional shares from the warrant.
- You could also start with your investment amount, $200K, multiply that by the coverage percentage (50%) to get $100K, and divide that by the price per share, $2.50, to arrive at 40K.

Logically, this makes sense. You were offered 50% warrant coverage, or the right to buy an additional number of shares equal to half the shares you purchased when your note converted. What type of shares you get to buy and what price depends on the terms of the warrant as mentioned above. Typically the warrant coverage is for the type of shares sold in the next round, at the next round's price. However, if no next round occurs, you will need a "default" class of shares to convert into, which might be common stock or a new series of preferred stock described in the warrant.

17.4.3 TAX ISSUES WITH WARRANTS

If you buy a note with a warrant, be aware that special tax issues arise.

Original Issue Discount

Assume you invest $100K for a note with a principal amount of $100K and a warrant. The IRS will view the note and the warrant together as one investment "unit." It will deem that the $100K you invested must be allocated between the note and the warrant. This will result in the note having what is referred to in the tax law as the original issue discount (OID).[135] OID must be included in taxable income on an accrual basis.

For example, assume the IRS determines that the fair market value of the warrants received is $20K. This would mean that you would have $20K of OID in the note, and would have to include that in taxable income over some period of time. It will be phantom income on which you have to pay tax. This tax issue is one reason note and warrant financings have fallen

---

135. https://www.law.cornell.edu/uscode/text/26/1273

out of favor. More common today are note financings without warrants. Instead of warrants, notes have conversion discounts.

Investment Warrants vs. Services Options

There is a significant tax difference between warrants issued in connection with an investment transaction, and warrants or options issued in consideration for services rendered.

If you receive a warrant or a stock option in exchange for service rendered, then the same rules for nonqualified stock options apply:

- Section 409A applies, which means that if they are priced below fair market value the optionee will be subject to 20% penalty taxes and interest upon the vesting of the options.
- If priced at fair market value on grant, the receipt of the option is not taxable.
- If priced at fair market value on grant, the vesting of the option does not give rise to tax.
- On exercise, ordinary income tax is owed on the difference between the fair market value of the stock received and the exercise price.

On the other hand, if you acquire a warrant in connection with and as part of an investment, then the exercise of the warrant does not give rise to any taxable income, even if at the time of exercise there is a significant spread (meaning, the fair market value of the stock at the time of exercise is greater than the exercise price).

17.4.4 WHAT ABOUT A WARRANT FINANCING?

It is rare, but we have seen circumstances where someone will want to buy just a warrant in a company. Warrants are typically not purchased alone, so a "warrant financing" is atypical. Why? Think of it this way. Why would you invest in a security that only entitles you to become a stockholder if you later "exercise" the warrant? A warrant does not make you a creditor of the company, because a warrant is not a promissory note. Nor does a warrant make you a stockholder of the company, because it has to be exercised before it is converted to stock.

If you have the opportunity to buy a warrant, standing alone, and you want to go ahead, make sure the warrant has the terms that you desire, including, at least: (i) a lengthy term (like 10 years); (ii) an automatic exercise prior to termination if in the money: (iii) adjustment provisions in the event of a stock split; (iv) a net exercise provision; (v) an attorneys' fees provision (and if possible, a favorable venue clause).

18   General Investment Terms

In the sections so far covering the different investment vehicles, each section has included terms that are unique to or typically associated with that investment type. This section includes the general investment terms that could show up on any term sheet, regardless of the investment vehicle. We have touched on many of these terms already, but in this section we will go deeper.

We have grouped the terms into subsections, and you can use this chapter as a reference whenever you come across one of these concepts.

18.1   *Economic Rights*

The rights in this section address how you can participate in or get impacted by future investment rounds. For example, if the company has to raise money in the future at a lower valuation, you do not want to get your ownership stake heavily diluted or "washed out." If the company is doing well, you may want to ensure that you have the right to keep investing.

18.1.1   PARTICIPATION RIGHTS

Investors may want the right to continue to invest and thereby minimize their dilution as much as possible as the company grows.

◇ CAUTION Sometimes investors ask to never be diluted below a certain percentage of a company. For example, an investor might offer to buy 5% of a company but want the company to obligate itself to never dilute the investor below 5% of the company. This is an unsophisticated and impractical request. There is no realistic, practical way to accomplish this in a company that expects to raise multiple rounds of funding. Remember, *everyone* gets diluted, including the founders.

To help you protect the value of your stock from dilution, you can negotiate for participation rights.

Participation rights (or preemptive rights) allow investors to invest in subsequent rounds to maintain their pro rata share. **Super participation rights (or gobble up rights)** allow you to buy *more* than your pro rata share, meaning the right to invest more if other investors do not exercise their participation rights in full.

Depending on how the provisions are drafted, you may not only have the right to buy your pro rata share but also shares covered by the pro rata rights of other stockholders who elect not to participate.

There are a few key components to a participation or preemptive rights provision:

- The definition of pro rata.[136]
- How much notice you are given.
- If others don't exercise, can you participate in their share as well?
- What are the carve-outs?

There are a variety of typical carve-outs from participation rights, including:

- stock option grants;
- issuances of equity to banks or commercial lenders;
- issuances of equity to joint venture partners, or similar persons, the purpose of which is other than to raise capital.

Regardless of these carve-outs, if the provisions are correctly put together, on the next round you will be able to buy enough shares to restore your pro rata position. Realize though that in the future the valuation might get too high for you to continue to participate in any meaningful way.

Another option, if you are one of the very early investors, is to negotiate that your investment for X% of the company not be calculated until the company has raised at least some specified amount of money from third parties in a preferred stock financing. This is what accelerators and incubators frequently do in their contracts.

---

136. For example of how you might define pro rata, see the participation in the NVCA Investor Rights Agreement.[137]

137. https://nvca.org/wp-content/uploads/2019/06/ NVCA-Model-Document-Investor-Rights-Agreement.docx

18.1.2 **RIGHT OF FIRST REFUSAL**

A **right of first refusal** gives the investors the right to buy the founder's shares if a founder is going to sell them to a third party.

If you are very bullish on the company and want the opportunity to increase your investment, then this type of term can be useful. It is less common in angel deals than in venture deals, where founders may be looking to cash out some of their equity.

Sometimes, companies will want to impose a right of first refusal on investor shares. In such cases, you may want to ask for a right of first refusal and co-sale right on founder shares. Right of first refusal agreements often go together with co-sale rights, which give the investors the right to sell some of their stock if the founders are selling stock.

18.2 *Control and Governance*

Control and governance refers to how the company is controlled (hiring and firing officers, issuing equity, M&A transaction approval) and who controls it. The primary control mechanism is the board of directors and protective provisions. We covered a number of protective provisions within our discussion of preferred stock.[§16.4] Drag-along agreements are worth mentioning because they impact who is *not* in control of a transaction (potentially you).

18.2.1 **BOARD SEATS**

If you are a significant investor, you may want to negotiate a board seat. We cover boards of directors and boards of advisors in detail in Boards and Advisory Roles.[§26]

If you do take a board seat, as part of the term sheet, you may want to insist that the company obtain directors and officers insurance to protect you in the event of a lawsuit. In addition, it is always a good idea to have a lawyer who is familiar with these insurance policies to work with company management and the company's broker to make sure that you are getting a policy with the coverages you want and without exclusions that might leave you unprotected.

18.2.2 **DRAG ALONG**

A **drag-along agreement (or take-along agreement)** requires those who sign it, ideally all of the company's stockholders, to vote in favor of change of control transactions—to go along with the sale of the company or a sale of all of the interests in the company, including yours, even if you do not agree with the proposed sale and would otherwise refuse to go along or vote for it.

◇ CAUTION Larger investors like drag-along agreements; as an angel investor, you would prefer not to be subject to a drag-along agreement. If you are presented with a drag-along agreement, make sure it has some checks and balances in it. You can see a drag-along provision with the appropriate investor protection in the Series Seed Stock Investment Agreement.[138]

18.3 *Information and Access*

What if you made an investment in an early-stage company and never heard from them again; or only received documents to sign when they wanted to authorize more stock? Many investors like to know what is going on with their investments, and the rights described in this section make sure that you as an investor can get regular updates and access to management if you want that.

18.3.1 **INFORMATION RIGHTS**

Information rights are the rights to receive certain information about the company at specified times—for example, the right to receive quarterly and annual financial statements, the right to receive an updated capitalization table from time to time, and the right to receive the company's annual budget. Sometimes, information rights are only made available to investors who invest a certain amount in a financing (typically referred to in the investment documents as a "major investor").

◇ IMPORTANT Companies that go dark, or that do not communicate with their investors on a regular basis, can be a significant source of angst for investors. If an entrepreneur or lead investor (who might be a major investor while you are not) pushes back on inclusion of all investors in

---

138. https://www.seriesseed.com/

information rights, you can stress that there is no additional work required by the company. The documents are already being prepared, and they just need to add you to the electronic distribution list.

18.3.2 INSPECTION RIGHTS

Inspection rights are the rights to visit the business premises, meet with management, and review the company's books and records. Companies may have a legitimate reason to push back on giving all investors inspection rights, as it could be a significant drain on management's time if they were obligated to meet with or entertain at their office a large number of individual investors.

You can find example inspection rights language in Section 3 of the NVCA example Investor Rights Agreement.[139]

The reasons to push for these terms mirrors the reasons to push for information rights. However, because of the potential business disruption, inspection rights are usually reserved for major investors.

18.3.3 OBSERVER RIGHTS

Observer rights are rights to attend a company's board meetings as a guest, in a non-voting capacity. The ability to attend board meetings provides tremendous insight into what is happening at the company. However, often very sensitive information is discussed, and a company may be very reluctant to provide this right to anyone other than the lead investor for a particular round.

A company would typically prefer observer rights to include confidentiality language and the ability to exclude the observer to maintain attorney client privilege. An example of an observer agreement can be found in the appendix.§30.7

18.4 *Liquidity*

Terms in this section impact how and when you might get cash back out of the investment. We discuss liquidation preferences in the section covering preferred stock,§16.4.1 since a liquidation preference is most typically a facet of a preferred stock financing.

---

139. https://nvca.org/wp-content/uploads/2019/06/
    NVCA-Model-Document-Investor-Rights-Agreement.docx

18.4.1 REDEMPTION RIGHTS

Redemption rights (or put right) are the rights to have your shares redeemed or repurchased by the company at the original purchase price or some multiple, usually after a period of time has passed (perhaps five years). It is also possible to prepare these provisions to allow redemption in the event the company fails to reach a milestone, or breaches a covenant.

◇ CAUTION Be aware, however, that even if you have redemption rights, if a company is insolvent it will not be able to legally satisfy a redemption demand. Under most states' corporate laws, corporations are disallowed from redeeming shares when the corporation is insolvent either on a balance sheet or ability to pay its debts as they come due, and directors are personally liable if they authorize a redemption when the corporation is insolvent.

Redemption rights are not common in angel deals. However, they can be appropriate and a good mechanism to employ if a business has the danger of becoming a lifestyle business for the entrepreneur. If you want to put redemption rights in place in order to avoid a lifestyle business outcome, you will probably also want to put in place covenants, such as restrictions on founder salaries—perhaps subject those to the approval of a compensation committee composed entirely of independent directors—to ensure that the redemption rights will have value and are enforceable when they come due.

18.4.2 REGISTRATION RIGHTS

A **registration rights agreement** is an agreement of the company to register securities with the Securities and Exchange Commission so that the holder of the securities can sell them. When investors demand the company register the investors' shares, it is so the investors can sell those shares on the public market and get liquidity—the liquidity goes to the investors, not the company.

Registration rights are not common in angel deals. However, it would be perfectly appropriate for an angel to ask to have the same registration rights granted to a future investor. The following language would suffice to achieve this:

> The company agrees that in the event that the company enters into a registration rights agreement with future investors in the company, the company shall include the Investors with the coverage thereof to the same extent and with the same rights as such future investors.

You can find an example of a registration rights agreement in the Investor Rights Agreement at NVCA.[140]

18.4.3 CO-SALE OR TAG-ALONG RIGHT

The **co-sale right (or tag-along right)** is the right to participate alongside another stockholder, typically a founder, when that stockholder is selling their shares.

If the value of a company's stock has gone up significantly, but it is still far from a liquidity event, and the founders are selling some of their shares to an outside investor, you may want to sell some of your stock and realize a gain. This right is useful if you are concerned that the founder might find a buyer for his or her shares and leave you behind.

In a world in which it can take ten years for a company to go public, it is reasonable that founders would want to sell some of their shares to take some money off the table and improve their lifestyle. As an early investor, you would like to do the same thing if they have found a buyer, which is why you want a co-sale right.

18.5 *Representations and Warranties*

Representations (or reps) and **warranties** can cover a broad range of topics in a financing transaction and they typically get more thorough as the amount of money gets bigger. In general terms, a representation is an assertion that the information in question is true at the time of the financing, and the warranty is the promise of indemnity if the representation

---

140. https://nvca.org/wp-content/uploads/2019/06/
     NVCA-Model-Document-Investor-Rights-Agreement.docx

turns out to be false. For example, a company might rep that they have no unpaid salaries, or that they are not currently being sued. We address two more specific reps below.

If you want to get a taste of probably the most typical sort of representations and warranties companies give in private financings, you can review the representations and warranties in the Series Seed documents.[141]

18.5.1 CAP REP

A capitalization rep or cap rep is a representation and warranty in a securities purchase agreement in which the company makes assurances to you about its ownership and capital structure. For example, the company may represent and warrant that it has authorized 10M shares of common stock and that it only has 2M shares outstanding. If they are wrong, the investor can sue for damages and remedies.

The cap rep is critical in a fixed-price financing. If the company does not give you a cap rep, how do you know much of the company you will own? This is true even in a convertible debt financing, although a cap rep is less common in those documents because the amount of the company you will own as a result of those transactions will be governed by a valuation to be determined later, or a valuation cap set forth in the convertible note.

18.5.2 FINANCIAL STATEMENTS REP

Whenever you make an investment, you would prefer the company make a representation and warranty about the company's financial statements. As an aside, you should take a look at those statements to see how much cash is left in the bank and what if any outstanding debts exist.

18.6 *Key Definitive Document Agreements*

We've discussed some of the definitive documents specific to the different types of angel investment types above. Below are definitive document agreements that can be associated with a broad range of financings.

---

141. https://www.seriesseed.com/posts/documents.html

18.6.1 VOTING AGREEMENT

A **Voting Agreement** is an agreement between the voting stockholders of a company in which the parties agree to vote their shares in a particular fashion to ensure that certain persons or their designees are elected to the board of directors. The agreement must be signed by the stockholders, because under corporate law it is the shareholders who elect the directors of the company; if your agreement is just with the company your right will not be enforceable.

> ❯ EXAMPLE

A two-person company is owned 60% by one person and 40% by the other. The two parties could agree that they would each vote their shares to elect each other to the board of directors. This would ensure that the 60% owner cannot throw the 40% owner off the board.

> ❯ EXAMPLE

Suppose there is a company comprised of three equal owners. Absent a Voting Agreement, any two owners can throw the third owner off the board and out of the company. With a Voting Agreement, they can each agree to vote their shares to elect each other to the board. This wouldn't prevent the board, by a two to one vote, from terminating the employment of one of the owners, but it would prevent the one terminated owner from being thrown off the board of directors.

◇ CAUTION If a company agrees to appoint you to its board of directors, that agreement is probably not enforceable, because only the stockholders of a company can agree to elect you to its board of directors, not the company.

> ❯ EXAMPLE

You want to negotiate for a board seat of a company you are investing in. In the term sheet, the company agrees to enter into an agreement with you to appoint you to the board. Immediately after the closing, the existing board of directors passed a resolution increasing the size of the board by one person and appointing you to fill the vacancy. You got what you wanted; you are on the board. But at the next annual meeting of shareholders, a majority of the shareholders vote for an entirely different board, and you are thrown off. You go to your lawyer, and ask if he will start a lawsuit to enforce your right to a board seat. Your lawyer tells you: "Your agreement with the company is not enforceable. For it to be enforceable, you need that agreement to take the form of a Voting Agreement signed by a majority of the shareholders."

18.6.2 INVESTOR RIGHTS AGREEMENT

An **Investor Rights Agreement** typically includes covenants or ongong promises on the part of the Company to provide the investors with certain rights. Those rights could include registration rights, participation rights, information rights, observer rights, inspections rights, protective provisions, and other covenants. The voting agreement may be part of the Investor Rights Agreement.

A good example of an Investor Rights Agreement can be found at NVCA.[142]

The Investor Rights Agreement may contain **protective provisions**. Protective provisions are special voting agreement provisions which require a company, before it can take certain actions, to obtain the separate approval of a particular group of shareholders.

If you invest in Series Seed Preferred Stock, the typical protective provisions can be found in an example term sheet found at Series Seed.[143]

---

142. https://nvca.org/wp-content/uploads/2019/06/
NVCA-Model-Document-Investor-Rights-Agreement.docx

143. https://www.seriesseed.com/

PART IV: VALUATION, OWNERSHIP, AND DILUTION

Understanding how ownership percentages in a company are impacted by valuation, and diluted as the company raises money and hires employees is crucial to being a good investor and a smart entrepreneur. This section will walk through these key concepts as we tell the story of one fictional company.

19 The Interplay of Valuation, Ownership, and Dilution

19.1 *Pre-Money and Post-Money Valuation*

Valuation is how much a company is worth; valuation and value may be used interchangeably, or valuation may refer to the process of determining a company's value. A public company's value is expressed by how much people are willing to pay for the shares on the stock market. For a private company, the company's value is determined in negotiations between the founders raising money and the investors.

You may have heard of 409A valuations for startups.

The common stock in a private company can be valued through a formal process called a **409A valuation**. 409A valuations are done for purposes of granting compensatory equity (typically stock options); they have little or no bearing on how much angels or VCs are going to pay for preferred stock in a company.

The **pre-money valuation** is the agreed upon value of the company immediately prior to the investment. The pre-money valuation is the single most important factor, but not the *only* factor, in determining how much of the company you will own when you invest a specific amount of money.

We will get into the mechanics of determining your ownership below.§19.2 But first, how does this pre-money valuation get determined?

If a CEO is pitching their startup to accredited investors, they will have a slide near the end that describes their proposed financing, i.e. how much money they are planning to raise, and the pre-money valuation, in the case of a priced round. (In a convertible round, it would be the valuation cap and discount.) In a typical Series Seed preferred stock financing, a CEO may be looking to raise $1M with a pre-money valuation of $3M. That is the starting point for negotiation of the term sheet. If due diligence uncovers some issues, there will be pressure to bring the pre-money valuation down.

There are no hard and fast rules about how to calculate the pre-money valuation of a startup. A savvy CEO will understand how comparable startups have been valued. Seasoned investors will have an intuitive sense of a reasonable valuation based on other deals they have seen and the particulars of the company. Their assessment will depend on a range of factors, including:

- **Strength of the team.** A CEO with prior successful startup exits can command a higher pre-money valuation.
- **Traction in the market.** This can include number of customers, amount of revenue, and lead over the competition.
- **Assets.** This can include intellectual property like granted patents and trademarks.
- **Stage of the product.** Is it a beta product, a prototype, a fully functional product live in the marketplace with clear advantages?
- **Barriers to competition.** Does the company have exclusive distribution relationships, key partnerships, or other assets that will make it hard for followers to compete?
- **Macro funding environment.** Seasoned investors who have seen several cycles of pre-money valuations going up and then down across the board may be able to set appropriate valuations with more confidence.
- **Negotiating skill of the CEO and interest in the deal.** If the CEO is a great salesperson and negotiator, they may be able to get a stronger pre-money valuation absent strength in many of the factors above.

The earlier the stage of the company, the harder it may be to come up with a pre-money valuation that entrepreneurs and investors can agree on. That is part of the appeal of non-priced investment vehicles like convertible notes and convertible equity—they essentially delay the need to determine a specific pre-money valuation.

FOUNDER The entrepreneur would like to see as high a valuation as possible, because it means they have to give up less of the company to raise a certain amount of money—as our fictional company story will make clear. Savvy entrepreneurs will understand that the higher the valuation, the harder it will be to generate investor interest, and they will do some benchmarking by looking at other deals of comparable companies. If the entrepreneur asks for too high a pre-money valuation in the opinion of investors, and is not willing to negotiate, investors will walk away.

In short, you will see a big range of valuations proposed by entrepreneurs, and after a while, you will start to get a sense of "fair" pre-money valuations.

The **post-money valuation** is the value of a company immediately following the investment. For example, if the pre-money was $3M, and the investment was $1M, then the post-money valuation would be $4M. Convertible equity instruments such as convertible notes or SAFEs can be set up as either pre-money or post-money instruments. The SAFE currently published by Y Combinator is a post-money SAFE.

In this example, the investors and entrepreneurs came to an agreement that the company was worth $3M before the investment; immediately after the investment it is still worth $3M as a going concern, but now it has an additional $1M in the bank. Hence the post-money valuation of $4M.

In the simplest scenario, if the investors have paid $1M for the equity of a company that is now worth $4M, they should own 25% of the company, and that would be reflected in the capitalization table of the company in the relative share counts. We will discuss the divergence from the simplest scenario in detail below, including how the percentage of ownership for everyone immediately post financing is impacted by the topping up of the stock option pool.

19.2 *Calculating Ownership and Dilution*

⚒ FOUNDER It is useful for both entrepreneurs and investors to understand the mechanics of dilution, how dilution and ownership are calculated, and how the cap table will be impacted by investment.

Dilution is the decrease in ownership percentage of a company that occurs when the company issues additional stock, typically for one of the following reasons: to issue to a co-founder who came on after incorporation, to sell to investors, or to add to its stock option pool.

When a company is formed, the certificate or articles of incorporation states the total number of shares the company is authorized to issue, called **authorized shares**. If the company decides it needs more shares at some point, it will need to amend its certificate or articles of incorporation, and that typically requires approval of a majority of stockholders. Authorized shares can include common stock and preferred stock.

Issued and outstanding shares are the shares that have been issued to founders, employees, advisors, directors, or investors. Issued and outstanding shares do not include stock options that have been reserved in the option pool. Ownership percentage calculated on an **issued and outstanding basis** is determined by dividing the number of shares owned by an individual or entity by the total issued and outstanding securities.

Fully diluted shares take into account all issued and outstanding shares on an as-converted to common stock basis, assuming the conversion or exercise of all convertible securities, such as options, warrants, and convertible preferred stock. Sometimes fully diluted shares take into account not just issued options but the entire stock option pool share reserve. Investors prefer that the price per share be determined on a **fully diluted basis** because increasing the number of shares in the denominator in the formula above reduces the price per share.

Considering that a stock option pool can represent 15% or 20% of the shares of a company, the ownership difference resulting from the two definitions can be substantial.

If you are calculating dilution based on the number of issued and outstanding securities, then each time part of the stock option pool is allocated to an employee in the form of a stock option grant, your ownership percentage goes down slightly, since there are now more issued and outstanding securities (the additional stock options). If you are calculating dilution on a fully diluted ownership percentage (or simply put, a fully diluted basis), counting the entire option pool, then your ownership percentage doesn't change, since all of the stock options, either allocated to employees or not, were already in the denominator.

When a company hires an employee and gives them stock options as part of their compensation, they usually issue the options out of the company's stock option plan (not the company's authorized but unissued shares).

20 Company Setup and Initial Ownership

In this section we will begin our example of a fictional company to explain some more key concepts, and illustrate how valuation and dilution effect ownership as represented in the cap table, starting with the initial company setup.

> ❯❯ EXAMPLE
>
> Joe and Pete started a software company, Pext, Inc., which is developing an app to help pets send and receive texts. They retained a well-known startup lawyer who incorporated their company in Delaware and helped them assemble and execute all of the correct documents with respect to the formation and organization of the company. The corporation was initially authorized under its charter to issue a total of 30M shares, 25M shares of common stock and 5M shares of preferred stock. Thus, the company had a total of 30M authorized shares.

20.1 *The Stock Option Pool*

The **stock option pool** is a specified number of shares set aside and reserved for issuance on the exercise of stock options granted to employees under a **stock option plan** or an **equity incentive plan**. Equity incentive plans have more awards available under them to issue than stock options (they also have stock bonuses, restricted stock awards, and sometimes other types of awards as well). The shares reserved under an equity incentive plan should be reflected on the cap table. Options are granted out of the pool via grants that are approved by the board. Each grant reduces the remaining available pool, until it is topped up again by the board authorizing the reservation of additional shares under the plan from the authorized shares. The **strike price** is the exercise price of the stock option.

◇ IMPORTANT Because stock options can be executed to purchase stock, they need to be accounted for in the cap table; and the stock option pool impacts both the percentage ownership calculation and potentially the price per share, as we will see below.

※ FOUNDER When a company is founded, the founders are wise to set aside 10–15% of the equity in an option pool for future new hires, contractors, and advisors. Over the first few years that equity gets allocated to the new hires, members of the board of directors, advisors, and independent contractors. When the company goes to raise money, savvy investors will want to see that option pool topped up to 10% or 15% again in anticipation of the company hiring many more employees.

Why does the stock option pool need to be so big? The earlier the stage of the company and the more senior the employee, the more equity that employee will demand. Bringing in a seasoned CEO to a very early-stage company (if one of the founders is no longer going to be the CEO) may require giving them 10% of the equity, likely vesting over four years. That is the high end, but even an experienced senior engineering lead or sales executive might command 2%-3% of the equity.[144] Steve Ballmer received 8%[146] of Microsoft stock when he joined as the 30th employee, and now owns more of the company[147] than Bill Gates. Smart CEOs track a budget of equity for employees, directors, and advisors. That stock gets allocated via stock option grants approved by the board of directors. As the company matures it needs to give out less stock to each employee, even senior ones, but the number of employees it is hiring is also increasing.

---

144. Learn more about typical equity levels in the *Holloway Guide to Equity Compensation.*[145]

145. https://www.holloway.com/g/equity-compensation/sections/ typical-employee-equity-levels

146. https://www.forbes.com/sites/georgeanders/2014/09/30/ long-ago-twist-yielded-ballmer-a-fortune-in-microsoft-stock/#138771db36a5

147. https://www.computerworld.com/article/2487340/ gates-will-surrender-microsoft-shareholder-crown-to-ballmer-in-2014.html

When investors are doing diligence on a company, one thing they check is how many shares (options) are left in the stock option pool. A case is often made that this pool needs to be topped up before the investment or as part of the investment. We will see the impact of this as we follow our example company.

> ❯❯ EXAMPLE

After agreeing on their relative proportionate stock ownership in the company (60% to Pete and 40% to Joe), Joe and Pete also set aside 15% in an equity incentive plan (commonly referred to as a stock option plan) for future advisors, contractors, and employees. Pete and Joe allocated a total of 10M shares to the cap table, including 1.5M for the stock option plan. They did not issue all of their authorized shares, because they needed to reserve out of the authorized but unissued shares at least enough shares to cover potential future co-founders, investment rounds, and a possible topping up of the stock option pool. Pete and Joe each bought their respective shares of stock from the company at a fraction of a penny per share. Immediately after these stock issuances, there were 8.5M issued and outstanding shares, and 10M shares on a fully diluted basis (counting the entire option pool share reserve).

20.1.1 **FIGURE 1: THE INITIAL CAP TABLE**

	SHARES OR OPTIONS	ISSUED AND OUTSTANDING[148]	FULLY DILUTED[149]
Pete	5,100,000	**60.00%**	51.00%
Joe	3,400,000	**40.00%**	34.00%
Issued and Outstanding	**8,500,000**	100.00%	
Option Pool	1,500,000		**15.00%**
Total Fully Diluted	10,000,000		100.00%

You can see in the table the difference in the ownership percentages based on the two different ways to calculate it (bold numbers represent the inputs driving the calculations). The first column represents calculating a founder's ownership as a percentage of shares outstanding; the second

---

148. Ownership percentage calculated on an issued and outstanding basis.
149. Ownership percentage calculated on a fully diluted basis, including pool.

column shows the calculation on a fully diluted basis taking into account the option pool. While this may seem like a mundane distinction, we make a point to call it out because it comes up in terms sheets for priced rounds. You do not measure someone's percentage ownership by reference to the total number of shares the corporation is authorized to issue. The various different approaches to calculating ownership will come up when discussing how much of the company investors are going to own after they put their collective money in. Thus, the fact that the company is authorized to issue as many as 25M shares of common stock is irrelevant to determining a founder's percentage ownership. The company could be authorized to issue 1B shares; it would not matter.

20.2 *Dilution From Adding a Co-Founder*

The simplest example of dilution comes from adding another co-founder. This is different from adding another employee, which we will explore below. It is similar to the impact of selling shares in a priced round, but we will save that discussion for further on in our example so that we don't tackle too many variables at once!

> ❭ EXAMPLE

Joe and Pete decide to add a technical co-founder, Rachel. After negotiation, the parties agree that Rachel will receive 15% of the company. Rachel buys her shares directly from the company out of the corporation's authorized but unissued shares.

20.2.1 FIGURE 2A: CO-FOUNDER GETS 15% OWNERSHIP CALCULATED AS A PERCENTAGE OF ISSUED AND OUTSTANDING SHARES

This is what the cap table looks like after Rachel purchases stock from the company such that she owns 15% of the issued and outstanding shares.

	SHARES OR OPTIONS	ISSUED AND OUTSTANDING	FULLY DILUTED
Pete	5,100,000	51.00%	44.35%
Joe	3,400,000	34.00%	29.57%
Rachel	1,500,000	**15.00%**	13.04%
Issued and Outstanding	10,000,000	100.00%	

	SHARES OR OPTIONS	ISSUED AND OUTSTANDING	FULLY DILUTED
Option Pool	1,500,000		13.04%
Total Fully Diluted	11,500,000		100.00%

Note that the number of shares Rachel is issued to reach 15% is calculated prior to taking into account the dilution of the option pool. If Rachel was super savvy on dilution, she might have tried to negotiate a 15% ownership after taking into account the option pool—that is, on a fully diluted basis. Or, in other words, she could have asked Pete and Joe to bear the dilution from the option pool—not her. Smart investors often ask for their ownership to be calculated on a fully diluted basis (meaning, for the pre-existing owners to take the dilution hit for the option plan shares set aside). You can see the impact of this change in the calculation below.

20.2.2 FIGURE 2B: CO-FOUNDER GETS 15% OWNERSHIP ON A FULLY DILUTED BASIS

	SHARES OR OPTIONS	ISSUED AND OUTSTANDING	FULLY DILUTED
Pete	5,100,000	49.68%	43.35%
Joe	3,400,000	33.12%	28.90%
Rachel	1,765,000	17.19%	**15.00%**
Issued and Outstanding	10,265,000	100.00%	
Option Pool	1,500,000		12.75%
Total Fully Diluted	11,765,000		100.00%

Rachel ends up with an additional 265,000 shares by changing how she defines her 15% ownership. This is exactly how it works with investors as well. The advantage that Rachel gets in this latter calculation comes at the disadvantage of the other (prior) owners.

Since Pete and Joe are savvy negotiators too, they make the point that it makes sense that all founders should be subject to dilution from the option pool. So our example will continue on from Figure 2A.

As you can see from this simple example so far, when the company issues additional stock to founders or (later) investors out of its authorized stock, it dilutes the ownership of the existing stockholders. They own the same number of shares, but their percentage ownership of the company goes down.

Dilution occurs when a company issues new shares (other than in connection with a stock split or other adjustment affecting all shareholders in the same way). Shares may be issued for any of the following reasons:

- An additional founder may join who will get a significant share of the company.
- Shares may be purchased by investors.
- The company may increase the number of shares reserved for issuance under its equity incentive plan, or adopt one or more new equity incentive plans.
- The company may issue shares or other convertible securities to lenders, strategic partners, landlords, and similar persons.

20.3 *Dilution From Adding an Employee*

When a company hires an employee and gives them stock options as part of their compensation, they usually issue the options out of the shares reserved for issuance under the company's stock option plan (not the company's authorized but unissued shares).

Joe and Pete hire a very experienced head of marketing and give them a stock option to purchase 3% of the company.

To translate the 3% of the company into a number of shares, Pete and Joe multiply 3% by the company's issued and outstanding shares plus its entire stock option pool reserve. They are calculating the ownership on a fully diluted basis. This way, if they issue 3% to another executive the next week, that executive would get the same number of shares. Effectively, you don't want each employee to dilute the next employee, especially since the board of directors may be approving option grants to five employees at the same time. This is how most companies translate negotiated percentages into share numbers; it does not have to be done this way, but it is the most common way.

20.3.1 FIGURE 3: FIRST EMPLOYEE STOCK OPTION

Picking up from Figure 2A,[§20.2] the first employee is granted an option to purchase 345,000 shares (3% multiplied by 11,500,000), which represents

3% of the sum of the issued and outstanding shares and the entire stock option pool reserve.

	SHARES OR OPTIONS	ISSUED AND OUTSTANDING	FULLY DILUTED
Pete	5,100,000	49.30%	44.35%
Joe	3,400,000	32.87%	29.57%
Rachel	1,500,000	14.50%	13.04%
Employee 1	345,000	3.33%	**3.00%**
Issued and Outstanding	10,345,000	100.00%	
Option Pool Available	1,155,000		10.04%
Total Fully Diluted	11,500,000		100.00%

345K shares were issued out of the option pool for Employee 1, the marketing director, which had several impacts (compare to Figure 2A):

- It decreased the remaining option pool, which now represents a smaller percentage of shares.
- It increased the total number of issued and outstanding shares and securities convertible into shares, which diluted all existing shareholders when their ownership is measured as a percentage of issued and outstanding securities.
- It did not change the fully diluted ownership (which includes the option plan in the denominator) of the existing shareholders, because those shares were already in the option pool.

21 Dilution From Selling Priced Shares to Investors

What follows is a simple example of how ownership gets diluted with the selling of shares. In the next section, we'll bring it all together and talk about how those shares get priced.

In a priced round, the company issues shares out of its authorized stock, either common stock, or more typically preferred stock. A specific number of those shares are sold to investors at a specific price. This new stock gets added to the cap table, which increases the number of issued and outstanding shares. All the existing shareholders (founders, prior investors, employees with stock options, advisors) have the same number of shares or options they had before the transaction, so they are all diluted in their ownership by the increase in the denominator (total number of shares).

✻ FOUNDER Every time founders raise more money or issue stock options for new employees, they dilute their ownership. Prior investors are also diluted by these activities. The degree of dilution is determined largely by the ratio between the amount of money being raised and the pre-money valuation. If the founders raise too much money before they can justify a high valuation, they give up too much of the company too early.

◇ IMPORTANT The 50% ownership mark is an important threshold for founders. Those who control more than 50% of the company's stock have a lot of control over the company. Any significant corporate activity around issuing more stock or how the board is structured, for example, can ultimately be controlled by owning a majority of the stock—unless the founders have agreed to specific control provisions[§12.3.3] for investors. Once the founders have sold off more than 50% of their stock to investors, they have essentially lost control of the company they founded. Because of this, you may see resistance among founders to going below the 50% threshold too early.

✻ FOUNDER A good rule of thumb for entrepreneurs is not to sell off more than 20% of the company in any single financing round. Pete has seen naive entrepreneurs pitch a financing of $400K on a $600K pre-money valuation. The result would be selling off 40% of the company in the first investment round. Future rounds will continue to dilute the founders and early investors. You don't want founders to get to a low percentage ownership early in the process or they may not see a lot of upside and lose motivation.

◇ IMPORTANT To manage ongoing dilution, the pre-money valuation for each successive round has to grow dramatically. This is why it is so important that startups hit their operational milestones (improving the product, getting customers, et cetera) and do as much as possible with the money they raise at each step.

Let's take another step with Pext, Inc. and see how the amount of money raised and the pre-money valuation impact how much the founders own at the end of two rounds under two different sets of assumptions.

21.1 *Scenario A: Raising $250K*

> ⟫ EXAMPLE

Pext, Inc. raises its first external round as a priced round, closing a $250K raise with a $1M pre-money valuation. (If you have been reading carefully, you would rightly object to a priced round for a raise of only $250K, and suggest a SAFE or convertible note instead, but bear with us so we can illustrate the dilution!) If the pre-money is $1M, the post-money valuation in this case will be $1.25M (pre-money valuation plus amount raised), and the percentage of the company sold will be 20% ($250K/$1.25M). Let's say that our savvy investors insist that their ownership should be calculated on a fully diluted basis.

21.1.1 FIGURE 3S: SUMMARY CAP TABLE PRIOR TO ANY INVESTMENTS

Consolidating the cap table above (Figure 3[§20.3.1]) to aggregate founders and employees prior to investment:

	SHARES OR OPTIONS	ISSUED AND OUTSTANDING	FULLY DILUTED
Founders	10,000,000	96.67%	86.96%
Employee 1	345,000	3.33%	3.00%
Issued and Outstanding	10,345,000	100.00%	
Option Pool Available	1,155,000		10.04%
Total Fully Diluted	**11,500,000**		100.00%

21.1.2 FIGURE A1: IMPACT OF RAISING $250K ON $1M PRE-MONEY VALUATION, FULLY DILUTED BASIS

	SHARES OR OPTIONS	ISSUED AND OUTSTANDING	FULLY DILUTED
Founders	10,000,000	75.64%	69.57%

	SHARES OR OPTIONS	ISSUED AND OUTSTANDING	FULLY DILUTED
Employees	345,000	2.61%	2.40%
Round 1 Investors	2,875,000	21.75%	**20.00%**
Issued and Outstanding	13,220,000	100.00%	
Option Pool	1,155,000		8.03%
Total Fully Diluted	14,375,000		100.00%

Let's assume that $250K lasts a year (founders are taking minimal salary), and Pext has made great progress. They now have a fully functioning app in the Apple app store with 10K downloads and great early customer engagement numbers. They want to hire a full time app developer and a full time marketing person. Based on the customer engagement and their execution to date overall, they raise another $750K round of funding, and convince investors that they are worth $3M pre-money. Again, they will be selling another 20% of the company: (750K/(3M + 750K)) = 20%. This would be a typical scenario.

The post-money valuation after the first round was $1M + $250K = $1.25M. So this is a great progress in the valuation from one round to the next ($1.25M post to $3M pre-money), and is called an "up-round."

21.1.3 **FIGURE A2: IMPACT OF THEN RAISING $750K ON $3M PRE-MONEY VALUATION, FULLY DILUTED BASIS**

	SHARES OR OPTIONS	ISSUED AND OUTSTANDING	FULLY DILUTED
Founders	10,000,000	59.48%	55.65%
Employees	345,000	2.05%	1.92%
Round 1 Investors	2,875,000	17.10%	16.00%
Round 2 Investors	3,593,750	21.37%	**20.00%**
Issued and Outstanding	16,813,750	100.00%	
Option Pool	1,155,000		6.43%
Total Fully Diluted	17,968,750		100.00%

At this point, everything is going well and the founders own almost 56% of the stock on a fully diluted basis. The Round 1 investors have been diluted from their initial 20% down to 16% by the Round 2 investors.

21.2 *Scenario B: Raising $500K*

For comparison now, let's look at scenario B, where the founders raise $500K instead of $250K on the same $1M pre-money valuation. Now they are giving up a third of the company in the first external round.

21.2.1 FIGURE B1: IMPACT OF RAISING $500K ON A $1M PRE-MONEY VALUATION, FULLY DILUTED BASIS

	SHARES OR OPTIONS	ISSUED AND OUTSTANDING	FULLY DILUTED
Founders	10,000,000	62.13%	57.97%
Employees	345,000	2.14%	2.00%
Round 1 Investors	5,749,138	35.72%	**33.33%**
Issued and Outstanding	16,094,138	100.00%	
Option Pool	1,155,000		6.70%
Total Fully Diluted	17,249,138		100.00%

In scenario A, the founders owned roughly 70% after the first raise, in scenario B, they only own 58%. They have given up 12% of the company for the extra $250K. They would have to make a lot more progress on that extra $250K in order to bring up the pre-money valuation for the next round well beyond what they could have done with only $250K.

🏴 FOUNDER Raising a large round relative to the pre-money valuation is brutal on the existing stockholders—both the founders and any existing equity investors. (Careful readers will point out that raising money is a big distraction for a company and ask if it isn't better to raise as much as possible each time? This is a tension for the founders.[150])

Following scenario B for a final illustration, let's assume that the company didn't make as much progress with the $500K (they spent a lot of time finding a cool office and buying expensive furniture, bought a pricey

---

150. https://www.holloway.com/g/venture-capital/sections/determining-how-much-to-raise

domain name, hired a well-known design firm to do a cool logo, and they over-hired and over-spent in marketing before the product was ready.[151])

When they went to raise another round, they could only convince investors that the pre-money was $1.5M. The post-money valuation from the first round was $1.5M ($1M pre + $500K = $1.5M). This is a "flat round," where the pre-money valuation has not grown. An even worse scenario is a "down round" where the pre-money valuation goes down from the previous post-money valuation.[152]

21.2.2 **FIGURE B2: IMPACT OF RAISING $750K ON A $1.5M PRE-MONEY VALUATION, FULLY DILUTED BASIS**

	SHARES OR OPTIONS	ISSUED AND OUTSTANDING	FULLY DILUTED
Founders	10,000,000	40.46%	38.65%
Employees	345,000	1.40%	1.33%
Round 1 Investors	5,749,138	23.26%	22.22%
Round 2 Investors	8,623,275	34.89%	**33.33%**
Issued and Outstanding	24,717,413	100.00%	
Option Pool	1,155,000		4.46%
Total Fully Diluted	25,872,413		100.00%

In scenario B, the founders give up another one third of the company on a fully diluted basis and now own less than 39% of the company. They have less than 50% of the voting shares and have lost a large degree of control of the company. The Round 1 investors have also seen a lot of dilution, from 33.33% to 22.22% ownership of the company.

⚶ FOUNDER The key takeaways are that raising too much money relative to the pre-money valuation causes excessive dilution, and not increasing the pre-money valuation enough as the company needs to raise bigger rounds *also* causes excessive dilution.

◇ IMPORTANT Once you have invested, you suffer the same relative dilution as the founders in successive rounds, so you are aligned in your motiva-

---

151. Pete has seen all of these and more.
152. You can also think of this as the stock price.

tion to quickly increase the value of the company before the company has to raise money again.

These two scenarios were crafted to illustrate the impacts of the dilution resulting from the ratio of the amount raised to the pre-money valuation. We could have written a scenario about a company that raised too little ($250K), burned through it in six months and spent the next six months investing all their time raising money again instead of growing the company. As we noted above, determining the right amount of money to raise should be a carefully considered decision. To reiterate the benefits of convertible notes early on in the fundraising process, the company can raise money more cheaply with less negotiations on terms, and without even setting a pre-money valuation.

21.3 *Setting the Price Per Share*

In the dilution examples above, we determined ownership percentage and the number of shares to be sold to the investors without ever calculating the price per share. We did that by first calculating the percentage being bought by the investors using the pre-money valuation and the investment amount:

$$\% \text{ Purchased} = \frac{\text{Investment Amount}}{\text{Pre-Money Valuation} + \text{Investment Amount}}$$

To calculate the number of shares, we had to decide which total share number we were going to use (issued and outstanding or fully diluted); and because we wanted as many shares as possible, we chose fully diluted. The formula for getting to the number of shares is:

$$\text{Shares Purchased} = \frac{\% \text{ Purchased}}{1 - \% \text{ Purchased}} \times \text{Fully Diluted Shares Pre-Investment}$$

If you are calculating the number of shares based on *issued and outstanding shares only*, you would substitute the issued and outstanding shares total for the fully diluted share total in the formula above.

Expressing the post investment ownership percentage in the term sheet is a valid way to ensure that there are no surprises. For example, the term sheet might say:

> Immediately following the new investment, the purchasers of the Preferred Stock will own X% of the Company, calculated on a fully-diluted basis, including all issued and outstanding shares of stock on an as-converted to common stock basis, all convertible securities outstanding, and an available option pool of [10]%.

If you are going to make an offer to invest in a company through a term sheet, and you don't know how many securities it has outstanding, and you want to assure yourself of your desired percentage after your money comes in, you will probably express the price per share on a post-money basis.

The basic share price calculation is:

$$\text{Price Per Share} = \frac{\text{Pre-Money Value}}{\text{Total Shares Pre-Investment}}$$

As we explain in Calculating Ownership and Dilution,[§19.2] there are two running share totals and it is possible to use either one in the calculation. The price per share in a fixed price round may be calculated by dividing the pre-money valuation by either the number of shares outstanding—the issued and outstanding shares—or the issued and outstanding shares on a fully diluted basis.

21.4 *Price Per Share in Scenario A*

⟩ EXAMPLE

Let's look at the difference in the two approaches using our cap table from our scenario A example just above, where the Round 1 investors are buying 20% of the company for $250K at a $1M pre-money.

21.4.1 FIGURE 3S: CAP TABLE PRIOR TO INVESTMENT

	SHARES OR OPTIONS	ISSUED AND OUTSTANDING	FULLY DILUTED
Founders	10,000,000	96.67%	86.96%

	SHARES OR OPTIONS	ISSUED AND OUTSTANDING	FULLY DILUTED
Employees	345,000	3.33%	3.00%
Issued and Outstanding	10,345,000	100.00%	
Option Pool	1,155,000		10.04%
Total Fully Diluted	**11,500,000**		100.00%

Using the fully diluted basis, the price per share is $1M/11,500,000 or $.087 per share. When this company IPOs at $17 per share, you'll have a 20X return! Checking the math, 2,875,000 shares purchased by the investors (see the post investment cap table in Figure A1) at $.087 each is $250K.

If the investment was instead defined as 20% ownership post investment based on the issued and outstanding shares, the price would be calculated as $1M/10,345,000 = $.097 each. The shares are more expensive, and so the investors only receive 2,586,385 shares for their $250K. That's 288,615 fewer shares, or roughly 10% less.

◇ IMPORTANT As an investor, you clearly want to use as large a pre-investment share total as possible in calculating the price per share (large denominator), so you want the price per share based on the *fully diluted* calculation. And pay attention to the definition of fully diluted, as it can vary.

21.5 *The Impact Of The Option Pool On Dilution and Price Per Share*

As we saw in the pricing discussion above, the difference between a calculation based on issued and outstanding shares versus fully diluted shares can be significant. The option pool is typically the biggest component of the difference between issued and outstanding and fully diluted shares, and so the size of that option pool tends to get a lot of scrutiny at the time of any investment.

As a company hires employees, it issues grants of options on the stock that is reserved for the stock option pool, thereby slowly depleting that pool. It is common that a company has to top up its stock option pool several times as it grows from no employees to dozens, to hundreds, to potentially thousands. It increases the pool by allocating shares from the company's authorized stock. When the company adds more shares to the option pool, it dilutes all the existing stockholders (when using the fully diluted ownership calculation). It is a round of dilution without directly bringing in any money (the way a stock sale to investors does). So companies aren't anxious to top up the pool by themselves.

Savvy investors know that the company should have a healthy stock option pool so it can motivate the new employees it wants to hire with the money it is raising. So as part of almost any priced investment round there is a discussion about how big the pool should be and who is going to take the dilution hit. New investors want to allocate additional shares to the pool in a way that dilutes the existing equity holders before the new investors come in. The company would prefer if the option pool were topped up *after* the new money came in, as the dilution to the founders and prior investors would be less because the new investors would be sharing in that dilution.

> ⟫ EXAMPLE

Below is an example of how Figure A2 would change if the Round 2 investors had insisted that they are buying 20% for their $750K, and they still agree to the $3M pre-money, but now they also insist that the stock option pool be topped up to 15%. If you look back to Figure A2, you will see that the stock option pool is down to 6.43% post investment if it is not addressed. Because the investors have established their 20% post investment ownership (on a fully diluted basis) as part of their investment terms, the full burden of the dilution in this case is borne by the founders and existing investors (and existing employees). The founders go from 55.65% ownership post investment to 49.17%. A big difference. The investors for their part get more shares, 473,942 more, because they require 20% of a larger total of fully diluted shares now.

21.5.1 **FIGURE A3: $750K INVESTMENT FOR 20% OWNERSHIP POST INVESTMENT, INCLUDING TOPPING UP THE OPTION POOL TO 15% POST INVESTMENT**

	SHARES OR OPTIONS	ISSUED AND OUTSTANDING	FULLY DILUTED
Founders	10,000,000	57.84%	49.17%
Employees	345,000	2.00%	1.70%

	SHARES OR OPTIONS	ISSUED AND OUTSTANDING	FULLY DILUTED
Round 1 Investors	2,875,000	16.63%	14.14%
Round 2 Investors	4,067,692	23.53%	**20.00%**
Issued and Outstanding	17,270,000	100.00%	
Option Pool	3,050,000		**15.00%**
Total Fully Diluted	20,337,692		100.00%

Because the investors are now buying more shares for their $750K, the price per share goes down. Another way to think about this is that the investors insisted that the option pool be topped up before they invested. Topping it up required more shares. The option pool prior to the investment had to be increased to 18.75%, so that after the dilution of that option pool by the 20% ownership stake from Round 2, it would be 15%. The price per share in this example is

$$\frac{\$750K}{4,067,692 \text{ shares}} = \$0.184$$

This is what the investors are paying divided by the number of shares they are receiving; or, using our standard formula of the pre-money valuation divided by the number of fully diluted shares immediately before they invest (after the top up):

$$\frac{\$3M}{16,270,000 \text{ shares}} = \$0.184$$

The good news is, despite all the dilution suffered by the founders and the Round 1 investors by the savvy Round 2 investors, the price per share has more than doubled from $.087 at Round 1 to $.184 at Round 2. This is a function of the company hitting its milestones and driving up the pre-money valuation.

As an investor, you would like the company to top up the option pool before you invest. We hope that with this understanding of the impact on founders and the prior investors (which may include you or your fellow angels), you will appreciate why the existing stockholders want the new investors to share the burden of increasing the option pool.

22 Dilution and Conversion

So far, we've walked through the story of a company that goes straight to raising a priced round, and explored a couple of scenarios to demonstrate some key concepts and mechanics. In this section, we're going to pick up the story of the same company back after they added their first employee.[§20.3] Instead of going straight to a priced round, the company first raises a convertible note, then a preferred stock round. How will this series of events affect the cap table and investor ownership?

Let's find out!

22.1 *Convertible Note to Priced Round*

> ❯ EXAMPLE

After adding their first employee,[§20.3] Pext, Inc. decides to raise a small amount of external capital, $400K, in order to pay some contract developers for the MVP of the product and to cover some marketing expenses to do early customer acquisition testing. Because they are raising less than $500K, and want to minimize the legal costs, they raise capital in the form of a convertible note. The note has the following key terms:

- valuation cap of $3M
- discount of 20%
- qualified financing for mandatory conversion must be a preferred stock offering of at least $1M
- interest at 5%

There are no shares sold during a convertible note offering, since it is debt, and therefore there is no change to the cap table.

A year later the company has made great progress and decides to raise $2M. They do this in the form of a Series Seed Preferred Stock financing.

Because a preferred stock round will be a priced round, the company will have to negotiate a valuation for the company. The founders and the existing note holders ideally don't want to give up more than 20% of the company in this round in return for the new infusion of $2M. A quick calculation suggests that the pre-money valuation would have to be $8M for that to be the case:

$$\frac{\$2M}{\$2M + \$8M} = 20\%$$

This financing will trigger the mandatory conversion of the convertible notes from the prior financing because it meets all of the criteria. That conversion of debt to equity will impact the cap table as well.

As we discussed at length above, the option pool will need to be addressed as well as part of this financing. Let's start by taking another look at our summary cap table Figure 3S, where we have a single line item for Founders and one for Employees.

22.1.1 **FIGURE 3S: SUMMARY VERSION OF FIG 3**

	SHARES OR OPTIONS	ISSUED AND OUTSTANDING	FULLY DILUTED
Founders	10,000,000	96.67%	86.96%
Employees	345,000	3.33%	3.00%
Issued and Outstanding	10,345,000	100.00%	
Option Pool Available	1,155,000		10.04%
Total Fully Diluted	11,500,000		100.00%

The preferred stock investors feel that the $8M pre-money is at the high end of what they are comfortable with, so they insist that the terms be written such that they own 20% of the company on a fully diluted basis post investment and that the option pool be topped up to 15% of the final cap table post investment.

There are a lot of unknowns here, so we'll take it a step at a time. We can think about this as three separate transactions:

1. The convertible note holders convert at the valuation cap. (We will check later if it would have been beneficial to convert at the discount.)

This will dilute the founders and employees and reduce the relative size of the option pool.

2. The option pool will get topped up.
3. The preferred investors will come in.

22.2 *Effects of Note Conversion on Dilution*

While note conversion terms can be written in slightly different ways, for our purposes, we will use a simple example where the stock price using the valuation cap conversion option was specified to be calculated as follows: Valuation cap divided by the issued and outstanding securities immediately prior to the sale of the preferred. The valuation cap was $3M. The number of issued and outstanding securities was 10,345,000 per the cap table in Figure 3. The price per share is therefore $3M/10,345,000 or $0.28999517.

The 5% interest on the $400K in notes would have generated an additional $20K in the intervening year, so the convertible note investors will be converting $420K into shares at $0.28999517. Running the math, the convertible note holders will get $420K/$0.28999517 = 1,448,299 shares. So the conversion of the notes before any other actions would have the cap table looking like this:

22.2.1 FIGURE 4: CAP TABLE ACCOUNTING FOR THE CONVERSION OF THE CONVERTIBLE NOTES

	SHARES OR OPTIONS	ISSUED AND OUTSTANDING	FULLY DILUTED
Founders	10,000,000	84.79%	77.23%
Employees	345,000	2.93%	2.66%
Convertible Note Investors	**1,448,299**	12.28%	11.19%
Issued and Outstanding	11,793,299	100.00%	
Option Pool Available	1,155,000		8.92%
Total Fully Diluted	12,948,299		100.00%

22.3 *Option Pool Top-Up*

Now the option pool has to get topped up such that it will be 15% of the fully diluted shares after the dilutive effect of the preferred stock sale. Because the preferred stock sale will cause a 20% dilution (selling 20% of the company) across the board, the option pool must be 18.75% prior to being diluted by the preferred stock:

$$18.75\% \times 0.8 = 15.00\%$$

22.3.1 FIGURE 5: CAP TABLE ACCOUNTING FOR THE INCREASE IN THE OPTION POOL

	SHARES OR OPTIONS	ISSUED AND OUTSTANDING	FULLY DILUTED
Founders	10,000,000	84.79%	68.90%
Employees	345,000	2.93%	2.38%
Convertible Note Investors	1,448,299	12.28%	9.98%
Issued and Outstanding	11,793,299	100.00%	
Option Pool Available	2,721,531		**18.75%**
Total Fully Diluted	14,514,830		100.00%

The stock option pool must be increased from 1,155,000 to 2,721,531 in order for each to reach 18.75% of the total fully diluted shares. From Figure 5 above, it is clear that all equity and option owners have shared the burden of the increase in the stock option pool when calculated on a fully diluted basis.

22.4 *Sale of Preferred Stock*

The terms of the stock sale stipulated that the preferred stock investors would own 20% of the company on a fully diluted basis, and that at that time the option pool would represent 15% of the company on a fully diluted basis. Those conditions result in the cap table represented in Figure 7 below.

22.4.1 FIGURE 6: CAP TABLE AFTER THE PREFERRED STOCK SALES

	SHARES OR OPTIONS	ISSUED AND OUTSTANDING	FULLY DILUTED
Founders	10,000,000	64.84%	55.21%
Employees	345,000	2.24%	1.90%
Convertible Note Investors	1,448,299	9.39%	7.98%
Preferred Stock Investors	3,628,708	23.53	**20.00%**
Issued and Outstanding	15,422,007	100.00%	
Option Pool Available	2,721,531		15.00%
Total Fully Diluted	18,143,538		100.00%

You can see that our 18.75% option pool in Figure 5 has been diluted by the new investment as well, and is now at the target 15%.

So what is the price per share that the preferred stock investors paid? They spent $2M for 3,628,708 shares, or $0.55116 per share.

22.5 *Checking the Convertible Note Conversion*

We started working through the impact of the preferred stock investment on the cap table by assuming that the note holders would be better off with the valuation cap conversion than the discount conversion, but let's check.

If the noteholders had converted their $420K at the 20% discount, they would be paying $0.55116 multiplied by $0.80 per share, or $0.44093 per share. And $420K divided by $0.44093 is 952,532 shares.

Converting at the valuation cap generated 1,448,299 shares, so that was clearly the more advantageous conversion option.

23 Dilution From the Departure of a Founder

After two years with the company, Joe, one of the founders, has become restless and decides to leave the company to become a crabapple farmer in New Zealand. Because the company was set up by competent attorneys, the founders were on four year vesting schedules. Joe is exactly halfway through his vesting schedule, so upon his departure, the company will buy back 50% of his shares, or 1,700,000 shares. These shares were purchased by Joe as part of the company setup for a fraction of a penny per share, let's say $0.001 per share. Joe would have originally bought his shares two years ago for $3,400, and will sell half back for $1,700. But aren't Joe's 1,700,000 shares, which represent 9.37% of the company—which a year ago had a post-money valuation of $10,000,000—worth close to a million dollars? They might be, but the terms of stock purchase agreement and the vesting schedules therein would have stipulated that upon departure the company has the right to buy back any unvested shares at the issuing price, in this case $0.001 per share. This is a bummer for Joe, but he is, after all, walking away with the 50% of his stock ownership which he had vested. When the stock is repurchased by the company it is typically retired or returned to the treasury, so for all practical purposes, it is removed from the cap table.

The good news for the other stock owners is that by removing a large chunk of the issued and outstanding stock from the cap table, their ownership stakes go up.

23.0.1 **FIGURE 7A: CHANGE IN OWNERSHIP STAKE AFTER A FOUNDER DEPARTURE**

	SHARES OR OPTIONS	ISSUED AND OUTSTANDING	FULLY DILUTED
Founders	8,300,000	60.49%	50.48%
Employees	345,000	2.51%	2.10%
Convertible Note Investors	1,448,299	10.55%	8.81%
Preferred Stock Investors	3,628,708	26.44%	22.07%
Issued and Outstanding	13,722,007	100.00%	
Option Pool Available	2,721,531		16.55%
Total Fully Diluted	16,443,538		100.00%

Because the number of founders' shares has gone down, all other stock or option holders' ownership stakes have gone up. In fact, Pete and Rachel's ownership stakes have also gone up, but the founders' ownership as a group has gone down.

23.0.2 **FIGURE 7B: DETAIL ON FOUNDER OWNERSHIP FROM FIGURE 8A**

	SHARES OR OPTIONS	ISSUED AND OUTSTANDING	FULLY DILUTED
Pete	5,100,00	37.17%	31.02%
Joe	1,700,000	12.39%	10.34%
Rachel	1,500,000	10.93%	10.34%
Employees	345,000	2.51%	2.10%
Convertible Note Investors	1,448,299	10.55%	8.81%
Preferred Stock Investors	3,628,708	26.44%	22.07%
Issued and Outstanding	13,722,007	100.00%	
Option Pool Available	2,721,531		16.55%
Total Fully Diluted	16,443,538		100.00%

If you refer back to Figure 1,[20.1.1] you can see that Pete's original owner-ship was 60% of issued and outstanding shares, or 51% on a fully diluted basis. After bringing on Rachel as an additional co-founder, selling con-vertible notes, and then topping up the option pool and selling preferred shares, Pete's ownership share was down to 33.07% of issued and outstand-ing shares, and 28.11% on a fully diluted basis (not shown in table.) After Joe's departure, Pete's ownership stands at 37.17% of issued and outstand-ing shares, and 31.02% on a fully diluted basis.

Note, that we have not accounted for the likely hiring of additional employees throughout the course of the two years. If more employees had been hired, it would have used up some of the option pool, which would have reduced the ownership percentages on an issued and outstanding basis, but not on a fully diluted basis.

PART V: CORPORATE STRUCTURE AND TAX ISSUES

24 What Angels Need to Know About Business Entities and Taxes

In Part III: Financings and Term Sheets,[14] we covered the most common investment scenarios. In this section, we will review the most common types of entities in which you might consider investing, as well as the relevant tax issues that arise.

Angel investing involves a number of different tax issues for investors. You might wonder, for example, when can you recover your investment in a company for tax purposes? Can you deduct your investment in the year you make the investment? Is there a tax credit for making the types of investments you are making?

The tax consequences of any particular investment will depend on *the type of entity* in which you invest—typically either a C corporation, S corporation, or LLC taxed as a partnership—and *how* you invested—stock purchase, convertible debt or convertible equity, interest in an LLC taxed as a partnership, and so on.

24.1 *Investing in C Corporations*

The most common type of entity in which you will likely invest will be a Delaware C corporation.

A **C corporation** is a type of business entity which is taxed for federal income tax purposes under Subchapter C of the Internal Revenue Code. C corporations pay the taxes that are due on their income; their shareholders are not taxed on and not liable for taxes on the corporation's income (in contrast to S corporations and limited liability companies, which are taxed as partnerships).

As we discussed in Legal Due Diligence for Angel Investments,[§12] Delaware is the most popular place for early-stage companies to incorporate because of the state's corporate law history and the business-friendly legal precedents there. Delaware corporate law is also the most familiar to the investment community.

24.1.1 TAX ISSUES WITH INVESTMENTS IN C CORPORATIONS

Investors prefer C corporations because the C corporation pays its own taxes, and the investor is not taxed on the income of the company. If you invest in an S corporation or an LLC taxed as an S corporation or partnership, you will be taxed on the income of the entity, even if the entity doesn't distribute cash to you to pay the tax.

◇ **IMPORTANT** When you invest in a C corporation, you generally do not get a tax break or a tax credit or tax deduction at the time of your investment. Unfortunately, for federal income tax purposes, when you buy stock in a C corporation, your purchase price goes into the cost basis of the stock you acquire. You don't get to recover[153] that basis until you sell the stock or the stock becomes completely and totally worthless.

Qualified Small Business Stock

There *are* special tax breaks for investing in certain types of startups, however. For example, Section 1202[154] and Section 1045[155] of the Internal Revenue Code are designed to encourage investment in C corporations engaged in qualified trades of businesses with less than $50M in gross assets (both before and after the investment).

Section 1202 provides a special incentive for investments in **qualified small business stock (or QSBS)**. QSBS is stock of a C corporation actively engaged in a "qualified" trade or business issued to an investor when the C corporation had less than $50M in gross assets (both before and after the

---

153. By recover, we mean either deduct or amortize or offset the amount of your investment against the proceeds from selling the investment. For example, if you invest $100 in an asset, when do you get to deduct the $100? If you buy $100 in corporate stock, you *never* get to deduct it. It goes into your cost basis and will offset the amount realized on sale to determine gain. But what about if the company goes out of business? When do you get to write off or recover your basis in the asset? The rule regarding worthless stock has historically been that the stock has to be completely worthless to tax your investment in it as a loss.

154. https://www.investopedia.com/terms/s/section-1202.asp

155. https://www.law.cornell.edu/uscode/text/26/1045

investment). "Qualified" trades or businesses are generally not service-based businesses. Under Section 1202, if you hold the QSBS for more than five years, you get a tax break on your long-term capital gains tax rate.

The statute refers to "qualified trade or business" as "any trade or business other than":

(a) any trade or business involving the performance of services in the fields of health, law, engineering, architecture, accounting, actuarial science, performing arts, consulting, athletics, financial services, brokerage services, or any trade or business where the principal asset of such trade or business is the reputation or skill of 1 or more of its employees,

(b) any banking, insurance, financing, leasing, investing, or similar business,

(c) any farming business (including the business of raising or harvesting trees),

(d) any business involving the production or extraction of products of a character with respect to which a deduction is allowable under section 613 or 613A, and

(e) any business of operating a hotel, motel, restaurant, or similar business.

◇ **IMPORTANT** The The tax break is currently a 100% exclusion from federal income tax entirely,[156] on up to the greater of either $10M in gain or 10x the aggregate adjusted basis of QSBS issued by the corporation and disposed of by the taxpayer during the taxable period. Basis for 1202 purposes is not less than the fair market value of property exchanged for QSBS. This is a very significant tax break. But it is only available to investments in C corporations, not S corporations or entities taxed as partnerships, such as multi-member LLCs that haven't elected S or C corporation status.

If you sell QSBS before holding it for five years, you can roll over your gain under Section 1045 into another qualified small business, provided you make the rollover investment within 60 days. Section 1045 is potentially very helpful, but the 60-day rollover window might be hard to make. It usually takes much longer than 60 days to find an investment. One suggestion to Congress to improve the law is to allow for more than 60 days to make a rollover investment.

---

156. https://www.law.cornell.edu/uscode/text/26/1202

24.2 *Investing in S Corporations*

You might be interested in investing in an S corporation.

Shareholders in **S corporations** can generally only be individuals who are U.S. citizens or lawful permanent residents. Shareholders cannot be other business entities or organizations. When a venture capital firm invests in an S corporation, that companies loses their S corporation status and convert automatically to a C corporation.

◇ CAUTION   S corporations can only have one economic class of stock. Meaning, you will only be able to buy common stock; you won't be able to buy preferred stock.

An S corporation can divvy up governance rights as long as the economic rights$^{\S 18.1}$ of all of the shares is the same (for example, an S corporation can have voting and non-voting stock, as long as the voting and non-voting stock have the same economic rights).

24.2.1 TAX ISSUES WITH S CORPORATIONS

◇ CAUTION   If you invest in an S corporation, you will be taxed on your proportionate share of the entity's income, even if the company does not distribute any cash to you with which to pay the tax. (In contrast, to repeat, C corporations pay tax at the corporate level and thereby shield you from any direct tax consequences.)

If you want to make sure that the company distributes cash to you so that you will be able to pay the tax on the entity's income that you are taxed on, you will have to enter into an agreement with the company that expresses this, and it should be part of your term sheet. One positive aspect of investing in S corporations is that if the company has an operating loss, you will be allocated some portion of those losses to report on your individual tax return.

◇ CAUTION   However, be aware your losses may be limited by the passive activity loss rules.

⚠ DANGER   Another thing to watch out for: If you invest in an S corporation that does business across a number of states, you might have to pay income tax, or, in the event of an operating loss, still file a tax return in those states even if you don't live in or visit them.

24.3 *Investing in LLCs*

Sometimes founders form LLCs as an easy way to get started. **Limited liability companies (or LLCs)** can be simpler to form than corporations. LLCs also have the benefit of being pass-through entities for tax reasons by default. Meaning, the losses flow through to the personal tax returns of the owners, unless an election to be taxed as a corporation is made.

◇ IMPORTANT The financial and tax consequences of your investment depend on how the LLC is taxed for federal income tax purposes. This is a legal and business due diligence point$^{\S12.4}$ you will want to run down right away.

It is not uncommon for founders to have forgotten what their tax accountant did when they formed the company. If you are considering investing in a business organized as an LLC, you must confirm the tax classification of the LLC. It is preferable to do this sooner rather than later. Don't assume that because the company is formed as an LLC that it is taxed as a partnership. For federal income tax purposes, an LLC can be classified as either:

- a disregarded entity (if it is owned by one person);[157]
- a partnership;
- an S corporation; or
- a C corporation.

◇ CAUTION You will want to know the tax classification of the entity sooner rather than later in your investment process because investments in pass-through entities give rise to a number of issues that you might not want to spend time confronting.

If the LLC is taxed for federal income tax purposes as a partnership, but it intends to convert to a C corporation later, you may want to require the LLC to convert to a C corporation prior to your investment. If you invest in an LLC taxed as either a partnership or an S corporation, you will be taxed on the LLC's income even if no cash is distributed to you to pay the tax. In

---

157. A disregarded entity is treated as a division of its owner for federal income tax purposes. If you are an individual, you report the LLCs income, gain, loss, et cetera, on Schedule C of your Form 1040, just like you would in the case of a sole proprietorship.

other words, investing in an LLC can unnecessarily complicate your personal tax situation. See the tax issues section below.

You may, however, want to invest in an LLC taxed as a partnership that intends to stay an LLC taxed as a partnership. In addition to the single layer of taxation and its ability to pass through losses, other advantages of retaining the LLC form include the abilities to:

- allocate income and losses in a manner disproportionate to ownership;
- spin off or split up assets or businesses in a tax-efficient manner; and
- consummate an asset sale and have the gain largely qualify as capital gain.

It is not always the case that investing in an LLC is the wrong choice. But be careful, because it frequently is. Below we will discuss some of the challenges with investing in LLCs and some things to watch out for.

24.3.1 TAX ISSUES WITH LLCS TAXED AS PASS-THROUGH COMPANIES

LLCs with multiple owners who do not make any special elections are taxed as partnerships for federal income tax purposes. Under the federal tax law, partnerships do not themselves pay the federal income tax on their income. Instead, their owners pay the federal income tax on their share of the income allocated to them. This can be problematic for an angel investor for a number of reasons. See the discussion about investing in S corporations.§24.2

◇ CAUTION In this section we discuss the potential problems of investing in an LLC taxed as a pass-through company:

- **Pass-through taxation.** If you invest in an LLC taxed as a pass-through company (meaning, either as an entity taxed as a partnership or as an S corporation), the LLC itself, as an entity, will not pay any federal income taxes. Instead, its owners will have to report on their tax returns and pay the tax on the income that the LLC generates—even if the LLC does not distribute any cash to its owners. Most angel investors do not want to invest in a company that will cause them to have to pay tax on the entity's income, regardless of whether any cash is actually distributed to them.

  - Investors in LLCs should consider ensuring that the LLC agreement requires the LLC to distribute sufficient cash to owners so that you may pay the tax on the LLC's income allocated to you. However, some LLC agreements do not mandate tax distributions.

- **State income taxes.** LLCs are also problematic for state income tax purposes. If you invest in an LLC, you might become liable for state income taxes in states in which the LLC does business but in which you are neither a resident nor a visitor. For example, an investor who is a resident of a state such as Washington, which does not have income tax, may become subject to income taxation if they invest in an LLC doing business in a state with income tax, such as California. This could be a very unwelcome and expensive surprise.
- **No qualified small business stock benefit.** Another negative aspect of investing in LLCs is that LLCs cannot issue qualified small business stock. Qualified small business stock is advantageous because it may qualify for special reductions in long-term capital gains tax treatment on sale (including up to 100% of the gain being excluded from tax entirely). This is not possible with LLCs.
- **Difficulty with understanding allocations.** LLCs are also problematic because of the complex tax rules governing how income is allocated to the owners. You might receive a Schedule K-1[158] from an LLC, indicating your distributive share of the LLC's income, loss, expense, credit, and other tax items—and not understand what it is you were allocated or why.
- **Delay in tax documents.** If an LLC sends you a Schedule K-1 for your taxes, you may not receive that document until September following the end of the tax year.

24.3.2 **CHALLENGES AS A MINORITY INVESTOR IN AN LLC**

Voting Rights

Another problem with LLCs is that the LLC agreement may contain a variety of provisions that are detrimental to the LLC's minority owners. For example, because the LLC agreement is a contract in which the LLC members can essentially agree on anything (to waive fiduciary duties, for example), it has to include an amendment provision specifying how the agreement can be modified.

---

158. https://www.irs.gov/forms-pubs/about-form-1065#collapseCollapsible1654639160736

◇ CAUTION Companies are not going to want to have an amendment provision that requires unanimity, because that would hamstring the company and give any one member the right to hold the company up. As a result, if you are a minority investor in an LLC, you are probably going to be asked to sign an agreement that says it can be amended without your consent. This might make you uncomfortable.

You may want to ask for protective provisions, meaning special voting rights of just the investors, just as you can when investing in a corporation. It is possible to negotiate for just about any type of special voting rights you want in an LLC.

At the very least in these situations, you should ask that the amendment provision be written such that no amendment can single out or treat any member differently from the group, or require any one member but not others to put in additional capital, guarantee any debt, or otherwise cause any member to have a personal liability. Additionally, you may want to specify what types of amendments require your consent—such as requiring the members to contribute additional capital.

Potential For Capital Calls

◇ IMPORTANT As alluded to above, an LLC agreement could specify that a manager or a majority of the members can require capital contributions from all members. Review the agreements carefully to insure that you will not be on the hook to make a larger financial commitment than you had intended. Make sure your investment documents don't obligate you to put more money into the company. This is not an uncommon provision in an LLC agreement.

》 EXAMPLE

Joe knew an investor who invested in a bar, and the LLC agreement obligated all of the members of the LLC to put additional capital in upon the majority consent of the members. This was basically a blank check the investor was signing up for!

Investor Protective Covenants

You can ask for all of the same investor protective covenants in the LLC context that you can ask for in the corporate context. Those might include:

- **Information rights.** For example, the rights to receive regular accounting reports, and have access to accounting information.
- **Disclosure and approval of conflicted transactions.** In other words, the investors must approve insider transactions[159] after disclosure of all material facts related to the insider transaction.
- **Right of first refusal.** Meaning, the right to be the first to purchase shares other members are selling.
- **Co-sale rights.** The right to sell your shares alongside the founders, if the founders are selling some or all of their shares.
- **Participation rights.** The right to buy more shares if the company sells more in an equity financing.

Withdrawal

⬦ **CAUTION** If the managers can indebt the LLC or require capital contributions, you may want to exit the LLC immediately. But frequently, LLC agreements preclude an owner from exiting or withdrawing.

If you invest in an LLC, you might want to negotiate for the right to withdraw from the LLC and convert your interest into the right to receive an amount of cash upon written notice from you under certain circumstances, such as:

- The LLC fails to give you the information you need to file your taxes in a timely manner.
- The LLC fails to observe your information rights or other rights you've negotiated.

Another approach is to invest through an LLC that you create and own specifically for making investments. With this approach, if your LLC becomes liable somehow to the portfolio company, then at least that liability will not become your personal liability, but will only be the liability of the LLC you formed to make the investment.

---

159. Any transactions where a director or executive does a deal directly with the company. (Like the CEO's $100M severance deal he approved himself!)

Non-Compete, Non-Solicitation Agreements

Frequently, LLC agreements will include non-compete and non-solicitation (of customers and potentially employees) provisions that attempt to:

- bind all owners regardless of whether the owner provides services to the company (this doesn't make sense, but is common), and
- broadly apply to any and all businesses whatsoever that the LLC is currently engaged with or becomes engaged with.

⬦ CAUTION These provisions can be problematic if you have investments across the industry. If you are not a service provider to the company, or if you were once but are no longer a service provider to the company, you should not be bound by a non-compete or non-solicitation agreement.

LLC Agreements Are Complex

LLCs are also problematic because LLC agreements can be long and difficult to understand. The statutes under which LLCs are created typically allow the parties to contractually agree on anything. This means LLC agreements wind up covering a lot of different subjects. To give you a short list, your average LLC agreement will contain provisions addressing the following:

- economics
- governance
- tax allocations
- cash distribution
- new member admission
- transferability of units (more specifically, restrictions on transfers)
- amendment of the agreements
- withdrawal provisions.

LLC agreements may also contain buyout provisions.

24.3.3 SHORTLIST OF QUESTIONS FOR CONSIDERATION IN BECOMING A MINORITY MEMBER OF AN LLC

◇ IMPORTANT If you're considering becoming a minority member of an LLC, make sure you've asked and have received satisfactory answers to the following questions:

1. Are you on the hook for anything personally, or could you be on the hook for anything personally?
2. Do you have the right to withdraw from the LLC, or are you stuck?
3. Can the majority members amend the LLC agreement without your consent?
4. Does the LLC agreement bind you to a non-compete, or a non-solicit?
5. Have you confirmed the LLC's tax status? Did it check the box to be taxed as an S corporation?
6. If the LLC is taxed as a pass-through company, does the LLC have to distribute cash to you so that you can pay the taxes on the LLC's income?
7. Do you have voting rights? Are they meaningful or are you such a minority that it won't matter?

8. Does the LLC agreement say that conflicted interest transactions have to be approved by at least two independent managers or owners (members) who are not conflicted?
9. Do you have good information rights?
10. Are there transfer restrictions on your units? Can you sell your units? Can others sell theirs despite the fact that you can't sell yours?
11. Do you have co-sale rights?
12. Are your units subject to rights of first refusal?
13. Do you have participation rights in the company's next financing?
14. Are you subject to a drag-along agreement? Is it suitably drafted?
15. Have you confirmed that you will not be taxed as a result of your admission to the company?[160]

25 Tax Credits and Losses

⚠ DANGER Please always consult with your tax advisors regarding credits and losses and other tax matters. Tax law changes frequently and the summaries in this book may not accurately describe how the rules apply to your particular situation.

25.1 *Tax Credits*

The federal income tax law does not, in 2020, provide a tax credit for investing in startups. However, the state in which you live, if it has an income tax, might. You should consult your local tax CPA to find out what incentives your state might offer.

25.2 *Tax Issues With Losses*

What happens if you invest in a company and the company fails? Can you deduct your loss? If you can deduct your loss, what sort of loss is it, capital or ordinary?

---

160. Sometimes when you invest in an entity taxed as a partnership, depending on the way your investment is structured, the act of the investment itself can give rise to what is referred to as a "capital shift," causing some investors to owe taxes merely as a result of the investment!

An ordinary loss is the best type of loss because it can be set off against ordinary income (your salary). Capital losses are only deductible against capital gains plus $3K of ordinary income per year. If you don't have much in the way of capital gain, because of this $3K per year limitation, it might take you years to fully deduct your losses.

In general, investments in corporations result in capital losses only when the corporation's stock is completely worthless. The "completely worthless" test can require that the company be completely dissolved and wound up.[161] Even if the corporation is nearly dead, it still may not be dead enough for you to take a loss. One way to take the loss on a nearly defunct company is to assign the shares for $1 to an unrelated third party. Some angel groups set up programs to facilitate these types of assignments.

While capital losses are problematic because they are only deductible against capital gains and then up to $3K of ordinary income per year, Section 1244[162] of the tax code converts some capital losses into ordinary losses. In order to take advantage of Section 1244, your stock must be Section 1244 stock,[163] which is generally stock that represents the first $1M invested in a company. But Section 1244 is limited, to $50K for individual taxpayers and $100K for married couples filing jointly.

25.2.1 DON'T INVEST THROUGH A NON-ROTH IRA

⚠ DANGER Sometimes angels will want to invest in a company through an IRA. This does not usually make sense. Why? Because an angel investment, if it is a good one, should result in a long-term capital gain or be tax-free under Section 1202 (if the investment was in qualified small business stock), but if you make this investment through a non-Roth IRA you will convert these gains to ordinary income (distributions through a traditional IRA are taxed as ordinary income).

If an investment is a loser, if you made the investment through an IRA you won't be able to take the loss. This can be a terrible thing because your losses can shelter your gains. Remember also that if your investment was part of the first $1M invested in a company, the loss may be deductible as

---

161. "Wound up" means taking all the various actions to fully and finally put a company to bed: paying all bills, closing all accounts, filing all final tax returns, and so on. You may see this referred to as "winding up" or "winding down."

162. https://www.law.cornell.edu/uscode/text/26/1244

163. https://www.investopedia.com/terms/s/section-1244-stock.asp

an ordinary loss as opposed to a capital loss. It would be a real shame to invest in such a way that you cheated yourself out of a valuable tax benefit which Congress enacted to encourage investments in small businesses.

Second, many IRA custodians will refuse to go along. They won't want to let you invest your IRA in a private company whose offering materials do not include a private placement memorandum.

PART VI: STAYING ENGAGED

26 Boards and Advisory Roles

As an angel investor, you may be asked or choose to negotiate a board seat or advisory position with a company you invest in. We've mentioned boards a few times throughout this book, so let's dig in to the details.

26.1 *Board of Directors*

In a corporation, the **board of directors (or BOD)** controls the company. It is typically made up of one or more founders, investors from each round, and one or more advisors. The board's authority is expansive: it can fire the CEO and the other officers of the company; approve all equity issuances, including all stock option grants to employees and all equity financing rounds (including convertible note rounds); approve leases and other significant financial commitments; approve or deny the sale of the company or decide to shut the company down. On the board of directors, each director has one vote.

If you are on the board of directors, you are said to have a *board seat*. Sometimes, angel investors might want to have a board seat so that they can more closely monitor their investment. At other times, a company might want to give you a board seat for reasons of reputation or risk management.

In an early-stage company, the board of directors should be small. It is often made up initially of just the founders or a subset of the executive founders if there are more than three. Sometimes the founders will have added an industry veteran to the board to provide credibility and advice. The CEO is always a member of the board. Typically, the lead for each round of investment or their representative is added to the board, allowing them a small measure of control as well as visibility into the progress of the company. As the board grows, the founder board members, other than the CEO, may be replaced with representatives of the new investors.

Board representation is typically negotiated as part of each investment round. Because the board of directors is so powerful, you should expect entrepreneurs to be careful about adding members.

The Delaware corporations code expression of this power is pretty typical. It says: "The business and affairs of every corporation organized under this chapter shall be managed by or under the direction of a board of directors, except as may be otherwise provided in this chapter or in its certificate of incorporation."

◇ **IMPORTANT** Directors of for-profit corporations—that is, members of the board of directors—have two primary fiduciary duties: a duty of care and a duty of loyalty. A duty of care means your conduct will be held to a certain standard. And the duty of loyalty means you have to be careful with how you handle conflicts of interest. Becoming a member of the board of directors of a company is not a matter to be taken lightly.

◇ **CAUTION** You should always approach the decision of negotiating or accepting a board seat with caution—with great power comes great responsibility. Directors are fiduciaries to all of the shareholders and it is never a risk-free role.

In addition, a board seat will not give you control unless you can build a coalition with other board members to form a majority in the event that things are going sideways or the CEO is being problematic.

Being a board member also takes time. There are regular board meetings to attend and prepare for, and members may be called on ad hoc to help address strategic issues. In addition to the formal duties and responsibilities of the board, board members may be called upon to help with fundraising, sourcing and hiring key employees, business development, and sales leads.

◇ **IMPORTANT** If you accept a board seat, know that by accepting it you are accepting potential personal liabilities. We'll explain that below.§26.1.2 In contrast, a board observer does not have these fiduciary duties.

A **board observer** has the right to attend board meetings, they can participate in board discussions, and so can frequently influence board decisions as if they are a voting member of the board. A board observer has no vote in board decisions, and so they get access to all the information, but without the fiduciary duties and risk of liability. Board observer status for a member of a group of investors would normally be negotiated as part of the term sheet under observer rights. This might be appropriate, for example, for a large investor in a round who is not the lead investor.

If you are taking a board seat, we suggest getting a copy of the American Bar Association's Corporate Director's Guidebook,[164] a very good guide to the duties of a director.

26.1.1 DO DIRECTORS SIGN AGREEMENTS?

Because a director's duties arise by operation of law (the law fills in the blanks on what these duties are, rather than the duties being laid out in a contract), it is not necessary for a director to sign a confidentiality and IP assignment agreement. If you are only a director, you do not need to sign any agreement with the company save maybe an agreement on how they are going to pay you (such as stock option plan agreements, and you might also prefer an indemnification agreement). Of course, if you are also providing services as an executive officer, or as a consultant, then you should expect to sign an agreement with confidentiality, IP assignment, and potentially non-compete and non-solicitation provisions as well (if such provisions are enforceable in your jurisdiction).

◇ IMPORTANT In general, if you agree to serve as a director of a company, you *will* want to enter into an indemnification agreement with the company. These agreements can be very important, as there is risk of personal liability as a board member.

---

164. https://www.amazon.com/Corporate-Directors-Guidebook-Seventh-Committee/dp/
1641055928/

An **indemnification agreement** is a contract between a company and a director or officer in which the company agrees to indemnify, defend, and hold harmless a director or officer if the director or officer is sued as a result of being a director or officer of the company.

You can find a sample indemnification agreement at NVCA.[165]

26.1.2 PERSONAL LIABILITY AS A BOARD MEMBER

⚠ DANGER You risk personal liability as a board member, meaning that you can be sued personally in certain circumstances. Personal liability of a board member can arise in a number of different ways, including but not limited to:

- A breach of fiduciary duty.
- The company fails to pay wages due to employees, and the employees sue. Under some state laws, directors can be personally liable for willful nonpayment of wages, failure to pay tax withholdings, and similar items. In some states, the damages for these claims, which can be recovered personally from directors and officers in certain cases, include treble damages[166] and attorneys' fees. These numbers can add up fast.
- The company fails, and creditors of the company sue, contending that once the company was insolvent you didn't do anything to protect them, and in fact made things worse. Under most state laws, once a company becomes insolvent, then the directors' duties shift from the stockholders to the corporation's creditors.
- The company otherwise engages in transactions that give rise to a shareholder lawsuit (for example, the company sells securities, while investors lose their money and sue).

◇ IMPORTANT There are several ways to protect yourself if you become a board member.

- Make sure that the company has directors and officers liability insurance, often referred to as D&O insurance.[167]
- Enter into an indemnification agreement with the company.

---

165. https://studylib.net/doc/8198417/nvca-model-indemnification-agreement

166. https://en.wikipedia.org/wiki/Treble_damages

167. https://www.investopedia.com/terms/d/directors-and-officers-liability-insurance.asp

- Make sure the company has competent legal counsel and is using that counsel in appropriate circumstances.
- Make sure that the company is following good accounting practices, such as using a third party for payroll tax accounting, and has a good finance person on the team who can generate financial statements.
- If you accept a board seat, you will want to review the company's financial performance and condition as a part of your regular board meetings.

26.1.3 KEEPING MINUTES (IT'S NOT HARD)

If you are on the board, take care to make sure someone attending the meetings "takes minutes"—that is, documents what happens in the meeting. Minutes do not have to be long. In fact, they can and should be short. At a minimum, minutes need to capture the following:

- When the meeting started.
- Who was present and if a quorum was reached.
- If not all of the directors were present, who could not attend, and did they receive notice of the meeting.
- Who acted as chair of the meeting, and who acted as secretary.
- Topics discussed, such as:

  - the company's financial position and financial trends;
  - a discussion of sales or other business matters;
  - the performance of management.[168]

- When the meeting adjourned.

If the board will approve stock options at the meeting, additional detail will be required. You can find template board minutes in the appendix.§30.9

26.2 *The Board of Advisors*

Sometimes companies establish advisory boards to advise the senior management of the company (sometimes just the CEO) on strategic matters.

---

168. Topics are usually left at high levels like these, without a lot of detail, because you don't want minutes to reflect anything negative about the business operations if they are reviewed in hindsight. They are typically kept short, reflecting mainly that everyone is doing their jobs.

Serving as a member of an advisory board for a company can be a great way to get to know the company in depth and keep track of what is happening. It will also help you develop a deeper relationship with the CEO and gain insight into the disruption of an industry. If you have useful domain expertise and the time to be an advisor, you may be able to increase the likelihood of success of your investment through your advice.

Being an active advisor can take time, and like BOD members, you will likely be asked to help with introductions to potential customers and sources of future funding, as well as recruiting of key employees, in addition to any domain-specific advice you may be able to offer.

🖐 **CONFUSION** Advisory boards are not governing boards. That means that advisory board members do not have fiduciary duties. Nor are companies bound to observe the recommendations of an advisory board.

The advisor responsibilities and compensation are codified in the **advisor agreement (advisory agreement or advisory board agreement)**. Advisor agreements will typically lay out the duration of the agreement, the amount of equity vested over the course of the agreement, and the vesting schedule.

As an advisor, despite not having fiduciary duties, you still might like to ask that your advisory board agreement include an indemnification obligation on the part of the company, in which the company agrees to indemnify you if you are sued as a result of your involvement with the company. If you would like to review an example advisory board agreement, the Founder Institute makes one publicly available.[169]

26.2.1 ADVISOR COMPENSATION

You will likely get an equity kicker to your investment in the form of common stock or common options. Cash compensation for advisors is not typical, except perhaps for reimbursement of some minor expenses.

The amount of equity may depend on how impactful you think you can be, the stage of the company, and your ability to negotiate. The low end of the range might be 0.15% vesting over four years, while the high end might be 1% or more and might vest in only two years. You can find suggested equity ranges for advisors at differing stages of development on the Founder Institute FAST agreement.[170] Typical vesting schedules are either

---

169. https://fi.co/contents/206
170. https://fi.co/fast

monthly or quarterly and can include cliffs similar to employee vesting agreements.

Equity compensation for advisors is almost always in the form of non-qualified stock options[171] (NSOs or NQSOs) on common stock, similar to employee compensation. The advisory agreement will state that the board of directors will issue a stock option grant to the advisor, and ideally it should be clear as to the time frame in which the stock option grant will be executed. In a timely manner, if not coincident with the agreement, the board of directors should issue the stock option grant. That grant will state the number of options and the strike price of those options. The strike price should be the fair market value at the time of the option grant. It should also state that the stock will be subject to the stock incentive or stock option plan.

🔒 CONFUSION If you receive an option you will want to make sure it gives you more than 90 days to exercise the option once you stop performing services. Companies can extend option exercise periods to as long as ten years from the date of the grant of the option.

Tax Consequences for Advisors

⚠ DANGER If you are receiving equity compensation as an advisor, it is advisable to be aware of the tax consequences:

- If you receive stock, you usually have to pay tax on the value of the shares you receive when you receive them. If the shares are fully vested upon receipt, they are taxable upon receipt at their fair market value. For tax purposes, you are treated as if you received cash equal to the fair market value of the shares, and that you then used the cash to purchase the stock. If the shares are subject to vesting, you would typically want to file an 83(b) election[172] so that you could pay tax on the value of the shares at the time of receipt instead of in the future, when the value of the shares might be even higher and the tax consequences even more severe.
- If you receive a stock option, as long as the stock option has an exercise price equal to the fair market value of the shares of stock underlying the option, you will not owe tax on the receipt of an option.

---

171. https://www.holloway.com/g/equity-compensation/sections/kinds-of-stock-options
172. https://www.holloway.com/g/equity-compensation/sections/83b-elections

27 What To Do When One of Your Startups Is Struggling

🌿 FOUNDER A majority of your startup investments will likely fail to return your investment. Understanding why startups can fail will make you a better angel investor. This section should be helpful for founders as well.

The fact that the majority of companies don't get acquired or execute an IPO doesn't mean that you should just accept it when you have a portfolio company in trouble. While your legal options to take action are often very limited, you may be able to help with your own efforts and expertise and by rallying your fellow investors. First, we'll look at common reasons startups fail, and then discuss how you can get involved in a struggling startup should you choose to.

27.1 *Warning Signs of Troubles Ahead*

CBInsights[173] looked into more than 110 stories, and listed the top 12 reasons they found that startups had not succeeded. Let's take a look at the top three reasons and the implications for things to watch out for.

27.1.1 RAN OUT OF CASH (38%)

Some might argue that running out of cash is not the reason a company failed, but a symptom of another problem, like a lack of paying customers. That might be true for a company that has already raised its first round and cannot convince investors to put in more money. What is relevant to this discussion is that fundraising takes time and is best achieved when a company is making good progress and has hit its milestone goals promised in the prior round.

How to avoid this scenario. Make sure that the company is raising enough money to reach its next key milestone and will have a minimum of 12–18 months of runway. Keeping in touch with your investments' cash burn rate and bank balance can help a lot, so negotiate for information rights at a minimum, and ideally observer rights to board meetings. The company should start looking for its next round no later than when it still has at least four months of cash in the bank.

---

173. https://www.cbinsights.com/research/startup-failure-reasons-top/

⚘ **FOUNDER** You can also direct founders to the Determining How Much to Raise[174] section of the *Holloway Guide to Raising Venture Capital.*

27.1.2 NO MARKET NEED (35%)

Another very common reason startups don't make it is *lack of demand for the product.* This is nearly completely avoidable if a startup is following lean startup[175] principles. With this approach, the team should have really strong validation about what customers want and are willing to pay for *before* they build the product. If you are not conversant in lean startup methodology, read the book that launched the movement: *The Lean Startup,*[176] by Eric Ries. (There is even a 58-page summary ebook version for Kindle on Amazon.com for less than $3!)

How to avoid this scenario. In addition to making sure the startup you are thinking of investing in is following "lean" techniques, look at the customer traction[§11.3] closely for validation that there are paying customers (a market) for the product. To be clear, they may not have paying customers yet, or even customers, or even a product. But they should have talked to lots of potential customers to understand their needs and pain points deeply and validate that the features the entrepreneurs have in mind will be seen as valuable.

27.1.3 NOT THE RIGHT TEAM (14%)

This can be a bit of a catch-all. Was there a functional gap in the team, like marketing or engineering leadership? Were the key founders not all fully committed? Did someone leave when the going got tough? Did they not work well together? Did they lack domain expertise?

How to avoid this scenario. We talked a lot about the importance of the startup team in Evaluating Opportunities,[§10.1] and beat the drum again in Business Due Diligence for Angel Investments.[§11.1] If you've taken steps to evaluate the team and are not convinced that this team is uniquely suited to achieve success in their market, this might not be the right investment.

---

174. https://www.holloway.com/g/venture-capital/sections/determining-how-much-to-raise

175. https://en.wikipedia.org/wiki/Lean_startup

176. https://www.amazon.com/Lean-Startup-Entrepreneurs-Continuous-Innovation/dp/0307887898

27.2 *Staying Informed*

The best hope to avoid a complete failure of a startup you have invested in is to stay informed and keep up-to-date on how the company is doing. A good startup CEO will send out regular communications to the investors. This should cover good news, bad news, and how the investors can help the company. If you are getting these reports, you should definitely read them, and you should have an idea of whether the company is executing well, when it is thinking about raising another round, whether the company is struggling to fill a key slot on the executive team, or failing to land key customers.

If you are not getting updates, be proactive in reaching out to the CEO or the lead investor in your financing round or other investors in the round who may be connected to the company.

Negotiating for information rights and board observer rights can be really useful, because being informed of problems early gives you the best opportunity to do something about it before the company runs out of runway.

27.3 *Digging In*

Assuming you discover that things are not going well, you need to decide how much time and energy you want to invest to try to get things back on track. Part of being engaged as an angel investor is helping where you can when a portfolio company needs it, and if you have focused your investments in domains that you know well, there should be plenty of opportunities to help, including:

- **Talent gaps.** It is very common for angels to get involved in helping a startup source and recruit key talent. Many active investors have strong networks, and they may even know seasoned executives and consultants that they can bring in on an interim basis if necessary to get companies "over the hump" on whatever issue is holding them back. This can be an effective stop-gap solution while the company continues to recruit for a permanent executive.
- **Specific execution challenges.** Founding teams are necessarily small, and young entrepreneurs often have gaps in their business experience. For example, strong technical founders may need help driving

customer growth, which might be slow due to poor positioning, ineffi-
cient marketing, ineffective pricing, or a poor initial user experience.
Arrange a working session with the team and spend several hours digging into a specific issue. You may be surprised how effective your own
business experience, domain expertise, and seasoned perspective can
be in overcoming challenges.

Angels can help with product feedback, finances, and introductions to
potential customers or marketing/distribution partners as well.

In short, many problems that might otherwise cause a startup to fail
are solvable if the company still has enough runway to execute and the
investors are willing to get involved. The key is to keep track of what is
going on with the company and rally your co-investors as necessary.

⚠ **DANGER** At the same time, don't go too far. Do not, for example, offer
or agree to become a guarantor of the company's debt. Sometimes companies will want to issue you a warrant or give you other compensation
to guarantee their debt. Just say no. The scenario that some creditor will
come after you to pay off the company debt is one you want to avoid. The
downside here is much bigger than losing your investment.

≫ EXAMPLE

In an ironic personal twist, Pete invested in an LLC with an individual who had guaranteed a debt in another LLC. That other LLC
failed, and this individual had to declare personal bankruptcy. As a
result, the LLC Pete invested in was shut down.

27.4 *The Pivot*

Not having a market for the product or service is the number one reason
startups fail.

A **pivot**, a term popular in startup culture, happens when a company
realizes that their current product or business strategy is not going to work
and they change course to a new product and/or business model. A classic pivot scenario is that a company is struggling to sell their product,
while potential customers keep asking them if they can solve a different
but related problem.

≫ EXAMPLE

A company may be struggling to sell a digital advertising network product. Their sales prospects don't see the need, since the existing solutions are sufficient; but they keep saying that what they really need is an ad network analytics product to inform them on how the advertising networks they are using already are performing. The company uses the same team and pivots its product strategy to an analytics product.

The history of successful startups is full of pivots: Twitter started out as a podcast directory; Pinterest was initially a shopping app called Tote. Some successful startups have pivoted multiple times, in some cases to completely new product categories. So if your portfolio company is simply not finding paying customers for its current product in its current market, perhaps they need to pivot. You can be helpful by encouraging that exploration and acting as a sounding board for new ideas.

Pivots work best when there is significant runway (more than three months!) left in the company and the team can apply some aspects of its team and technology directly to the new market. It takes time to evaluate the new market and get a detailed enough understanding of the new customer set to be able to build new features with confidence. It also takes time to build those features, update the website and all the marketing, start prospecting for sales, et cetera. The more the team can leverage their existing assets, the more likely they are to succeed. The more the team stays within its domain expertise, per the example above, the more likely it can save time in customer discovery and have some existing relationships that it can leverage for early sales.

◇ IMPORTANT Pivots are not to be taken lightly—it is akin to hitting the restart button. Suddenly, the company has no product, and it has no customers for the new product they don't yet have. There are times, however, when the new idea is so compelling and it comes directly out of the company's experience with its existing business that the entrepreneurs can convince existing investors to provide some additional interim financing to get the company to a significant milestone on the new business. Then it will be in a position to raise an external round with new investors.

28 Common Wisdoms and Painful Lessons

In writing this book, we wanted you to benefit from our collective wisdom. With Joe's extensive legal experience working with startup financings, and Pete's experience as a startup founder and executive of successful and failed companies, and as an angel investor in Seattle, we believe our perspective will help you avoid the mistakes we've made along the way, and look forward to successes.

Keep in mind that when you start angel investing, it is all great. You invest in smart teams chasing big opportunities, and you are getting in early. But the sad fact is that most startups fail. It is only after a few years that you will start to see which of your portfolio companies are doing well and which are underperforming.

We have found that we learn more from the failures than the successes, so we're passing along some of those painful lessons. By following the guidance in this book and doing your due diligence, you will hopefully decline to invest in a lot of companies with poor prospects, and get the most out of the investments you do make that succeed. Below are some of the keys we've found to unlock a great angel investing journey.

28.0.1 DON'T INVEST TOO FAST

◇ IMPORTANT   We frequently see angel investors invest all of the funds they have set aside for angel investments too quickly, even within a year. If you are going to start angel investing, don't get so excited you deploy all of your angel capital too quickly. It is only after you see a dozen or more pitches that you can start to get a feel for what is a really interesting opportunity. It usually takes years for your investments to start returning capital. So if you invest the allocable portion of your portfolio that you set aside for angel investments in the first couple of years of your investing, you might be out of the game for quite a while if you have to wait for a liquidity event to start investing again.

28.0.2 CONSIDER AN ANGEL INVESTOR BOOTCAMP OR FUND

These are becoming more popular, and there are now two in Seattle. John Sechrest runs the Seattle Angel Conference,[177] which educates twenty or so aspiring angel investors per class on how to do due diligence and evalu-

---

177. https://www.seattleangelconference.com/

ate opportunities. They screen something like forty companies who apply and over the course of the first two weeks they see all the pitches; over the next ten weeks, they break into due diligence teams, share information, and reduce the forty companies down to the four finalists who present at the Seattle Angel Conference event. Each investor commits $5K at the beginning of the class, and the winning company takes home a $100K investment in the form of a convertible note.

As a participating investor, you get lectures, you get to see forty companies, you get to see diligence performed on twenty companies and to participate in the process yourself. Pete was part of the first class of Seattle Angel Conference, and the company that won is still alive and growing today. There are many other formats, including angel investment funds where members participate in due diligence and make small investments across many companies. SeaChange Fund[178] in the Pacific Northwest is one example.

28.0.3 BUILD A PORTFOLIO OF INVESTMENTS

◇ IMPORTANT We refer to your "portfolio" of angel investments throughout this book, and let's be very clear about why: You don't want to rely on just one startup panning out, but build a portfolio, or collection, of many companies to maximize the likelihood that you'll see a return! Rather than putting $100K into each of two investments, put $25K into eight companies. You don't want all of your eggs in one or two baskets. Ideally, you have enough capital to build a portfolio of ten investments or more. All you need is one big win out of that portfolio to make money overall.

Another way to extend your portfolio of investments cheaply is to invest in a fund that allows you to participate in a large number of angel investments. For example, the Alliance of Angels has a "sidecar" fund that co-invests along with individual angels when more than three members invest in a single deal. By participating in the fund, one can invest in all of the popular deals that come through the group. The angels who invested directly in those deals did the due diligence, so if you have confidence in your fellow angels it is an easy way to diversify your portfolio.

---

178. https://seachangeventures.com/

28.0.4 DON'T OVERINVEST IN ONE COMPANY

◇ IMPORTANT Similar to the lesson about having a large, diverse portfolio of investments, do not invest too much in any one company. This can be hard, especially when you are highly confident you have found a winner. Know this: it is very hard to predict winners when you are making early-stage company investments.

> ❯ EXAMPLE
>
> Pete's first investment was into a company that looked like it couldn't lose. Through personal relationships of the founders, the company had locked up an exclusive distribution deal in the telecom space that looked like it would just print money. The founder was a real salesman, and Pete put in $75K as his first formal angel investment. Two very frustrating years later that company was bankrupt. If he had put $25K into each of three different investments, he would have learned more, had more fun, and had three times the chance of a positive outcome.

28.0.5 DON'T THROW GOOD MONEY AFTER BAD

Most startups fail, but they don't all fail quickly. Companies that are struggling will often need to raise money again without having hit the success milestones they pitched in their last round. You will see requests for bridge financing, which is when a company asks for more money to get them to a near-term milestone (like a product launch or big customer signing) that they believe will allow them to raise more money on better terms not far down the road. They know that their best bet for raising money in a challenging situation is from existing investors who already have skin in the game. They often offer incentives to participate, like warrants or a big discount to the next round if it will be a convertible note financing.

Pete has seen two of these requests from companies he invested in. In both cases, many investors participated, but Pete declined. (Not because Pete is such a smart investor, but because he is a nervous investor, and looks for reasons not to invest!) Both companies eventually failed.

Those opportunities can work out for investors, but you should be very cautious. Your opportunity cost for spending $25K bridging a struggling company is investing in the next really exciting opportunity you see.

There is a great McKinsey & Company article[179] about how software and services companies grow fast or die slowly. You don't want to be funding that slow death.

28.0.6 DON'T LET FLATTERY SWAY YOU

"You are obviously super smart and have awesome experience; we would love to have you on our advisory board if you invest. You'd be vesting another 0.1% of the company essentially for free!"

Pete's embarrassed to admit he was swayed by flattery like this to make an investment he was only marginally excited about. That company is still alive, but they are on a slow growth trajectory and the CEO has changed twice. The advisory board met a couple of times in the first year.

Flattery can be tremendously appealing, and an advisory role means you likely have more insight into the company's progress and you can help them succeed. In reality, there is very little in most cases that a single advisor can do to sway the outcome of a company. If you think you can materially contribute, you should do that out of your interests as an investor anyway, and only after you have fully vetted the company before investing.

28.0.7 STAY WITHIN YOUR DOMAIN

If possible, stay within your area of expertise, as we discussed in Finding Opportunities.§9 For example, Pete has no idea how to evaluate medical device companies. He doesn't understand the steps in the FDA approval process or the distribution channels or pricing for that market. He doesn't go near medical device investments!

28.0.8 DON'T NEGOTIATE TOO AGGRESSIVELY

⚠ DANGER Negotiating deal terms too aggressively can have major downsides for the company down the road, and set a bad precedent for future deals. A classic example: you negotiate for a multiple liquidation preference and participating preferred. This might be great for you, but when the next round comes in and those investors put more money in and get the same multiple and participation you got, you might not be too happy.

---

179. https://www.mckinsey.com/industries/technology-media-and-telecommunications/our-insights/grow-fast-or-die-slow

Additionally, once you have invested, you are all on the same side. You don't want to poison the relationship with the entrepreneurs by being too aggressive. (We debated titling this section "Don't be a dick," but didn't want to offend our sensitive readers. But it's a good rule.)

28.0.9 DON'T ACCEPT A BOARD SEAT LIGHTLY

⬦ CAUTION Do not accept a board seat unless you are willing to take the risk. Make sure that the company can afford directors and officers liability insurance; make sure the company has good indemnity provisions in its documents (have your lawyer review); and make sure the company gives you an indemnification agreement. Even if all of the above are in place, seriously consider whether you have the time and want the responsibility.

28.0.10 REMEMBER, IT'S NOT YOUR COMPANY

It can be a challenge for some angels who have backgrounds as successful CEOs or operating executives to be in a position of being an observer and not a decision maker. There may be a temptation to jump in and help to fix a problem or close a key deal. You've found the right marketing executive for them, why won't they just hire her!?

It's important to remember that you have invested *in the entrepreneur's company*. It is not your company, and you are not the CEO. You can advise, and make introductions to prospective customers and key hires, and help in lots of ways. But you bet on this horse and you have to let it run the race. Or if you are not into gambling on innocent animals... you invested because you had confidence in the CEO and the team. Now cheer them on.

29 Final Thoughts

> *"I have enjoyed every conversation I have had with an entrepreneur, whether I thought their idea was brilliance or lunacy. If you are a curious person and like to learn about new industries and technologies, and how intelligent, motivated, energetic people are trying to solve big problems, angel investing is incredibly satisfying. If you are fascinated by the entrepreneurial journey because you have lived it yourself (or aspired to), it is fun and fascinating to follow your portfolio*

companies' successes… and challenges, along with many other companies that you can follow through your angel investor colleagues. Angel investors tend to be smart, successful people who share the same excitement and passion for startups. It has been a great way to meet people and make new friends. Don't do it just for the payout. As much as the destination of a big payout appeals, it's the journey that makes becoming an angel investor really worth it."

— Pete Baltaxe

"Remember, this book is meant to be a helpful reference guide, not an encyclopedia. Don't be afraid to reach out for help. Rely on your mentors, your friends, your colleagues, get a good lawyer, and come back here when you need a reference. Always remember that angel investing is optional. Keep your objectivity. Don't get emotional, don't. Getting too excited over a deal can keep you from properly performing due diligence. Move slowly. Don't think negatively, but think neutrally.[180] *There's no opportunity so great that it's worth writing a $25K check without knowing what's going on or how it's going to affect you down the road. At the same time, don't get so caught up in the minutiae of the deal terms that it becomes a source of angst or stress. All of the rules, advice, and admonitions found in this book or anywhere else only have value in the right situations, and following these rules too closely can breed arrogance and even ignorance. You don't want to be so strung up on following 'rules' that you're gummed up on taking any action and miss out on a great deal. Remember that the best return I ever saw went to an angel who wasn't too stuffy to take a common stock deal—even though you wouldn't normally be advised to buy common stock! Angel investing is all about situational awareness. Don't lose your perspective, don't lose sleep, and don't invest money you can't afford to lose."*

— Joe Wallin

---

180. https://thriveglobal.com/stories/
  the-power-of-neutral-thinking-nfl-guru-trevor-moawads-5-secrets-of-high-performance-and-they-arent-what-you-think/

APPENDICES

30 Appendix A: Example Documents

30.1 *Example Convertible Note Term Sheet*

For your convenience, this template document is available as a Google Doc[181] to make it easier to copy and edit. All material here is provided for illustration only; please read the disclaimer[§4] before use.

[COMPANY]

Convertible Note Offering Term Sheet

This term sheet summarizes the principal terms pursuant to which [Company] , a [Delaware/etc.] _____ corporation (the "Company"), will raise up to $ _____ through the issuance of promissory notes (the "Notes") to a limited number of "accredited" investors. The Company will make available to each investor all information the investor reasonably requests so that the investor can familiarize him/her/itself with the Company's business. To the extent that these terms are inconsistent with the underlying legal documents (a Promissory Note), the terms of the Note control.

COMPANY:	[COMPANY] , A [DELAWARE] CORPORATION.
Interest Rate:	The Notes will bear interest at __ % per annum. Interest will accrue and be payable upon maturity.

---

181. https://www.holloway.com/ang-appendix

COMPANY:	[COMPANY] , A [DELAWARE] CORPORATION.
Conversion:	The Notes are convertible the next round of preferred stock issued by the Company in an equity financing in which the Company raises at least $ [2,000,000] (excluding debt that is converting to preferred stock) which closes before the Maturity Date (as defined below), at the lower of (i) a [15-20%] discount to the purchase price of the securities sold in such offering, or (ii) the price per share determined by reference to the Valuation Cap, on a fully-diluted basis (but not considering the conversion of this note and other similar notes).
Valuation Cap:	$ _____ .
Maturity Date:	The Notes will mature ___ (__) years after their date of issuance ("**Maturity Date**").
Minimum Investment:	$ _____ (waivable at the Company's discretion).
Use of Proceeds:	The proceeds of the offering will be immediately available to the Company for general working capital purposes.
Size of the Offering:	$ _____ . The Company reserves the right to raise a greater or lesser amount in its sole discretion.
Suitability:	An investment in the Notes is available to "accredited investors" who can bear the substantial risks involved and are willing to accept the lack of liquidity of their investment.
Subordination:	The Promissory Notes will be subordinated to other borrowings of the Company.
Closings:	There is no minimum amount required to be raised before the Company can accept subscriptions. The Company may hold any number of subsequent closings.
Amendment:	The Notes may be amended with the consent of the Company and holders of a majority in interest of the principal amount of the Notes outstanding.
Restricted Securities:	The Promissory Notes are not registered securities and are not transferable without the written approval of the Company.

THE FOREGOING SUMMARY DOES NOT PURPORT TO BE A COM-
PLETE SUMMARY OF THE PROMISSORY NOTES. EACH INVESTOR
SHOULD READ THE FORM OF PROMISSORY NOTE IN ITS
ENTIRETY. IN ADDITION, INVESTORS SHOULD CONSULT THEIR
TAX AND LEGAL ADVISORS AS TO THE IMPLICATIONS OF AN
INVESTMENT IN THE NOTES.

30.2 *Example Series A Preferred Term Sheet*

For your convenience, this template document is available as a Google Doc[182] to make it easier to copy and edit. All material here is provided for illustration only; please read the disclaimer[§4] before use.

[COMPANY]

Term Sheet

Series A Preferred Stock Offering

_____, 20__

COMPANY:	**[COMPANY] , A [DELAWARE] CORPORATION.**
Type of Security:	Series A Convertible Preferred Stock
Offering Size:	The Company intends to raise as much as $ _____ in this offering, although the Company may increase or decrease this amount in its sole discretion.
Price Per Share:	$ _____ per share
Minimum Investment:	$ _____ (may be waived by the Company in its sole discretion)
Shares Authorized To Be Sold in This Offering:	_____
Liquidation Preference:	On a liquidation of the Company, the Series A Preferred will be entitled to a return of their purchase price per share, and the remainder of the proceeds will be paid to the common shareholders (a 1x liquidation preference; non-participating preferred)
Anti-Dilution:	Standard, broad-based weighted average anti-dilution protection; customary carve-outs for stock options and other board-approved equity issuances other than for capital raising
Dividends:	Non-cumulative; when, as and if declared by the board

---

COMPANY:	**[COMPANY] , A [DELAWARE] CORPORATION.**
Voting Rights:	Series A Preferred will vote on an as-converted-to-common-stock basis and not as a separate class. Consent of holders of a majority of the Series A Preferred is required to amend or alter the rights, preferences and privileges of the Series A Preferred Stock
Conversion:	The Series A Preferred will be convertible into common stock on a 1:1 basis (unless the conversion ratio is adjusted as a result of an anti-dilution adjustment, or in the event of a stock split, etc.). Mandatory conversion in the event of (i) an IPO or (ii) upon the written consent of holders of a majority of the Series A
Investor Eligibility:	"Accredited Investors" only
Information:	The Company will provide additional information upon request
Closings:	One or more closings as the Company accepts subscriptions
Use of Proceeds:	Working capital; proceeds will be immediately available to the Company
Subscription Procedure:	Investors must execute a Stock Purchase Agreement, which will include a right of first refusal in favor of the Company on the Series A Stock purchased by the investor

Capitalization

(as of .... , 20__ , as adjusted for maximum Series A Offering)

	NO. OF SHARES	% ON FULLY-DILUTED BASIS
Issued and outstanding Common Shares:	--------	-------- %
Stock option pool to be reserved:	--------	-------- %
Series A to be sold in the offering:	--------	-------- %
	--------	100%

30.3 *Example Common Stock Term Sheet*

For your convenience, this template document is available as a Google Doc[183] to make it easier to copy and edit. All material here is provided for illustration only; please read the disclaimer[§4] before use.

[COMPANY]

Term Sheet

Common Stock Offering

_____, 20__

COMPANY:	[COMPANY] , A [DELAWARE] CORPORATION.
Type of Security:	Common Stock
Pre-Money Valuation	$ _____
Offering Size:	The Company intends to raise as much as $ _____ in this offering, although the Company may increase or decrease this amount in its sole discretion
Price Per Share:	$ _____ per share
Sale:	If the Company is sold before the conversion of the notes sold in the offering, holders of the notes will be entitled to be paid the greater of: (i) [3]X their note principal and accrued interest, or (ii) the amount they would have received had they converted to equity at the Valuation Cap
Minimum Investment:	$ _____ (may be waived by the Company in its sole discretion)
Shares Authorized To Be Sold in This Offering:	_____
Dividends:	When, as and if declared by the board. The Company has not paid dividends in the past and does not currently contemplate that it will pay dividends in the future
Voting Rights:	All shares have the same voting rights

183. https://www.holloway.com/ang-appendix

COMPANY:	[COMPANY] , A [DELAWARE] CORPORATION.
Investor Eligibility:	"Accredited Investors" only
Information:	The Company will provide additional information upon request
Closings:	One or more closings as the Company accepts subscriptions
Use of Proceeds:	Working capital; proceeds will be immediately available to the Company
Subscription Procedure:	Investors must execute a Common Stock Purchase Agreement, which will include a right of first refusal agreement in favor of the Company on any proposed transfers of Common Stock purchased in the offering

Capitalization

(as of .... , 20__ , as adjusted for maximum offering)

	NO. OF SHARES	% ON FULLY-DILUTED BASIS
Issued and outstanding Common Shares:	--------	-------- %
Stock option pool to be reserved:	--------	-------- %
Common stock to be sold in the offering:	--------	-------- %
	--------	100%

30.4 *Example Revenue Loan Term Sheet*

For your convenience, this template document is available as a Google Doc[184] to make it easier to copy and edit. All material here is provided for illustration only; please read the disclaimer[§4] before use.

Term Sheet for a Revenue Loan

This Term Sheet is non-binding, and is meant to try to capture the parties' intentions about the terms of a potential investment. However, neither of the parties have any obligations to one another until they enter into and sign definitive agreements.

---

184. https://www.holloway.com/ang-appendix

AMOUNT OF LOAN:	$ _____
Monthly Repayment Amount	_____ % of the borrower's preceding month's net revenue, due and payable on or before the [5th] day of each month.
"Net Revenue":	"Net Revenue" means all of the borrower's revenues and cash receipts, from all product or service sales, except customer returns and shipping charges.
Repayment Amount:	The note will be considered paid in full when the borrower has paid the lender [___ times] the amount of the loan, not including any penalties, attorneys' fees or similar items.
Maturity Date:	As soon as the borrower has paid the lender the Repayment Amount, or 5 years.
Security Interest:	The borrower will grant lender a first priority security interest in all of the borrower's property.
Acceleration of Repayment Amount:	The Repayment Amount will become immediately due and payable upon a change of control of the borrower, a sale of all or substantially all of the borrower's assets, or the borrower's insolvency or an event of default (as defined in the definitive documents).
Reporting:	The borrower will report to the lender its monthly Net Revenues each month. The borrower will also provide the lender customary information rights. In the event that the borrower underpays the lender, the borrower will pay the lender the deficiency plus a fee of 5% of the underpayment the lender's audit costs in uncovering such deficiency.
Success Fee:	On a sale of the borrower's business, the borrower will pay the lender a success fee in the amount of $ _____ or X% of the amount paid to the borrower's owners as a result of the sale.
Closing Fee:	The borrower will pay the lender closing fee of $ _____ .
Lender's Expenses:	The borrower will reimburse the lender's legal fees for documenting the loan.
Closing Conditions:	The loan will be subject to the lenders due diligence and the borrower's execution of the lender's standard loan documents. The loan documents will contain customary representations and warranties.
Negative Covenants:	The borrower may not incur additional indebtedness or grant additional security interests on any of its assets, make loans or advances, dispose of all or substantially all of its assets, or consummate a change in control without the consent of the lender.

AMOUNT OF LOAN:	$ ....
Accounting:	The loan will be treated as such on the borrower's balance sheet. In no event will the loan be treated or considered equity.
Confidentiality:	The borrower will hold this term sheet in strict confidence. This is a binding term.
Non-Binding:	Except for the paragraph titled Confidentiality, this term sheet is non-binding, and shall not imply any obligation to negotiate. Either party may terminate discussions at any time.

30.5 *Example Mutual Confidentiality Agreement*

For your convenience, this template document is available as a Google Doc[185] to make it easier to copy and edit. All material here is provided for illustration only; please read the disclaimer[§4] before use.

Mutual Confidentiality Agreement

This Agreement is made and entered into as of .... , 20 __ ("Effective Date"), by and between [Company], a .... corporation ("Company") and .... ("Other Party").

1. **Definition of Confidential Information.** *"Confidential Information"* as used in this Agreement shall mean information concerning a party's business, property or technology not generally known to the public which is disclosed by a party (a *"Disclosing Party"*) to the other (a *"Recipient"*) and which is either identified as "Confidential" at the time of disclosure or which under the circumstances surrounding the disclosure should reasonably be considered to be Confidential Information.

2. **Nondisclosure and Nonuse Obligation.** Recipient shall not in any way disclose any Confidential Information of the Disclosing Party to any third party, and shall only use Confidential Information of Disclosing Party in connection with its internal evaluations of the proposed transaction or business relation-

---

185. https://www.holloway.com/ang-appendix

ship between the parties. Recipient will treat all Confidential Information with the same degree of care as it accords its own Confidential Information, but in no case less than reasonable care. Recipient will disclose Confidential Information only to those of its employees and independent contractors who need to know such information and who have entered into written confidentiality agreements with Recipient which protect the Confidential Information.

3. **Exclusions from Nondisclosure and Nonuse Obligations.** Recipient's obligations under Paragraph 2 shall not apply to Confidential Information that Recipient can document (a) was in the public domain at or subsequent to the time communicated to Recipient by Disclosing Party through no fault of Recipient, (b) was rightfully in Recipient's possession free of any obligation of confidentiality at or subsequent to the time communicated to Recipient by Disclosing Party, or (c) was developed by employees or agents of Recipient independently of and without reference to any Confidential Information communicated to Recipient by Disclosing Party. A disclosure of any portion of Confidential Information either (i) in response to a valid order by a court or other governmental body, or (ii) otherwise required by law, shall not be considered to be a breach of this Agreement or a waiver of confidentiality for other purposes; provided, however, that Recipient shall provide prompt prior written notice thereof to Disclosing Party to enable Disclosing Party to seek a protective order or otherwise prevent such disclosure.

4. **Ownership.** All Confidential Information shall remain the property of the Disclosing Party, and no license or other rights to a Disclosing Party's Confidential Information are granted or implied hereby. Upon request from Disclosing Party at any time, Recipient will, at Disclosing Party's option, return or destroy all Confidential Information no later than five (5) days following such a request, and certify such destruction or return in writing.

5. **Independent Development.** Disclosing Party understands that Recipient may currently or in the future be developing information internally, or receiving information from other par-

ties that may be similar to Disclosing Party's Confidential Information. Nothing in this Agreement will be construed as a representation or inference that Recipient will not develop products or services, or have products or services developed for it that, without violation of this Agreement, compete with the products or services contemplated by Disclosing Party's Confidential Information.

6. **Disclosure of Third Party Information.** Neither party shall communicate any information to the other in violation of the proprietary rights of any third party.

7. **No Warranty.** Disclosing Party supplies Confidential Information "AS IS," and without express or implied warranties of any kind. Disclosing Party shall not be responsible or liable for any business decision made by Recipient in reliance on disclosures made pursuant to this Agreement.

8. **Injunctive Relief.** The parties acknowledge and agree that monetary damages would not be a sufficient remedy for any breach of obligations under this Agreement and that a Disclosing Party shall be entitled to injunctive relief as a remedy for any such breach by the Recipient. Such remedy will not be deemed the exclusive remedy for a breach of Recipient's obligations under this Agreement, but will be in addition to all other available legal and equitable remedies.

9. **Term.** This Agreement will govern all communications between Disclosing Party and Recipient from the Effective Date and remain in full force and effect for two (2) years; provided, however, that either party will maintain the trade secrets of the other party indefinitely.

10. **Binding Effect.** This Agreement will benefit and be binding upon the parties and their respective successors and assigns.

11. **Governing Law; Venue.** This Agreement shall be governed by, and construed in accordance with the laws of the State of _____ without giving effect to any conflict of laws principles to the contrary. Venue for any disputes arising under this Agreement will lie exclusively in the state or federal courts located in _____ County, _____ . The parties irrevocably waive any right to raise *forum non conveniens* or any other argument that _____ County, _____ is not the proper

venue, and irrevocably consent to personal jurisdiction in the state and federal courts of _____ .

12. **Attorneys' Fees.** The prevailing party in any such action will be entitled to recover its reasonable attorney fees and costs in such action and upon any appeals.

13. **Non-Waiver; Modification.** No failure or delay by either party in exercising any right, power, or remedy under this Agreement will operate as a waiver of any such right, power, or remedy. No waiver or modification of any provision of this Agreement will be effective unless in writing and signed by both parties.

14. **Entire Agreement.** This Agreement constitutes the entire agreement and understanding of the parties relating to the subject matter hereof and supersedes all prior and contemporaneous agreements, negotiations, and understandings between the parties, both oral and written.

IN WITNESS WHEREOF, the parties have executed this Agreement as of the date first written above.

[signature blocks omitted]

30.6 *Example Investor Side Letter Agreement*

> For your convenience, this template document is available as a Google Doc[186] to make it easier to copy and edit. All material here is provided for illustration only; please read the disclaimer[§4] before use.

[Company Letterhead]

[Date]

Re: Your investment in [Company] , a [Delaware] corporation

Dear Investor:

Thank you for your investment in [Name of Company] , a [Delaware] corporation (referred to as the *"Company"* or as *"us"* and *"we"* in this letter). We very much appreciate your support and trust. This letter agreement will confirm the agreement between us and you (*"you"* or the *"Investor"*), effective as of the execution of your securities purchase agreements with us. [Insert description of securities purchased.] In consideration for your investment in us, you are hereby entitled to the following rights, in addition to any other rights you are entitled to under law or as provided in the other agreements you entered into with us:

Information Rights.

Upon your request, the Company shall deliver to you, for so long as you hold our securities (unless this letter agreement otherwise terminates per below), [in each case to the extent that the Company has prepared such financial statements,] the following information:

(a) Copies of our balance sheet as of the end of such fiscal year and our statements of income, changes in financial position and shareholders' equity for such fiscal year, prepared in accordance with U. S. generally accepted accounting principles (*"GAAP"*) (all unaudited unless our financial statements are otherwise audited, in which case we will send you the audited statements);

(b) Copies of our balance sheet and statement of income for each quarter, prepared in accordance with GAAP and subject to routine year-end adjustments; and

---

186. https://www.holloway.com/ang-appendix

(c) Such other information relating to the financial condition, business or corporate affairs of the Company as you may from time to time reasonably request, including but not limited to information prepared by the Company for its quarterly Board of Directors meetings; provided, however, that the Company shall not be obligated under this Section 1 to provide information that (i) it deems in good faith to be a trade secret or highly confidential information, or (ii) the disclosure of which would adversely affect the attorney-client privilege between the Company and its counsel.

You agree to maintain the confidentiality of all of the information provided under this Section 1, and agree not to use such information other than for a purpose reasonably related to your investment in the Company or as requested by the Company.

Section 4(a)(7).

For so long as you hold our securities, upon request we agree to furnish promptly to you any information required for you to claim exemption for resale of the securities under Section 4(a)(7) of the Securities Act of 1933, as amended (or any successor or replacement provision thereto, the *"Resale Exemption"*), including, without limitation:

(a) The current address of the Company's executive offices;

(b) A current capitalization table of the Company reflecting the number of shares outstanding by class as of the end of the Company's most recent fiscal year prior to the date of the request;

(c) Name and address of the transfer agent, corporate secretary or other person responsible for transferring the Securities;

(d) A brief statement of the nature of the business of the Company and the products and services it offers;

(e) Names of the current officers and directors of the Company;

(f) Financial statements for the Company prepared in accordance with US generally accepted accounting principles [or IFRS for a non-US company] that satisfy the requirements of the Resale Exemption, including balance sheets and profit and loss or income statements, covering the 2 most recent prior fiscal years of operation (or such shorter period as the Company has been in operation) and any interim period that has been prepared by the Company; and

(g) Such other information relating to the Company as you may request that is reasonably necessary for you to transfer the securities in accordance with the Resale Exemption.

Pro Rata Rights.

You shall have the right (but not the obligation) to purchase your [pro rata share/up to $[insert dollar amount] of equity securities issued by the Company in the next financing in which we are raising capital (the *"Next Financing"*), on the same terms as such equity securities are offered to other investors who do not purchase such equity securities via the conversion of indebtedness; provided, however, that you will demonstrate to the Company's reasonable satisfaction that you are at the time of the proposed issuance of such equity securities an "accredited investor" as such term is defined in Regulation D under the Securities Act of 1933, as amended. For the avoidance of doubt, you shall not have a pro rata right in the Company's next convertible note or convertible equity financing.

Your *"pro rata share"* means, with respect to Next Financing securities, the sum of: (i) if you hold any convertible promissory notes issued by us, the ratio of the principal amount under any such notes to the pre-money valuation at which such Next Financing securities are issued, plus (ii) the ratio of the number of shares of capital stock of the Company then held by you (calculated on an as-converted to Common Stock basis) to the number of fully diluted shares immediately prior to the issuance of such Next Financing securities. Following the conversion or repayment in full of the outstanding amount under your Note, your "pro rata share" shall mean the ratio of the number of shares of capital stock of the Company then held by you (calculated on an as-converted to Common Stock basis) to the number of fully diluted shares immediately prior to the issuance of Next Financing securities. The number of fully diluted shares assumes full conversion and exercise of all options and other outstanding convertible and exercisable securities, calculated as of immediately prior to the issuance of the Next Financing securities. If we propose to issue equity securities covered under this pro rata right, we shall promptly give you written notice of our intention, describing the Next Financing equity securities, the price, the terms and conditions upon which we propose to issue the same, and your pro rata number of Next Financing equity securities (the "Notice"). [Our determination of your pro rata share of the Next Financing equity securities shall be binding on you.] In order to exercise this right, you must give the Company notice of your intent to exercise this right within ten (10) days of receiving the Notice and you shall invest and fund the purchase price for the equity securities and execute the principal financing documents for such Next Financing within ten (10) days after the initial closing of the Next Financing.

Most Favored Nation. You will be entitled to receive the benefit of any more favorable terms or conditions that we provide to other convertible debt lenders or convertible equity investors in any convertible debt or convertible equity financing that we consummate before your [note/SAFE] is converted into shares of our stock; provided, however, that if we are accepted into an accelerator or incubator program and in addition to any equity financing we obtain from such accelerator or incubator we are also provided substantial services, or space, any such equity financing will not be considered a convertible debt financing triggering this most favored nations clause.

Board Observer Right.

[As long as you own not less than ____ percent (___ %) of the shares of the [Series A] Preferred Stock you are purchasing under the Purchase Agreement (or an equivalent amount of Common Stock issued upon conversion thereof).]

[In the event of any breach of this letter agreement, a default under the note, or a breach or default of or under any agreement between you and us], then you or your representative shall thereafter have the right to attend all of our Board of Directors meetings in a non-voting observer capacity and, in this respect, we shall give you or your representative copies of all notices, minutes, consents, and other materials that we provide to our directors [at the same time and in the same manner as provided to such directors]; provided, however, that you and/or your representative shall agree to hold in confidence and trust and to act in a fiduciary manner with respect to all information so provided; and provided further, that we reserve the right to withhold any information and to exclude you and/or your representative from any meeting or portion thereof if access to such information or attendance at such meeting could adversely affect the attorney-client privilege between the Company and its counsel or result in disclosure of trade secrets or a conflict of interest, or if you or your representative is a competitor of the Company.

Attorneys' Fees.

The prevailing party in any action to enforce this letter agreement will be entitled to its attorneys' fees and costs.

Termination of this Letter Agreement.

The contractual rights set forth above shall terminate and be of no further force or effect upon (a) the consummation of the sale of the Company's securities pursuant to a registration statement filed by the Company under the Securities Act of 1933, as amended, in connection with the firm commitment underwritten offering of its securities to the general public; (b) the consummation of a merger or consolidation of the Company that is effected (i) for independent business reasons unrelated to extinguishing such rights and (ii) for purposes other than (A) the reincorporation of the Company in a different state or (B) the formation of a holding company that will be owned exclusively by the Company's stockholders and will hold all of the outstanding shares of capital stock of the Company's successor; (c) our liquidation and dissolution; or (d) when you cease holding the Convertible Promissory Note or after conversion of the Note you cease to hold at least 1% of our issued and outstanding stock.

Waiver and Amendments.

Any provision of this letter agreement may only be amended, waived or modified only upon the written consent of the Company and the Investor.

General.

To the extent that this letter agreement conflicts with any of the other documents or agreements entered into by and between the parties, including the [Convertible Promissory Note], this letter agreement will control. This letter agreement shall be governed by and construed in accordance with the laws of the State of [_____] (regardless of its or any other jurisdiction's choice-of-law principles). This letter agreement may be executed in counterparts, each of which shall be deemed an original, but all of which together shall constitute one and the same instrument. Sincerely yours, [Company]

_____   _____ , President

Agreed and Accepted:

_____

(print name of investor)

_____

Name: _____

Title: _____

30.7 *Example Observer Agreement*

> For your convenience, this template document is available as a Google Doc[187] to make it easier to copy and edit. All material here is provided for illustration only; please read the disclaimer[§4] before use.

OBSERVER AGREEMENT

THIS OBSERVER AGREEMENT (the "Agreement") is entered into as of _____ , 20 __ , by and between _____ ("Observer"), and _____ , Inc., a [Delaware] corporation (the "Company").

SECTION 1

OBSERVER RIGHTS

1.1 **Observer Rights.** As long as Observer owns at least ___ % of the issued and outstanding common stock of the Company, the Company shall invite [a representative of Observer / _____ , an individual] to attend all meetings of its board of directors in a non-voting observer capacity and, in this respect, shall give such representative copies of all notices, minutes, consents, and other materials that it provides to its directors and at the same time it provides such materials to its directors; *provided, however*, that such representative shall agree to hold in confidence and trust and to act in a fiduciary manner with respect to all information so provided; and *provided further*, that the Company reserves the right to withhold any information and to exclude such representative from any meeting or portion thereof if access to such infor-

---

187. https://www.holloway.com/ang-appendix

mation or attendance at such meeting could adversely affect the attorney-client privilege between the Company and its counsel or result in disclosure of trade secrets or a conflict of interest, or if the Observer or its representative is a competitor of the Company.

1.2 **Termination of Information and Observer Rights.** The covenants set forth in **Section 1.1** shall terminate and be of no further force or effect (i) immediately before the consummation of an underwritten public offering of the Company's common stock, or (ii) when the Company first becomes subject to the periodic reporting requirements of Section 12(g) or 15(d) of the Exchange Act, or (iii) upon the liquidation or dissolution of the Company, whichever event occurs first.

1.3 **Confidentiality.** The Observer agrees that the Observer and its representative will keep confidential and will not disclose, divulge, or use for any purpose (other than to monitor its investment in the Company) any confidential information obtained from the Company pursuant to the terms of this Agreement (including notice of the Company's intention to file a registration statement), unless such confidential information (a) is known or becomes known to the public in general (other than as a result of a breach of this *Section 1.3* by the Observer or its representative), (b) is or has been independently developed or conceived by the Observer without use of the Company's confidential information, or (c) is or has been made known or disclosed to the Observer by a third party without a breach of any obligation of confidentiality such third party may have to the Company; *provided, however,* that an Observer may disclose confidential information (i) to its attorneys, accountants, consultants, and other professionals to the extent necessary to obtain their services in connection with monitoring its investment in the Company; (ii) to any prospective purchaser of securities from the Observer, if such prospective purchaser agrees to be bound by the provisions of this *Section 1.3;* (iii) to any existing or prospective affiliate, partner, member, stockholder, or wholly owned subsidiary of the Observer in the ordinary course of business, provided that the Observer informs such person that such information is confidential and directs such person to maintain the confidentiality of such information; or (iv) as may otherwise be required by law, *provided that* the Observer promptly notifies the Company of such disclosure and takes reasonable steps to minimize the extent of any such required disclosure.

SECTION 2

MISCELLANEOUS

2.1 **Miscellaneous.** The Observer may not assign its rights under this Agreement. This Agreement shall be governed by and construed under the internal laws of the State of _____ as applied to agreements among _____ residents entered into and to be performed entirely within _____ , without reference to principles of conflict of laws or choice of laws. This Agreement may be executed in two or more counterparts, each of which shall be deemed an original, but all of which together shall constitute one and the same instrument. The headings and captions used in this Agreement are used for convenience only and are not to be considered in construing or interpreting this Agreement. Any term of this Agreement may be amended and the observance of any term of this Agreement may be waived (either generally or in a particular instance and either retroactively or prospectively), only with the written consent of the Observer and the Company. If one or more provisions of this Agreement are held to be unenforceable under applicable law, such provision(s) shall be excluded from this Agreement and the balance of the Agreement shall be interpreted as if such provision(s) were so excluded and shall be enforceable in accordance with its terms.

IN WITNESS WHEREOF, the parties hereto have executed this Agreement as of the date first above written.

[signature blocks omitted]

30.8 *Full Ratchet Side Letter Agreement*

This section is available in the digital edition at Holloway.com.

30.9 *Example Minutes of a Meeting of a Board of Directors*

For your convenience, this template document is available as a Google Doc[188] to make it easier to copy and edit. All material here is provided for illustration only; please read the disclaimer[§4] before use.

MINUTES OF MEETING OF THE BOARD OF DIRECTORS OF

_____ , INC.

_____ , 20 __

A meeting of the Board of Directors (the "**Board**") of _____ , Inc., a [Delaware) corporation (the "**Company**") was held at [insert location of meeting], on [insert date], commencing at [insert start time]. Directors in attendance included Messrs. [insert directors attending]. The following directors were not in attendance: [insert]. [Also in attendance was [_____ of legal counsel], and [insert others]. _____ was the Chairman of the meeting, and [_____] served as Acting Secretary for the meeting.

The Chairman called the meeting to order.

The first order of business was approval of minutes from the prior board meeting held on _____ . Upon motion duly made, seconded and approved, the board approved the minutes of the prior meeting [in the form presented/with certain changes].

The next item of business was [indicate which items of business were discussed].

If a motion is passed, say, "Upon motion duly made, seconded and adopted, the board approved..."

[If there are stock options to be issued, then more detailed resolutions are required.]

The board then discussed a variety of issues affecting the business, including [e.g., product development, marketing, product rollout and implementation, strategic relationships, media relations, staffing, the status of the certain significant contracts issues related thereto]. [The board then discussed financial issues, including the Company's current cash position, outstanding bills, payroll, budget, burn rate, and the status of the Company's stock

---

offering. Finally, the board discussed its meeting schedule for future meetings.]

There being no further business, the meeting was adjourned at [insert time]. Respectfully submitted,

_____ , Acting Secretary

Approved by:

_____ , Chair

30.10 *Annotated Convertible Note*

> For your convenience, this template document is available as a Google Doc[189] to make it easier to copy and edit. All material here is provided for illustration only; please read the disclaimer[§4] before use.

THIS CONVERTIBLE PROMISSORY NOTE HAS NOT BEEN REGISTERED UNDER THE SECURITIES ACT OF 1933, AS AMENDED. NO SALE OR DISPOSITION MAY BE EFFECTED EXCEPT IN COMPLIANCE WITH RULE 144 UNDER SAID ACT OR AN EFFECTIVE REGISTRATION STATEMENT RELATED THERETO OR AN OPINION OF COUNSEL FOR THE HOLDER SATISFACTORY TO THE COMPANY THAT SUCH REGISTRATION IS NOT REQUIRED UNDER THE ACT OR RECEIPT OF A NO-ACTION LETTER FROM THE SECURITIES AND EXCHANGE COMMISSION.

CONVERTIBLE PROMISSORY NOTE

Note Series: _____

Date of Note: _____

Principal Amount of Note: _____

For value received XYZ Inc., a [Delaware/other] corporation (the "**Company**"), promises to pay to the undersigned holder ("**Holder**") the principal amount set forth above with all accrued and unpaid interest thereon, each due and payable in the manner set forth below upon request of the Majority Holders[190] on or after

---

189. https://www.holloway.com/ang-appendix

190. Note that this Note does not allow any one note holder, unless they hold the majority in principal in amount of the notes, to unilaterally sue for their money back.

the second anniversary of the issuance of the first Note of the Note Series set forth above (the "**Maturity Date**").

1. **Basic Terms.**

   a. **Series of Notes.** This convertible promissory note (the "**Note**") is issued as part of a series of notes designated by the Note Series above (collectively, the "**Notes**") and issued in a series of multiple closings to certain persons and entities (collectively, the "**Holders**").

   b. **Payments**. All payments of interest and principal shall be in lawful money of the United States of America and shall be made pro rata among all Holders. All payments shall be applied first to accrued interest and thereafter to principal.

   c. **Interest Rate.** The Company promises to pay simple interest on the outstanding principal amount hereof from the date funds are received by the Company until payment in full, which interest shall be payable at the rate of ___ %[191] per annum or the maximum rate permissible by law, whichever is less. Interest shall be due and payable on the Maturity Date and shall be calculated on the basis of a 365-day or 366-day year, as the case may be, for the actual number of days elapsed.

   No Prepayment. The Company may not prepay this Note prior to the Maturity Date without the consent of the Majority Holders (as defined below).

2. **Conversion; Repayment Upon Sale of the Company.**

   a. **Conversion upon a Qualified Financing.** In the event that the Company issues and sells shares of its Equity Securities (defined below) to investors (the "**Investors**") on or before the date of the repayment in full of this Note in an arms-length equity financing resulting in gross proceeds to the Company, in one or more closings, of at least $250,000 (excluding the conversion of the Notes and any other debt) (a "**Qualified Financing**"), then the outstanding principal balance of this Note and any unpaid accrued interest shall automatically convert in whole without any further action by the Holder into such Equity Securities sold in the Qualified Financing at a conver-

---

191. Insert interest rate.

sion price equal to the lesser of (i) ____ %[192] of the price paid per share for Equity Securities by the Investors in the Qualified Financing or (ii) the price equal to the quotient of the valuation cap of $ _____ [193] (the "**Valuation Cap**") divided by the aggregate number of outstanding shares of the Company's common stock as of immediately prior to the initial closing of the Qualified Financing (assuming full conversion or exercise of all convertible and exercisable securities then outstanding, but excluding the shares of equity securities of the Company issuable upon the conversion of the Notes or any other debt). The issuance of Equity Securities pursuant to the conversion of this Note shall be upon and subject to the same terms and conditions applicable to the Equity Securities sold in such Qualified Financing, except as otherwise set forth herein (e.g., the conversion price); provided, however, that such documents have customary exceptions to any drag-along applicable to the Holder, including, without limitation, limited representations and warranties and limited liability and indemnification obligations on the part of the Holder. For the avoidance of doubt, the initial closing of the Qualified Financing is the first closing in which the Company accepts which funds which meet or exceed the Qualified Financing threshold.

b. **Maturity Date Conversion.** In the event that a Qualified Financing is not consummated prior to the Maturity Date, then, at the written election of the Majority Holders made at least five days prior to the Maturity Date, effective upon the Maturity Date, the outstanding principal balance and any unpaid accrued interest under this Note shall be converted into shares of the Company's common stock at a conversion price equal to the quotient of the Valuation Cap divided by the aggregate number of outstanding shares of the Company's common stock as of the Maturity Date (assuming full conversion or exercise of all convertible and exercisable securities then outstanding, but excluding the shares of equity securities of the Company issuable upon the conversion of the Notes or any other debt).

---

192. Insert discount percentage.
193. Insert the valuation cap.

c. **Sale of the Company.** Notwithstanding any provision of this Note to the contrary, if the Company consummates a Sale of the Company (as defined below) prior to the conversion or repayment in full of this Note, then (i) the Company will give the Holder at least five days prior written notice of the antic- ipated closing date of such Sale of the Company and (ii) at the closing of such Sale of the Company, in full satisfaction of the Company's obligations under this Note, the Company will pay the Holder an aggregate amount equal to the greater of (x) the aggregate amount of principal and unpaid accrued inter- est then outstanding under this Note or (y) the amount the Holder would have been entitled to receive in connection with such Sale of the Company if the aggregate amount of princi- pal and unpaid accrued interest then outstanding under this Note had been converted into shares of the Company's com- mon stock at a conversion price equal to the quotient of the Valuation Cap divided by the aggregate number of outstanding shares of the Company's common stock as of immediately prior to the closing of such Sale of the Company (assuming full con- version or exercise of all convertible and in-the-money exercis- able securities then outstanding, but excluding the shares of equity securities of the Company issuable upon the conversion of the Notes or other debt being converted or deemed to be converted in connection with such Sale of the Company).

d. **Procedure for Conversion.** In connection with any conver- sion of this Note into capital stock, the Holder shall surrender this Note to the Company and deliver to the Company any documentation reasonably required by the Company (includ- ing, in the case of a Qualified Financing, all financing docu- ments executed by other investors in connection with such Qualified Financing). The Company shall not be required to issue or deliver the capital stock into which this Note may con- vert until the Holder has surrendered this Note to the Com- pany and delivered to the Company any such documentation. Upon the conversion of this Note into capital stock pursuant to the terms hereof, in lieu of any fractional shares to which the Holder would otherwise be entitled, the Company shall pay the Holder cash equal to such fraction multiplied by the price at which this Note converts; provided, however, if such amount is less than $100.00, no such payment shall be required, and no fractional shares shall be issued. To secure the Holder's obligations to execute and deliver the documentation required by this Note, the Holder hereby appoints the Chief Executive Officer of the Company as the Holder's true and lawful attorney, with the power to act alone and with full power of substitution, to execute and deliver all such documentation required by this Note if, and only if, the Holder fails execute or deliver such documentation as required by this Note. The power granted by the Holder pursuant to this paragraph is coupled with an interest and is given to secure the performance of the Holder's duties under this Note, is irrevocable and will survive the death, incompetency, disability, merger or reorganization of the Holder.

e. **Interest Accrual.** If a Sale of the Company or Qualified Financing is consummated, all interest on this Note shall be deemed to have stopped accruing as of the signing of the definitive agreement for the Sale of the Company or Qualified Financing or an earlier date, determined by the Company, which may be as many as ten days prior to the signing of such definitive agreement.

f. **Certain Definitions.** For purposes of this Note:

i. "**Equity Securities**" shall mean the Company's preferred stock issued in the Company's next fixed-price financing, except that such defined term shall not include any security granted, issued and/or sold by the Company to any employee, director or consultant in such capacity. The Equity Securities may be sold in one more closings.

ii. "**Majority Holders**" shall mean the Holders holding Notes that represent a majority of the outstanding unpaid principal amount of all Notes.

iii. "**Sale of the Company**" shall mean (i) any consolidation or merger of the Company with or into any other corporation or other entity or person, or any other corporate reorganization, other than any such consolidation, merger or reorganization in which the stockholders of the Company immediately prior to such consolidation, merger or reorganization, continue to hold at least a majority of the voting power of the surviving entity in substantially the same proportions (or, if the surviving entity is a wholly owned subsidiary, its parent) immediately after such consolidation, merger or reorganization; (ii) any transaction or series of related transactions to which the Company is a party in which in excess of 50% of the Company's voting power is transferred; or (iii) the sale or transfer of all or substantially all of the Company's assets, or the exclusive license of all or substantially all of the Company's material intellectual property; *provided, however,* that a Sale of the Company shall not include any transaction or series of transactions principally for bona fide equity financing purposes in which cash is received by the Company or any successor, indebtedness of the Company is cancelled or converted, or a combination thereof.

3. **Representations and Warranties.**

a. **Representations and Warranties of the Company.** The Company hereby represents and warrants to the Holder, as of the date the first issuance of a note in this Note Series, as follows:

i. **Organization, Good Standing and Qualification.** The Company is a corporation duly organized, validly existing and in good standing under the laws of the state of its incorporation or organization. The Company has the requisite corporate power to own and operate its properties and assets and to carry on its business as now conducted and as proposed to be conducted. The Company is duly qualified and is authorized to do business and is in good standing as a foreign corporation in all jurisdictions in which the nature of its activities and of its properties (both owned and leased) makes such qualification necessary, except for those jurisdictions in which failure to do so would not have a material adverse effect on the Company or its business.

ii. **Corporate Power.** The Company has all requisite corporate power to issue this Note and to carry out and perform its obligations under this Note. The Company's Board of Directors (the "**Board**") has approved the issuance of this Note based upon a reasonable belief that the issuance of this Note is appropriate for the Company after reasonable inquiry concerning the Company's financing objectives and financial situation.

iii. **Authorization.** All corporate action on the part of the Company, the Board and the Company's stockholders necessary for the issuance and delivery of this Note has been taken.

iv. **Enforceability.** This Note constitutes a valid and binding obligation of the Company enforceable in accordance with its terms, subject to laws of general application relating to bankruptcy, insolvency, the relief of debtors and, with respect to rights to indemnity, subject to federal and state securities laws. Any securities issued upon conversion of this Note (the "**Conversion Securities**"), when issued in compliance with the provisions of this Note, will be validly issued, fully paid, nonassessable, free of any liens or encumbrances and issued in compliance with all applicable federal and securities laws.

v. **Governmental Consents.**

All consents, approvals, orders or authorizations of, or registrations, qualifications, designations, declarations or filings with, any governmental authority required on the part of the Company in connection with issuance of this Note has been obtained.

vi. **Compliance with Laws.** The Company is not in violation of any applicable statute, rule, regulation, order or restriction of any domestic or foreign government or any instrumentality or agency thereof in respect of the conduct of its business or the ownership of its properties, which violation of which would materially and adversely affect the business, assets, liabilities, financial condition, operations or prospects of the Company.

vii. **Compliance with Other Instruments.** The Company is not in violation or default of any term of its certificate of incorporation or bylaws, or of any provision of any mortgage, indenture or contract to which it is a party and by which it is bound or of any judgment, decree, order or writ, other than such violation(s) that would not individually or in the aggregate have an adverse effect on the Company. The execution, delivery and performance of this Note will not result in any such violation or be in conflict with, or constitute, with or without the passage of time and giving of notice, either a default under any such provision, instrument, judgment, decree, order or writ or an event that results in the creation of any lien, charge or encumbrance upon any assets of the Company or the suspension, revocation, impairment, forfeiture, or nonrenewal of any material permit, license, authorization or approval applicable to the Company, its business or operations or any of its assets or properties. Without limiting the foregoing, the Company has obtained all waivers reasonably necessary with respect to any preemptive rights, rights of first refusal or similar rights, including any notice or offering periods provided for as part of any such rights, in order for the Company to consummate the transactions contemplated hereunder without any third party obtaining any rights to cause the Company to offer or issue any securities of the Company as a result of the consummation of the transactions contemplated hereunder.

viii. **No "Bad Actor" Disqualification.** The Company has exercised reasonable care to determine whether any Company Covered Person (as defined below) is subject to any of the "bad actor" disqualifications described in Rule 506(d)(1)(i) through (viii), as modified by Rules 506(d)(2) and (d)(3), under the Securities Act of 1933, as amended ("**Disqualification Events**"). To the Company's knowledge, no Company Covered Person is subject to a Disqualification Event. The Company has complied, to the extent required, with any disclosure obligations under Rule 506(e) under the Securities Act of 1933, as amended (the "**Act**"). For purposes of this Note, "**Company Covered Persons**" are those persons specified in Rule 506(d)(1) under the Act; provided, however, that Company Covered Persons do not include (a) any Holder, or (b) any person or entity that is deemed to be an affiliated issuer of the Company solely as a result of the relationship between the Company and any Holder.

ix. **Offering.** Assuming the accuracy of the representations and warranties of the Holder contained in subsection (b) below, the offer, issue, and sale of this Note and any Conversion Securities are and will be exempt from the registration and prospectus delivery requirements of the Act, and have been registered or qualified (or are exempt from registration and qualification) under the registration, permit or qualification requirements of all applicable state securities laws.

x. **Use of Proceeds.** The Company shall use the proceeds of this Note solely for the operations of its business, and not for any personal, family or household purpose.

b. **Representations and Warranties of the Holder.** The Holder hereby represents and warrants to the Company as of the date hereof as follows:

i. **Purchase for Own Account.** The Holder is acquiring this Note and the Conversion Securities (collectively, the "**Securities**") solely for the Holder's own account and beneficial interest for investment and not for sale or with a view to distribution of the Securities or any part thereof, has no present intention of selling (in connection with a distribution or otherwise), granting any participation in, or otherwise distributing the same, and does not presently have reason to anticipate a change in such intention.

ii. **Information and Sophistication.** Without lessening or obviating the representations and warranties of the Company set forth in subsection (a) above, the Holder hereby: (A) acknowledges that the Holder has received all the information the Holder has requested from the Company and the Holder considers necessary or appropriate for deciding whether to acquire the Securities, (B) represents that the Holder has had an opportunity to ask questions and receive answers from the Company regarding the terms and conditions of the offering of the Securities and to obtain any additional information necessary to verify the accuracy of the information given the Holder and (C) further represents that the Holder has such knowledge and experience in financial and business matters that the Holder is capable of evaluating the merits and risk of this investment.

iii. **Ability to Bear Economic Risk.** The Holder acknowledges that investment in the Securities involves a high degree of risk, and represents that the Holder is able, without materially impairing the Holder's financial condition, to hold the Securities for an indefinite period of time and to suffer a complete loss of the Holder's investment.

iv. **Further Limitations on Disposition.** Without in any way limiting the representations set forth above, the Holder further agrees not to make any disposition of all or any portion of the Securities unless and until:

(1) There is then in effect a registration statement under the Act covering such proposed disposition and such disposition is made in accordance with such registration statement; or

(2) The Holder shall have notified the Company of the proposed disposition and furnished the Company with a detailed statement of the circumstances surrounding the proposed disposition, and if reasonably requested by the Company, the Holder shall have furnished the Company with an opinion of counsel, reasonably satisfactory to the Company, that such disposition will not require registration under the Act or any applicable state securities laws, provided that no such opinion shall be required for dispositions in compliance with Rule 144 under the Act, except in unusual circumstances.

(3) Notwithstanding the provisions of paragraphs (1) and (2) above, no such registration statement or opinion of counsel shall be necessary for a transfer by the Holder to a partner (or retired partner) or member (or retired member) of the Holder in accordance with partnership or limited liability company interests, or transfers by gift, will or intestate succession to any spouse or lineal descendants or ancestors, if all transferees agree in writing to be subject to the terms hereof to the same extent as if they were the Holders hereunder.

v. **Accredited Investor Status.** The Holder is an accredited investor as defined in Rule 501(a) of Regulation D promulgated under the Act. The Holder is an investor in securities of companies in the development stage and acknowledges that Holder is able to fend for itself, can bear the economic risk of its investment, and has such knowledge and experience in financial or business matters that it is capable of evaluating the merits and risks of the investment in this note. If other than an individual, Holder also represents it has not been organized for the purpose of acquiring this note. vi. **No "Bad Actor" Disqualification.** The Holder represents and warrants that neither (A) the Holder nor (B) any entity that controls the Holder or is under the control of, or under common control with, the Holder, is subject to any Disqualification Event, except for Disqualification Events covered by Rule 506(d)(2)(ii) or (iii) or (d)(3) under the Act and disclosed in writing in reasonable detail to the Company. The Holder represents that the Holder has exercised reasonable care to determine the accuracy of the representation made by the Holder in this paragraph, and agrees to notify the Company if the Holder becomes aware of any fact that makes the representation given by the Holder hereunder inaccurate.

vii. **Foreign Investors.** If the Holder is not a United States person (as defined by Section 7701(a)(30) of the Internal Revenue Code of 1986, as amended (the "**Code**")), the Holder hereby represents that he, she or it has satisfied itself as to the full observance of the laws of the Holder's jurisdiction in connection with any invitation to subscribe for the Securities or any use of this Note, including (A) the legal requirements within the Holder's jurisdiction for the purchase of the Securities, (B) any foreign exchange restrictions applicable to such purchase, (C) any governmental or other consents that may need to be obtained, and (D) the income tax and other tax consequences, if any, that may be relevant to the purchase, holding, redemption, sale, or transfer of the Securities. The Holder's subscription, payment for and continued beneficial ownership of the Securities will not violate any applicable securities or other laws of the Holder's jurisdiction.

viii. **Forward-Looking Statements.** With respect to any forecasts, projections of results and other forward-looking statements and information provided to the Holder, the Holder acknowledges that such statements were prepared based upon assumptions deemed reasonable by the Company at the time of preparation. There is no assurance that such statements will prove accurate, and the Company has no obligation to update such statements.

4. **Events of Default.**

a. Upon the occurrence and continuance of any Event of Default (as defined below), at the option and upon the declaration of the Majority Holders and upon written notice to the Company (which election and notice shall not be required in the case of an Event of Default under subsection (ii) or (iii) below), this Note shall accelerate and all principal and unpaid accrued interest shall become due and payable. The occurrence of any one or more of the following shall constitute an "**Event of Default**":

i. The Company fails to pay timely any of the principal amount due under this Note on the date the same becomes due and payable or any unpaid accrued interest or other amounts due under this Note on the date the same becomes due and payable (unless the Company cures such failure within 15 business days of notice thereof from the Majority Holders);

ii. The Company files any petition or action for relief under any bankruptcy, reorganization, insolvency or moratorium law or any other law for the relief of, or relating to, debtors, now or hereafter in effect, or makes any assignment for the benefit of creditors or takes any corporate action in furtherance of any of the foregoing; or

iii. An involuntary petition is filed against the Company (unless such petition is dismissed or discharged within 60 days under any bankruptcy statute now or hereafter in effect, or a custodian, receiver, trustee, assignee for the benefit of creditors (or other similar official) is appointed to take possession, custody or control of any property of the Company).

b. In any action to enforce the terms of this Note, the prevailing party will be entitled to an award of its reasonable attorneys' fees and other related costs.

5. **Tax Withholding.** If the Company is required to remit to any governmental authority an amount of money which represents a withholding from amounts paid or considered paid to the Holder, then the Holder agrees to provide the Company with the funds, in immediately available U.S. dollars, so that the Company has the funds to remit to such governmental authority. In all events, any amounts will be considered paid for the benefit of the Holder. The Holder hereby authorizes the Company to make any withholding required by law. The Holder agrees to provide to the Company a Form W-9 or comparable form as requested by the Company.

6. **Miscellaneous Provisions.**

a. **Waivers.** The Company hereby waives demand, notice, presentment, protest and notice of dishonor.

Further Assurances. The Holder agrees and covenants that at any time and from time to time the Holder will promptly execute and deliver to the Company such further instruments and documents and take such further action as the Company may reasonably require in order to carry out the full intent and purpose of this Note and to comply with state or federal securities laws or other regulatory approvals.

Transfers of Notes. This Note may be transferred only (i) in compliance with this instrument and (ii) upon its surrender to the Company for registration of transfer, duly endorsed, or accompanied by a duly executed written instrument of transfer in form satisfactory to the Company. Thereupon, this Note shall be reissued to, and registered in the name of, the transferee, or a new Note for like principal amount and interest shall be issued to, and registered in the name of, the transferee. Interest and principal shall be paid solely to the registered holder of this Note. Such payment shall constitute full discharge of the Company's obligation to pay such interest and principal.

Market Standoff. The Holder hereby agrees that the Holder shall not sell, dispose of, transfer, make any short sale of, grant any option for the purchase of, or enter into any hedging or similar transaction with the same economic effect as a sale of, any shares of common stock (or other securities) of the Company held by the Holder (other than those included in the registration) during the 180-day period following the effective date of the initial public offering of the Company (or such longer period, not to exceed 34 days after the expiration of the 180-day period, as the underwriters or the Company shall request in order to facilitate compliance with NASD Rule 2711 or NYSE Member Rule 472 or any successor or similar rule or regulation). The Holder agrees to execute and deliver such other agreements as may be reasonably requested by the Company or the managing underwriters that are consistent with the foregoing or that are necessary to give further effect thereto. In addition, if requested by the Company or the representative of the underwriters of common stock (or other securities of the Company), the Holder shall provide, within ten days of such request, such information as may be required by the Company or such representative in connection with the completion of any public offering of the Company's securities pursuant to a registration statement filed under the Act. The obligations described in this paragraph shall not apply to a registration relating solely to employee benefit plans on Form S-1 or Form S-8 or similar forms that may be promulgated in the future, or a registration relating solely to a transaction on Form S-4 or similar forms that may be promulgated in the future. In order to enforce the foregoing covenant, the Company may impose stop-transfer instructions with respect to such common stock (or other securities of the Company) until the end of such period. The Holder agrees that any transferee of any of the Securities (or other securities of the Company) held by the Holder shall be bound by this paragraph. The underwriters of the Company's stock are intended third-party beneficiaries of this paragraph and shall have the right, power and authority to enforce the provisions hereof as though they were a party hereto.

e. **Amendment and Waiver.** Any term of this Note may be amended or waived with the written consent of Company and the Majority Holders.

f. **Governing Law; Venue.** This Note shall be governed by and construed under the laws of the State of _____ , as applied to agreements among _____ residents, made and to be performed entirely within the State of _____ , without giving effect to conflicts of laws principles. The venue for any dispute arising out of or related to this Note will lie exclusively in the state or federal courts located in King County, Washington, and the parties to this Note irrevocably waive any right to raise forum non conveniens or any other argument that King County, Washington is not the proper venue. The parties to this Note irrevocably consent to personal jurisdiction in the state and federal courts of the state of Washington.

g. **Waiver of Jury Trial.** THE HOLDER HEREBY IRREVOCABLY WAIVES, TO THE FULLEST EXTENT PERMITTED BY APPLICA-

BLE LAW, ANY RIGHT IT MAY HAVE TO A TRIAL BY JURY IN ANY LEGAL PROCEEDING DIRECTLY OR INDIRECTLY RELATING TO THIS NOTE OR THE TRANSACTIONS CONTEMPLATED HEREBY, WHETHER BASED ON CONTRACT, TORT, OR ANY OTHER THEORY.

h. **Binding Agreement.** The terms and conditions of this Note shall inure to the benefit of and be binding upon the respective successors and assigns of the parties. Nothing in this Note, expressed or implied, is intended to confer upon any third party any rights, remedies, obligations, or liabilities under or by reason of this Note, except as expressly provided in this Note.

i. **Counterparts.** This Note may be executed in two or more counterparts, each of which shall be deemed an original, but all of which together shall constitute one and the same instrument. This Note may also be executed and delivered by facsimile signature, PDF or any electronic signature complying with the U.S. federal ESIGN Act of 2000 (e.g., www.docusign.com[194]).

j. **Titles and Subtitles.** The titles and subtitles used in this Note are used for convenience only and are not to be considered in construing or interpreting this Note.

k. **Notices.** All notices, requests, or other communications required or permitted to be delivered hereunder shall be delivered in writing, in each case to the address specified below or to such other address as such party may from time to time specify in writing in compliance with this section. Notices (i) if mailed by certified or registered mail or sent by hand or overnight courier service shall be deemed to have been given when received or (ii) if sent by email or other electronic means shall be deemed received upon receipt by the sender of an acknowledgment from the intended recipient.

l. **Expenses.** The Company and the Holder shall each bear its respective expenses and legal fees incurred with respect to the negotiation, execution and delivery of this Note and the transactions contemplated herein.

---

194. https://www.docusign.com/

m. **Delays or Omissions.** It is agreed that no delay or omission to exercise any right, power or remedy accruing to the Holder, upon any breach or default of the Company under this Note shall impair any such right, power or remedy, nor shall it be construed to be a waiver of any such breach or default, or any acquiescence therein, or of or in any similar breach or default thereafter occurring; nor shall any waiver of any single breach or default be deemed a waiver of any other breach or default theretofore or thereafter occurring. It is further agreed that any waiver, permit, consent or approval of any kind or character by the Holder of any breach or default under this Note, or any waiver by the Holder of any provisions or conditions of this Note, must be in writing and shall be effective only to the extent specifically set forth in writing and that all remedies, either under this Note, or by law or otherwise afforded to the Holder, shall be cumulative and not alternative. This Note shall be void and of no force or effect in the event that the Holder fails to remit the full principal amount to the Company within five calendar days of the date of this Note.

n. **Entire Agreement.** This Note constitutes the full and entire understanding and agreement between the parties with regard to the subjects hereof and no party shall be liable or bound to any other party in any manner by any representations, warranties, covenants and agreements except as specifically set forth herein.

o. **Exculpation among Holders.** The Holder acknowledges that the Holder is not relying on any person, firm or corporation, other than the Company and its officers and Board members, in making its investment or decision to invest in the Company.

p. **Senior Indebtedness.** The indebtedness evidenced by this Note is subordinated in right of payment to the prior payment in full of any Senior Indebtedness in existence on the date of this Note or hereafter incurred. "**Senior Indebtedness**" shall mean, unless expressly subordinated to or made on a parity with the amounts due under this Note, all amounts due in connection with (i) indebtedness of the Company to banks or other lending institutions regularly engaged in the business of lending money (excluding venture capital, investment banking or similar institutions and their affiliates, which sometimes engage in lending activities but which are primarily engaged in investments in equity securities), and (ii) any such indebtedness or any debentures, notes or other evidence of indebtedness issued in exchange for such Senior Indebtedness, or any indebtedness arising from the satisfaction of such Senior Indebtedness by a guarantor.

q. **Broker's Fees.** Each party hereto represents and warrants that no agent, broker, investment banker, person or firm acting on behalf of or under the authority of such party hereto is or will be entitled to any broker's or finder's fee or any other commission directly or indirectly in connection with the transactions contemplated herein. Each party hereto further agrees to indemnify each other party for any claims, losses or expenses incurred by such other party as a result of the representation in this section titled "Broker's Fees" being untrue.

r. **Confidentiality.** The Holder shall not in any way disclose any Confidential Information of the Company that the Holder may receive from time to time to any third party, and shall not use the Confidential Information of the Company for any purpose other than to monitor its investment in the Company. The Holder will treat all Confidential Information with the same degree of care as it accords its own Confidential Information, but in no case less than reasonable care. Notwithstanding the foregoing, the Holder may disclose the Company's Confidential Information to its attorneys, accountants or other professionals who are bound by confidentiality, to the extent necessary to obtain their services in connection with monitoring the Holder's investment in the Company. "**Confidential Information**" means information concerning a party's business, finances, property or technology not generally known to the public which is either identified as "Confidential" at the time of disclosure or which under the circumstances surrounding the disclosure should reasonably be considered to be Confidential Information.

s. **California Corporate Securities Law.** THE SALE OF THE SECURITIES WHICH ARE THE SUBJECT OF THIS AGREEMENT HAS NOT BEEN QUALIFIED WITH THE COMMISSIONER OF COR-

PORATIONS OF THE STATE OF CALIFORNIA AND THE ISSUANCE OF SUCH SECURITIES OR THE PAYMENT OR RECEIPT OF ANY PART OF THE CONSIDERATION THEREFOR PRIOR TO SUCH QUALIFICATION OR IN THE ABSENCE OF AN EXEMPTION FROM SUCH QUALIFICATION IS UNLAWFUL. PRIOR TO ACCEPTANCE OF SUCH CONSIDERATION BY THE COMPANY, THE RIGHTS OF ALL PARTIES TO THIS AGREEMENT ARE EXPRESSLY CONDITIONED UPON SUCH QUALIFICATION BEING OBTAINED OR AN EXEMPTION FROM SUCH QUALIFICA-TION BEING AVAILABLE.

Notice Regarding Oral Commitments under Washington Law. ORAL AGREEMENTS OR ORAL COMMITMENTS TO LOAN MONEY, EXTEND CREDIT, OR TO FORBEAR FROM ENFORCING PAYMENT OF A DEBT ARE NOT ENFORCEABLE UNDER WASHINGTON LAW.

[Signature pages follow]

31 Appendix B: C Corps, LLCs, and S Corps

31.1 *Choice of Entity*

✦ FOUNDER If you are going to start a company, one of the first legal decisions you will have to make is what type of entity to form. This can be a more complex question than you might think.

In general, for federal income tax purposes, there are three types of entities to choose from:

- C Corporations,
- S Corporations, or
- LLCs taxed as partnerships.

(This outline doesn't consider other potential entity choices, like public benefit corporations, social purpose corporations, cooperatives, et cetera.)

What primarily differentiates these business entities from one another is their federal income tax characteristics:

- **C Corporation.** A C Corporation is an entity that, in contrast to an S Corporation or an LLC taxed as a partnership, *is* subject to federal income tax and pays federal income taxes on its income. Its shareholders are not subject to tax unless the corporation pays amounts to them in the form of dividends, distributions, or salary.
- **S Corporation.** An S Corporation is not subject to federal income tax. Instead the company's shareholders pay federal income tax on the taxable income of the S Corporation's business based on their pro rata stock ownership.
- **LLC.** LLCs, like S Corporations, are "pass-through" entities, which means that their owners (referred to as members) pay the tax on the income of the LLC that is allocated to them based on the LLC agreement. For a sole member, unless an election is made to be taxed as a corporation, the LLC is treated as a "disregarded entity," meaning that the sole member reports the LLC's income or loss on his or her tax return just like a sole proprietorship, or division in the case of a corporate owner. For purposes of this discussion, when we talk about LLCs we are talking about LLCs that have more than one member and haven't made any elections to be taxed as C corporations or S corporations, but instead are taxed as partnerships for federal income tax purposes. For LLCs with multiple members, the LLC is treated as a partnership and must file the IRS Form 1065 (unless the entity elects to be taxed as a corporation). The members of the LLC are treated as partners for federal income tax purposes and each receives a Form K-1 reporting their share of the LLC's income or loss for the members to report on their federal income tax return.

31.2 *C Corps vs. S Corps*

31.2.1 C CORPORATION ADVANTAGES/S CORPORATION DISADVANTAGES

- **Investors generally prefer C corporations.** If you plan to raise money from investors, then a C corporation is probably a better choice than an S corporation. Your investors may not want to invest in an S corporation because they may not want to receive a Form K-1 and be taxed on their share of the company's income. They may not be eligible to invest in an S corporation. Thus, if you set yourself up as a C corporation, you will be in the form most investors expect and desire, and you will avoid having to convert from an S corporation or an LLC to a C corporation prior to a fund raise.

- **Only C corporations can issue qualified small business stock.** C corporations can issue qualified small business stock. S corporations cannot issue qualified small business stock. Thus S corporation owners are ineligible for qualified small business stock benefits. Currently, the QSBS benefit is a 100% exclusion from from tax on up to the greater of either $10M of gain or 10X the adjusted basis of qualified small business stock issued by the corporation and sold during the year, QSBS held for more than five years, and the ability to roll over gain on the sale of qualified stock into other qualified stock. This is a significant potential benefit to founders and one reason to not choose to form as an S corp.
- **Traditional venture capital investments can be made.** C corporations can issue convertible preferred stock, the typical vehicle for a venture capital investment. S corporations cannot issue preferred stock. An S corporation can only have one class of economic stock; it can have voting and non-voting common stock, but the economic rights of the shares (as opposed to the voting characteristics), have to be the same for all shares in an S corporation.
- **Retention of earnings/reinvestment of capital.** Because a C corporation's income does not flow or pass through to its shareholders, C corporations are not subject to pressure from their shareholders to distribute cash to cover their shareholders' share of the taxable income that passes through to them. An S corporation's pass-through taxation may make conservation of operating capital difficult because S corporations typically must distribute cash to enable shareholders to pay the taxes on their pro rata portion of the S corporation's income (S corporation shareholders are taxed on the income of the corporation regardless of whether any cash is distributed to them).
- **No one class of stock restriction.** S corporations can only have one class of stock; S corporations cannot issue preferred stock, for example. But this restriction can arise in other situations unexpectedly, and must be considered whenever issuing equity, including stock options or warrants.

- **Flexibility of ownership.** C corporations are not limited with respect to ownership participation. There is no limit on the type or number of shareholders a C corporation may have. S corporations, in contrast, can only have a limited number of shareholders, generally cannot have non-individual shareholders, and cannot have foreign shareholders (all shareholders must be U.S. residents or citizens).
- **More certainty in tax status.** A C corporation's tax status is more certain than an S corporation's tax status. For example, a C corporation does not have to file an election to obtain its tax status. S corporations must meet certain criteria to elect S corporation status, must then elect S corporation status, and then not "bust" that status by violating one of the eligibility criteria.

31.2.2 S CORPORATION ADVANTAGES/C CORPORATION DISADVANTAGES

- **Single level of tax.** S corporations are pass-through entities: their income is subject to only one level of tax, at the shareholder level. A C corporation's income is subject to tax, and any "dividend" distributions of earnings and profits to shareholders that have already been taxed at the C corporation level are also taxable to the shareholders (i.e., income is effectively taxed twice). This rule is also generally applicable on liquidation of the entity.
- **Pass-through of losses.** Generally, losses, deductions, credits, and other tax benefit items pass through to a S corporation's shareholders and may offset other income on their individual tax returns (subject to passive activity loss limitation rules, at-risk limitation rules, basis limitation rules, and other applicable limitations). A C corporation's losses do not pass through to its shareholders.
- **Simplicity of structure.** S corporations have a more easily understandable and simpler corporate structure than LLCs. S corporations can only have one class of stock—common stock—and their governing documents, articles, and bylaws are more familiar to most people in the business community than LLC operating agreements (which are complex and cumbersome and rarely completely understood).

31.3 *C Corps vs. LLCs Taxed as Partnerships*

31.3.1 C CORPORATION ADVANTAGES/LLC DISADVANTAGES

- **Traditional venture capital investments can be accepted.** The issuance of convertible preferred stock by C corporations is the typical vehicle for venture capital investments. Venture capitalists typically will not invest in LLCs and may be precluded from doing so under their fund documents.

- **Traditional equity compensation is available.** C corporations can issue traditional stock options and incentive stock options. It is more complex for LLCs to issue the equivalent of stock options to their employees. Incentive stock options also are not available to LLCs.

- **Ability to participate in tax-free reorganizations.** C corporations can participate in tax-free reorganizations under IRC Section 368. LLCs cannot participate in tax-free reorganizations under IRC Section 368. This means that if you think your business may get acquired by a company in exchange for the acquiror's stock, a C corporation would be a good choice of entity.

- **Qualified small business stock benefits.** C corporations can issue qualified small business stock. LLCs cannot issue qualified small business stock. Thus, LLC owners are ineligible for qualified small business stock benefits, which is the 100% gain exclusion of up to $10 million on the sale of qualified stock held for more than five years, and the ability to roll over gain on the sale of qualified stock into other qualified stock.

- **Self-employment taxes.** C corporation shareholders are not subject to self-employment taxes on the corporation's income. An LLC's members are generally subject to self-employment tax on their distributive share of the LLC's ordinary trade and business income.

- **Retention of earnings/reinvestment of capital.** A C corporation's income does not flow or pass through to its shareholders; this makes it easier to retain and accumulate capital because a C corporation will never have to distribute cash to its stockholders so that they can pay the tax on the entity's income. LLC's pass-through taxation can make conservation of operating capital difficult. LLCs typically distribute cash to enable members to pay the taxes on their share of the LLC's income (LLC members are taxed on the income of the LLC allocated to them regardless of whether any cash is distributed to them).

- **Fringe benefits.** C corporations have more favorable treatment of fringe benefits. LLC members cannot be considered "employees" for federal income tax purposes and therefore must pay self-employment taxes; fringe benefits of LLC members are generally included in income.
- **State income tax return filing requirements.** Each member of the LLC may be required to file a tax return in multiple states. This is not the case with C corporations.
- **Complexity/uncertainty.** The flexible nature of LLCs makes them more complex. Partnership tax is also substantially more complex than C corporation tax. The relatively new nature of the LLC form and limited amount of case law make LLC transactions more complex and uncertain than their corporate counterparts.
- **Tax rates.** Individual income tax rates can be higher than the highest stated corporate tax rates. At the time of this writing, the top C corp tax rate was 21%, and the top individual income tax rate was 37%.
- **Administrative burdens.** Partnership tax accounting is more complex than C corporation accounting.
- **Withholding on foreign members' distributive shares.** An LLC has to withhold taxes on certain types of income allocated to foreign persons, regardless of whether distributions are made. C corporations are not subject to this requirement.

31.3.2 LLC ADVANTAGES/C CORPORATION DISADVANTAGES

- **Single level of tax.** LLCs are pass-through entities: their income is subject to only one level of tax, at the member level. A C corporation's income is subject to tax, and any "dividend" distributions of earnings and profits to shareholders that have already been taxed at the C corporation level are also taxable to the shareholders (i.e., income is effectively taxed twice).
- **Pass-through of losses.** Generally, losses, deductions, credits, and other tax benefit items pass-through to an LLC's members and may offset other income on their individual tax returns (subject to passive activity loss limitation rules, at-risk limitation rules, basis limitation rules, and other potential limitations). A C corporation's losses do not pass-through to its shareholders.
- **Tax-free distributions of appreciated property.** An LLC can distribute appreciated property (e.g., real estate or stock) to its members with-

out gain recognition to the LLC or its members, facilitating spin-off transactions. A C corporation's distribution of appreciated property to its shareholders is subject to tax at the corporate level and possibly tax at the shareholder level as well. (It is for this reason that entities formed to invest in real estate or the stock of other companies should not be C corporations).

- **Tax-free formation.** Appreciated property can generally be contributed to LLCs tax-free under one of the broadest nonrecognition provisions in the IRC (IRC Section 721). Tax-free capitalizations for C corporations must comply with the more restrictive provisions of the IRS to be tax free (i.e., IRC Section 351) (although this is not usually a problem).

31.4 *S Corps vs. LLCs Taxed as Partnerships*

31.4.1 S CORPORATION ADVANTAGES/LLC DISADVANTAGES

- **Sales of equity.** S corporations can more easily engage in equity sales (subject to the one class of stock and no entity shareholder restrictions, generally) than LLCs. For example, because an S corporation can only have one class of stock, it must sell common stock in any financing (and this makes any offering simpler). An LLC will have to define the rights of any new class of stock in a financing, and this may involve complex provisions in the LLC agreement and more cumbersome disclosures to prospective investors. In addition, an S corporation does not have to convert to a corporation to issue public equity (although its S corporation status will have to be terminated prior to such an event). As a practical matter, an LLC will likely need to convert to a corporation before entering the public equity markets, because investors are more comfortable with a "typical" corporate structure.

- **Traditional equity compensation available.** S corporations can adopt traditional stock option plans; in addition, they can grant incentive stock options. It is very complex for LLCs to issue the equivalent of stock options to their employees (although they can more easily issue the equivalent of cheap stock through the issuance of profits interests—see below). Incentive stock options also are not available for LLCs.

- **Ability to participate in tax-free reorganizations.** S corporations, just like C corporations, can participate in tax-free reorganizations under IRC Section 368. LLCs cannot participate in a tax-free reorganization under IRC Section 368.
- **Ease of conversion to C Corporation status.** It is typically easier for an S corporation to convert to a C corporation than it is for an LLC to convert to a C corporation. For example, upon accepting venture capital funding, an S corporation will automatically convert to a C corporation. For an LLC to convert to a state law corporation taxed as a C corporation, it is necessary to either convert the LLC to a corporation pursuant to a state law conversion statute, or form a new corporate entity to either accept the assets of the LLC in an asset assignment or into which to merge the LLC. Also, converting an LLC to a C corporation may raise issues relating to conversions of capital accounts into proportionate stockholdings in the new corporation that are not easily answerable under the LLC's governing documents.
- **Simplicity of structure.** S corporations have a more easily understandable and simpler corporate structure than LLCs. S corporations can only have one class of stock—common stock—and their governing documents, articles and bylaws, are more familiar to most people in the business community than LLC operating agreements (which are complex and cumbersome and rarely completely understood).
- **Self-employment taxes.** S corporation shareholders are not subject to self-employment taxes. S corporation shareholders who are employees are taxed as employees and receive a Form W-2, not a Form K-1. An S corporation structure may result in the reduction in the overall employment tax burden. LLC members are generally subject to self-employment tax on their distributive share of the LLC's ordinary trade or business income. LLC members cannot be employees for federal income tax purposes and thus cannot receive Forms W-2.
- **Fringe benefits.** Only 2% or greater shareholders of S corporations have to include certain fringe benefits in income; generally all fringe benefits of LLCs are included in the income of the members, regardless of their percentage of ownership.

31.4.2 ADVANTAGES OF LLCS TAXED AS PARTNERSHIPS/S CORPORATION DISADVANTAGES

- **Flexibility of ownership.** LLCs are not limited with respect to ownership participation. There is no limit on the number of members an LLC may have. S corporations, in contrast, can only have a limited number of shareholders. Similarly, LLCs may have foreign members (although upon becoming a member of an LLC, a foreign member may suddenly become subject to the U.S. tax laws and have to file a U.S. tax return filing; additionally, an LLC will have to withhold on any income allocated to a foreign member; S corporations cannot have foreign shareholders (all shareholders must be U.S residents or citizens). As a practical matter, however, an LLC is not a viable choice of entity for a company that will have foreign investors or investors that are themselves pass-through entities with tax-exempt partners, because such investors may refuse or not be able to be members of an LLC.

- **Special allocations of tax attributes.** An LLC has flexibility to allocate tax attributes in ways other than pro rata based on stock ownership. An S corporation's tax attributes must be allocated to shareholders based on the number of shares they own.

- **Debt in basis.** An LLC member's basis for purposes of deducting pass-through losses includes the member's share of the entity's indebtedness. This is not the case with S corporations.

- **More certainty in tax status.** S corporations must meet certain criteria to elect S corporation status; they must then make an election; they must then not "bust" that status by violating one of the eligibility criteria. LLCs generally do not have to worry about qualifying or continuing to qualify for pass-through treatment.

- **Tax-free distributions of appreciated property.** An LLC can distribute appreciated property (e.g., real estate or stock) to its members without gain recognition to the LLC or its members, facilitating spin-off transactions. An S corporation's distribution of appreciated property to its shareholders results in the recognition of gain by the S corporation on the appreciation, which gain then flows or passes through to the S corporation's shareholders.

- **Profits interests.** It is possible to grant "cheap" equity to service providers through the use of "profits interests" under Rev. Proc. 93-27. See also Rev. Proc. 2001-43. It is more difficult for S corporations to issue cheap equity without adverse tax consequences to the recipients.

- **Payments to retiring partners.** Payments to retiring partners may be deductible by the partnership; payments in redemption of S corporation stock are not deductible.
- **Ease of tax-free formation.** Appreciated property can be contributed tax-free to LLCs under one of the most liberal nonrecognition provisions in the IRC. Contributions of appreciated property to S corporations in exchange for stock must comply with more restrictive provisions of the IRC to be tax-free (i.e., IRC Section 351) (although this is not usually a problem).

GLOSSARY

ACCELERATORS

Accelerators are institutions that take in cohorts of a dozen or so very early-stage startups, which go through a structured three or four month intensive program of education and mentoring. At the end of this period, there is typically a "demo day," where all the startups pitch to potential angel and institutional investors. These demo days may be how you find some of your deals.

ACCREDITED INVESTORS, NON-ACCREDITED INVESTORS

Startups raise money from **accredited investors**: either individuals or entities who meet the qualifications set by the Securities and Exchange Commission. According to the SEC, investors must meet a minimum level of income or assets (either high net worth or high income) in order to be accredited. The SEC rules make it challenging for companies to raise money from **non-accredited investors** who do not meet these standards.

ACQUISITION

Acquisition is a kind of liquidity event that occurs when a company buys at least a controlling interest in another company, for cash or stock of the acquiring company or a combination of the two. Being acquired by another company is the most common outcome for startups, excluding total failure. In 2018, 90% of the exits were acquisitions, while 10% were IPOs.[195]

ADVISOR AGREEMENT

The advisor responsibilities and compensation are codified in the **advisor agreement (advisory agreement or advisory board agreement)**. Advisor agreements will typically lay out the duration of the agreement, the amount of equity vested over the course of the agreement, and the vesting schedule.

---

195. https://nvca.org/wp-content/uploads/2019/08/NVCA-2019-Yearbook.pdf

ALL ACCREDITED INVESTOR RULE 506(B) OFFERINGS

The **All Accredited Investor Rule 506(b) offerings (or Rule 506(b))** is the most common way for private companies to raise money. Under Rule 506(b), companies cannot "generally solicit" or "generally advertise" their securities offerings. In a Rule 506(b) offering:

AMENDMENT PROVISIONS

Amendment provisions exist so that the investors and the startup can adjust the terms of their relationship as conditions change. It may be that a non-qualified financing opportunity comes along and the note holders want to convert. If this is not specifically addressed in other clauses within the note, the note could be amended to allow the investors to take that action. It is also possible that the lead investor in the upcoming priced round does not like some term in the note and wants to negotiate that with the note holders. The note investors may be willing to do that to get a deal to close on otherwise favorable terms.

ANGEL INVESTING GROUP

An **angel investing group (or angel group)** is a syndicate of angel investors that collaborate on deals. These groups can be large and formal (like Seattle's Alliance of Angels, which has over 140 members as of this writing), or small and informal (especially when not based in a major metropolitan area). They can help green investors learn the ropes of angel investing, improve access to deals, and share the work and potential costs of due diligence and negotiations.

ANGEL ROUND OR SEED ROUND

Whether or not a startup company comes out of an incubator or accelerator, the **angel round or seed round**, as it is usually called, is typically the first tranche of outside funding—that is, money from people the founders don't know. There is a tremendous range in the amount of money raised at this stage. Investments can take the form of debt (typically convertible notes) or a priced round in which the founders are selling shares of stock in the company. Seed rounds can vary from $100K to several million dollars.

ANTI-DILUTION PROTECTION, PURCHASE PRICE ANTI-DILUTION ADJUSTMENT PROTECTION

Anti-dilution protection, or, more precisely, **purchase price anti-dilution adjustment protection**, refers to provisions of stock, most typically preferred stock, that automatically adjust the conversion ratio of the stock to greater than 1:1 if the company sells shares in the future at a price less than what the investor paid.

AUTHORIZED SHARES

When a company is formed, the certificate or articles of incorporation states the total number of shares the company is authorized to issue, called **authorized shares**. If the company decides it needs more shares at some point, it will need to amend its certificate or articles of incorporation, and that typically requires approval of a majority of stockholders. Authorized shares can include common stock and preferred stock.

B2B COMPANIES, ENTERPRISE SALES

B2B companies (or business-to-business companies) sell their product or service to other companies, not individual consumers. B2Bs sell things like an inventory tracking app to restaurants, or a loyalty system for retail stores. A subset of B2B is **enterprise sales**, where companies sell to larger organizations like Microsoft, Intel, HP, or Procter & Gamble. B2B companies will usually have a list of existing customers, a number of trialing or beta customers, and a pipeline of deals.

B2C COMPANIES

B2C companies (or business-to-consumer companies) are offering a product or service to the general public.

BOARD OBSERVER

A **board observer** has the right to attend board meetings, they can participate in board discussions, and so can frequently influence board decisions as if they are a voting member of the board. A board observer has no vote in board decisions, and so they get access to all the information, but without the fiduciary duties and risk of liability. Board observer status for a member of a group of investors would normally be negotiated as part of the term sheet under observer rights. This might be appropriate, for example, for a large investor in a round who is not the lead investor.

BOARD OF DIRECTORS

In a corporation, the **board of directors (or BOD)** controls the company. It is typically made up of one or more founders, investors from each round, and one or more advisors. The board's authority is expansive: it can fire the CEO and the other officers of the company; approve all equity issuances, including all stock option grants to employees and all equity financing rounds (including convertible note rounds); approve leases and other significant financial commitments; approve or deny the sale of the company or decide to shut the company down. On the board of directors, each director has one vote.

BOOTSTRAPPING

Bootstrapping refers to the entrepreneurs self-funding, typically through a combination of savings and debt. In the bootstrapping phase, founders are doing their initial research, testing their hypotheses about product demand and features, and perhaps creating a minimum viable product (MVP) to get early customer feedback. The founders may be working full or part-time elsewhere and are drawing no salary for their work on the startup. Hopefully they have engaged a startup attorney and have executed the standard set of legal formation documents, invention assignment agreements, and so on.

BROAD-BASED WEIGHTED AVERAGE ANTI-DILUTION PROTECTION

Broad-based weighted average anti-dilution protection is a type of purchase price anti-dilution protection that has the effect of adjusting the conversion price of a class or series of preferred stock entitled to the protection if the company subsequently raises money by selling shares at a lower price per share than the price per share paid. This type of repricing takes into account the amount of shares the company sold at the lower price. The more the company raises at the lower your conversion price becomes.

BURN RATE

Burn rate is the amount of money a startup is spending every month. For a startup that is pre-revenue, this is considered the "monthly burn." For a startup with revenue, the burn rate is the monthly spend less any reasonably expected revenues.

C CORPORATION

A **C corporation** is a type of business entity which is taxed for federal income tax purposes under Subchapter C of the Internal Revenue Code. C corporations pay the taxes that are due on their income; their shareholders are not taxed on and not liable for taxes on the corporation's income (in contrast to S corporations and limited liability companies, which are taxed as partnerships).

CAPITALIZATION TABLE, STOCK LEDGER

The **capitalization table (or cap table)**, is a document showing each person who owns an interest in the company. Usually this is broken out by the name of each equity holder, and shows what type of equity instruments they hold. It is set up as a ledger, so that all share issuances and transfers can be tracked. Many companies use Excel or services like Carta to keep their capitalization table. They will create a worksheet for each type of equity security outstanding, such as common stock, Series A Preferred Stock, Series B Preferred Stock, and so on, including convertible debt and equity instruments that are issued. Included in the cap table is the **stock ledger**, showing all issuances of equity from the company to equity holders and all transfers of equity from one equity holder to another. There may be multiple ledgers for each type of stock or convertible security the company has ever issued.

CHARTER DOCUMENTS

In the corporate context, **charter documents** are a company's articles or certificate of incorporation, bylaws, and any other corporate agreements, such as shareholder agreements, voting agreements, and so on.

CLOSING

Closing refers to the moment at which you sign the definitive documents requiring your signature, and send the company your money, typically either in the form of a check or a wire transfer. The company signs the required documents and delivers to you the security purchased.

CO-SALE RIGHT

The **co-sale right (or tag-along right)** is the right to participate alongside another stockholder, typically a founder, when that stockholder is selling their shares.

COMMON STOCK

Common stock is stock that entitles the holder to receive whatever remains of the assets of a company after payment of all debt and all preferred stock priority liquidation preferences. Common stock does not usually have any of the special rights, preferences, and privileges of preferred stock (although it is possible to create a class of common that does, such as a class of common stock that has multiple votes per share, or is non-voting, or that has protective provisions).

COMPENSATORY EQUITY AWARDS

Compensatory equity awards are awards of stock, options, restricted stock units, and similar awards issued to service providers of a company. Under the securities laws, companies may issue compensatory equity to service providers without those service providers being accredited if they comply with another exemption, such as Rule 701.

CONFIDENTIALITY AGREEMENT

A **confidentiality agreement (or non-disclosure agreement of NDA)** prevents employees from discussing information pertaining to their work at the company, including the status of the company or its customers. The confidentiality agreement is typically included as part of an employment agreement.

CONVERSION DISCOUNT

A **conversion discount** provides that the holder of the note gets a purchase price discount when the note is converted into stock. Typically, the discount is 10%-20%, but discounts higher than that are not out of the question.

CONVERTIBLE DEBT

Convertible debt (or convertible note or convertible loan or convertible promissory note) is a short-term loan issued to a company by an investor or group of investors. The principal and interest (if applicable) from the note is designed to be converted into equity in the company. A subsequent qualified financing round or liquidity event triggers conversion, typically into preferred stock. Convertible notes may convert at the same price investors pay in the next financing, or they may convert at either a discount or a conversion price based on a valuation cap. Discounts and valuation caps incentivize investors for investing early and not setting a price on the equity when it would typically be lower. If a convertible note is not repaid with equity by the time the loan is due, investors may have the right to be repaid in cash like a normal loan.[196]

CONVERTIBLE EQUITY

Convertible equity is an entrepreneur-friendly investment vehicle that attempts to bring to the entrepreneur the advantages of convertible debt without the downsides for the entrepreneur, specifically interest and maturity dates. The convertible equity instrument the investor is buying will convert to actual equity (stock ownership) at the subsequent financing round, with some potential rewards for the investor for investing early. Those rewards are similar to the rewards for convertible debt, such as a valuation cap and/or a discount.

CUMULATIVE DIVIDEND

A **cumulative dividend** would accumulate every year, year over year, but be paid only "as and when" declared by the board. Cumulative dividends would be paid on liquidation, if not paid before. Cumulative dividends can be economically harsh on founders and junior investors and are not common in competitive deals.

CUSTOMER ACQUISITION COST

Customer acquisition cost (CAC) is a critical metric of the B2C startup. The company should be able to tell you about their most effective marketing channels, and what it costs on average to acquire a customer.

---

196. This definition has been adapted from the *Holloway Guide to Raising Venture Capital*[197].

197. https://www.holloway.com/g/venture-capital/sections/exits-and-returns

CUSTOMER LIFETIME VALUE

Customer lifetime value (or CLTV or CLV) is another critical metric. Entrepreneurs should understand (or at least have a model with assumptions around) the customer lifetime value and how long it takes for them to recover the cost of acquisition. For the company to be profitable, their CLTV has to dramatically exceed their customer acquisition cost (CAC). That may not be the case initially while they are experimenting and tuning their marketing mix and retention and pricing strategies—but they should have a hypothesis of how they are going to get there.

DEAL FLOW

Deal flow refers to the number of potential investment opportunities you review during a particular period. Ideally, if you are active, you will have the chance to review, if not all, a substantial portion of the investment opportunities in your particular area.

DEFINITIVE DOCUMENTS

Definitive documents are the legal contracts between the buyers (investors) and seller (the company) that spell out in detail the terms of the transaction, and are drafted by a lawyer. The definitive documents will set forth the entire understanding of the parties. Definitive documents can include an amended corporate charter and/or articles of incorporation that need to be filed with the secretary of state in the state in which the company is incorporated and would be available for the investor to review. The documents must be signed by all parties in order for a closing to be reached.

DILUTION

Dilution is the decrease in ownership percentage of a company that occurs when the company issues additional stock, typically for one of the following reasons: to issue to a co-founder who came on after incorporation, to sell to investors, or to add to its stock option pool.

DISCLOSURE SCHEDULES

Disclosure schedules are attachments to a stock purchase agreement in which the company discloses any items required to be disclosed on the schedule. If you are not familiar with stock purchase agreements, the representations and warranties are written in absolutes. The disclosure schedules are there to provide the details. Disclosure schedules are important to review as part of your diligence before signing the definitive documents.

DIVIDEND PREFERENCE

Preferred stock usually has a **dividend preference**, which means that dividends cannot be paid on the common stock unless a dividend is first paid on the preferred stock. A dividend preference might say that the preferred stock is entitled to a certain percentage dividend—say, 8% of the purchase price of the stock, per year, noncumulative, "as, if and when" declared by the board. The preference would go on to say that no dividends may be declared on the common unless and until the preferred dividend is paid.

DOMAIN EXPERTISE, FUNCTIONAL DOMAIN EXPERTISE

Domain expertise (or domain knowledge) means a thorough understanding of a particular field of study. In the context of angel investing, a deep knowledge of a particular industry's inner workings, including the ecosystem, market, competitors, and customers. Domain expertise can also refer to **functional domain expertise**, such as a deep understanding of social media marketing or iOS app development.

DOUBLE TRIGGER ACCELERATION, SINGLE TRIGGER ACCELERATION

Single trigger acceleration is 100% vesting upon one event—the change of control transaction. **Double trigger acceleration** is acceleration of vesting upon the occurrence of two events:

DRAG-ALONG AGREEMENT

A **drag-along agreement (or take-along agreement)** requires those who sign it, ideally all of the company's stockholders, to vote in favor of change of control transactions—to go along with the sale of the company or a sale of all of the interests in the company, including yours, even if you do not agree with the proposed sale and would otherwise refuse to go along or vote for it.

DUE DILIGENCE

Due diligence (or business due diligence) refers to the process by which investors investigate a company and its market before deciding whether to invest. Due diligence typically happens after an investor hears the pitch and before investment terms are discussed in any detail.

EMPLOYEE VESTING

Employee vesting refers to vesting on employee stock option grants. Sometimes investors will require that all employee option grants have to vest over a specified schedule (such as monthly over a 48-month period, but with a one-year cliff), unless approval is given by the investor's designee on the board or a majority of the investors.

EQUITY INCENTIVE PLAN, STOCK OPTION PLAN, STOCK OPTION POOL, STRIKE PRICE

The **stock option pool** is a specified number of shares set aside and reserved for issuance on the exercise of stock options granted to employees under a **stock option plan** or an **equity incentive plan**. Equity incentive plans have more awards available under them to issue than stock options (they also have stock bonuses, restricted stock awards, and sometimes other types of awards as well). The shares reserved under an equity incentive plan should be reflected on the cap table. Options are granted out of the pool via grants that are approved by the board. Each grant reduces the remaining available pool, until it is topped up again by the board authorizing the reservation of additional shares under the plan from the authorized shares. The **strike price** is the exercise price of the stock option.

EXEMPTION

An **exemption (or exempt offering)** is an offer and sale of securities that does not have to be registered with the SEC because the SEC has adopted an exemption from registration that you can qualify to use.

FIXED PRICE FINANCING

A **fixed price financing (or fixed price round or priced round)** is a type of financing where the investors buy a fixed number of shares at a set price (in a common stock or preferred stock round), as opposed to rounds in which the number of shares and the price of those shares will be determined later (such as convertible note or convertible equity rounds). The most common type of fixed price round are preferred stock deals, which often represent rounds larger than convertible rounds, greater than $500K for example, which justifies the legal cost of documenting the round.

FOUNDER VESTING

Founder vesting refers to a legal mechanism whereby founders have to continue to provide services for some period of time or have their shares potentially repurchased by the company. Founder vesting may follow a similar pattern to employee vesting, where the founder gains permanent ownership of their stock over the course of typically three or four years, with potentially a one-year mark for 25% ownership and monthly increases thereafter.

FULL RATCHET ANTI-DILUTION ADJUSTMENT PROTECTION

Full ratchet anti-dilution adjustment protection (or full ratchet) refers to a method of purchase price anti-dilution protection in which an adjustment is triggered upon the sale of stock at a lower price. Full ratchet rights entitle the holder to have their conversion adjustment formula reset in order to give them the number of common shares that they would have received had they purchased their shares at the lower price.

FULLY DILUTED BASIS, FULLY DILUTED SHARES

Fully diluted shares take into account all issued and outstanding shares on an as-converted to common stock basis, assuming the conversion or exercise of all convertible securities, such as options, warrants, and convertible preferred stock. Sometimes fully diluted shares take into account not just issued options but the entire stock option pool share reserve. Investors prefer that the price per share be determined on a **fully diluted basis** because increasing the number of shares in the denominator in the formula above reduces the price per share.

GENERAL SOLICITATION

General solicitation (or general advertising or public advertising) means using radio, TV, the unrestricted internet, and other means of soliciting investors. General solicitation and general advertising are defined in Rule 502(c) of Regulation D.

INCUBATOR

The term **incubator** generally refers to a company that generates its own startup ideas in-house. Using a resident team that is deeply versed in startup techniques, they will typically research the market, prototype the product or service, and test customer demand. If they see an idea getting traction, they look for a full-time CEO and help to build the core team of early employees. That team is then sent out to raise money as an independent entity. Incubators, which often refer to themselves as "labs," retain a significant ownership stake in the startups they help create.

INDEMNIFICATION AGREEMENT

An **indemnification agreement** is a contract between a company and a director or officer in which the company agrees to indemnify, defend, and hold harmless a director or officer if the director or officer is sued as a result of being a director or officer of the company.

INFORMATION RIGHTS

Information rights are the rights to receive certain information about the company at specified times—for example, the right to receive quarterly and annual financial statements, the right to receive an updated capitalization table from time to time, and the right to receive the company's annual budget. Sometimes, information rights are only made available to investors who invest a certain amount in a financing (typically referred to in the investment documents as a "major investor").

INITIAL PUBLIC OFFERING

An **initial public offering (IPO)** is the first sale of a company's stock to the public where the sale is registered with the Securities and Exchange Commission, specifies an initial trading price for the stock, and is generally financed by one or more investment banks.[198] This type of liquidity event is colloquially referred to as "going public."[199]

---

198. https://www.sec.gov/files/ipo-investorbulletin.pdf

INSPECTION RIGHTS

Inspection rights are the rights to visit the business premises, meet with management, and review the company's books and records. Companies may have a legitimate reason to push back on giving all investors inspection rights, as it could be a significant drain on management's time if they were obligated to meet with or entertain at their office a large number of individual investors.

INSTITUTIONAL INVESTOR

Institutional investor refers to an entity that is in the business of investing either its own money (like a family office) or other people's money. They are usually sophisticated in their legal knowledge and are savvy negotiators of early-stage deals, because they are in the business of making investments. In some cases they might be quite aggressive in the terms they seek from entrepreneurs.

INTELLECTUAL PROPERTY ASSIGNMENT AGREEMENT

The **intellectual property assignment agreement (or IP assignment agreement)** ensures that all the work produced by the employee belongs to the company, with customary exclusions that anything they do on their own time with their own equipment belongs to them, as long as it is not directly related to the business of the company. There is usually an addendum where the employee lists any of their own prior inventions or IP that they want excluded from the assignment.

INTEREST

Interest on a convertible note is not typically paid in cash while the note is outstanding. Most typically, it accumulates and is paid in stock on conversion. However, sometimes note holders negotiate for the right on conversion to have the interest paid in cash. Interest rates on convertible notes typically range from 4%-8%. Startups are very high risk, and the rate of interest typically would not adequately compensate an investor for that risk relative to alternatives; so it is best to think of the interest as a sweetener to the deal, since the main reason for buying the note is to end up with the equity when it converts.

---

199. This definition has been adapted from the *Holloway Guide to Raising Venture Capital*[200].

200. https://www.holloway.com/g/venture-capital/sections/exits-and-returns

INVESTOR RIGHTS AGREEMENT

An **Investor Rights Agreement** typically includes covenants or ongong promises on the part of the Company to provide the investors with certain rights. Those rights could include registration rights, participation rights, information rights, observer rights, inspections rights, protective provisions, and other covenants. The voting agreement may be part of the Investor Rights Agreement.

ISSUED AND OUTSTANDING BASIS, ISSUED AND OUTSTANDING SHARES

Issued and outstanding shares are the shares that have been issued to founders, employees, advisors, directors, or investors. Issued and outstanding shares do not include stock options that have been reserved in the option pool. Ownership percentage calculated on an **issued and outstanding basis** is determined by dividing the number of shares owned by an individual or entity by the total issued and outstanding securities.

LEAD INVESTOR

The **lead investor** is typically an experienced angel investor (or institutional investor) who negotiates the detailed terms of the deal with the entrepreneur, including the valuation. They also often have the thankless task of coordinating the due diligence efforts, working with the lawyer(s) representing the investors (including hiring and paying them, to be reimbursed later by the company), and reviewing the final documents. They may also be coordinating with other angel groups or investors on the closing date.

LEGAL DUE DILIGENCE

Legal due diligence refers to the process of reviewing a company's legal documents to ensure that the company has not made and is not making any legal errors that will put the investment at risk.

LIMITED LIABILITY COMPANIES

Limited liability companies (or LLCs) can be simpler to form than corporations. LLCs also have the benefit of being pass-through entities for tax reasons by default. Meaning, the losses flow through to the personal tax returns of the owners, unless an election to be taxed as a corporation is made.

LIQUIDATION PREFERENCE

A **liquidation preference** entitles the holder of the security with the liquidation preference to be paid before other stockholders on a sale of the company or all of its assets.

LIQUIDATION PREFERENCE OVERHANG

Liquidation preference overhang refers to how you might, if you invest in a convertible note or convertible equity instrument with a valuation cap or a discount (or both), ultimately might receive shares of preferred stock with a liquidation preference in excess of what you paid.

LIQUIDITY EVENT

In a **liquidity event (or exit)**, the company in which you invested is sold or the company goes public, allowing investors to cash out of their investment.

LOCKUP AGREEMENT

A **lockup agreement** is an agreement with the issuer of the securities (the company) that you will not sell your shares for some period of time, sometimes for as long as a year.

MATURITY

The **maturity** of the note—the length of time before it is due—typically ranges from 12–24 months. It is common that startups take longer to achieve their milestones then they or you expect. A shorter maturity date (12 months) is a ticking clock that might pressure an entrepreneur to raise money on unfavorable terms.

MINIMUM VIABLE PRODUCT

Minimum viable product (or MVP) refers to the product that the company has built which it believes it can sell and monetize. The product is far enough along to gauge whether customers will pay for it.

MOST-FAVORED NATIONS CLAUSE

A **most-favored nations clause (or MFN clause or MFN)** is a clause in a convertible note or convertible equity purchase agreement (or side letter agreement) that provides that the holder of the security is entitled to the benefit of any more favorable provisions the company offers to later investors. If you are an early investor in a convertible note round, an MFN clause can be a very good idea.

NARROW-BASED PURCHASE PRICE ANTI-DILUTION

In a **narrow-based purchase price anti-dilution** formula, the investors receive more shares on an as converted to common stock basis than with broad-based protection because in narrow-based you do not count the issued and outstanding options in "A" in the formula above, only the issued and outstanding stock. This results in a lower conversion price, making it less friendly to founders than broad-based. Narrow-based anti-dilution results in a greater adjustment than broad-based, weighted average anti-dilution adjustment provisions, but less than full ratchet adjustment provisions.

NON-PARTICIPATING PREFERRED

Non-participating preferred stock is preferred stock that entitles the holder on a liquidation to receive the *greater* of either (i) its liquidation preference, or (ii) what the preferred stock would receive if it converted to common stock.

NON-QUALIFIED FINANCING

A **non-qualified financing** is a financing that does not meet the definition of a qualified financing in your note, and thus does not cause your note to be automatically converted into shares of stock sold in the financing.

NONDISCLOSURE AGREEMENT

A **nondisclosure agreement (or confidentiality agreement or NDA)** is an agreement in which you agree to keep a company's confidential information confidential. In the broader business world, companies consider almost all their information confidential unless it is publicly available on their website, for example, or has been made public through press releases or financial filings. The startup world is a more specialized context, in which the investors will need to know a lot about a company before they consider investing, and will likely be pitching to groups of potential investors and sharing key details of the business in the process.

OBSERVER RIGHTS

Observer rights are rights to attend a company's board meetings as a guest, in a non-voting capacity. The ability to attend board meetings provides tremendous insight into what is happening at the company. However, often very sensitive information is discussed, and a company may be very reluctant to provide this right to anyone other than the lead investor for a particular round.

PARTICIPATING PREFERRED

Participating preferred stock is preferred stock that entitles the holder to a return of its liquidation preference, and then to participate with the common stock on an as-converted to common stock basis.

PARTICIPATION RIGHTS, SUPER PARTICIPATION RIGHTS

Participation rights (or preemptive rights) allow investors to invest in subsequent rounds to maintain their pro rata share. **Super participation rights (or gobble up rights)** allow you to buy *more* than your pro rata share, meaning the right to invest more if other investors do not exercise their participation rights in full.

PERFECT, SECURED, SECURITY INTEREST

When you say that a loan is **secured** by the company's assets, what you mean is that the company will grant the lender a security interest in its assets, which the lender may perfect.[201] A **security interest** is a direct interest in the assets of a company that the borrower grants to the lender. If the lender has a security interest in the company's assets, the lender can **perfect** its security interest by filing a financing statement (typically, a UCC-1) to ensure that subsequent creditors are behind it in line with respect to payment from proceeds of a sale of the assets. Once the lender does this, they have priority over subsequent creditors. A secured party can take action to seize the collateral and dispose of it in the event of a default on the loan.

PIVOT

A **pivot**, a term popular in startup culture, happens when a company realizes that their current product or business strategy is not going to work and they change course to a new product and/or business model. A classic pivot scenario is that a company is struggling to sell their product, while potential customers keep asking them if they can solve a different but related problem.

POST-MONEY VALUATION

The **post-money valuation** is the value of a company immediately following the investment. For example, if the pre-money was $3M, and the investment was $1M, then the post-money valuation would be $4M. Convertible equity instruments such as convertible notes or SAFEs can be set up as either pre-money or post-money instruments. The SAFE currently published by Y Combinator is a post-money SAFE.

PRE-MONEY VALUATION

The **pre-money valuation** is the agreed upon value of the company immediately prior to the investment. The pre-money valuation is the single most important factor, but not the *only* factor, in determining how much of the company you will own when you invest a specific amount of money.

---

201. Perfection[202] is a legal concept meaning you have done what you have to do to prevent someone who comes in later from getting ahead of you.

202. https://en.wikipedia.org/wiki/Perfection_(law)

PREFERRED STOCK, PREFERRED STOCK ROUNDS

Preferred stock rounds are the most common type of fixed price round for angel investments—in fact, when investors and founders refer to a *fixed price round* or a *priced round*, they usually mean a preferred stock financing, although common stock fixed price rounds are possible. **Preferred stock** is equity that has specified preferences relative to common stock and potentially to other classes of preferred stock. Those preferences are negotiated as part of the term sheet and documented in the definitive documents of the stock sale.

PRO RATA RIGHTS

Pro rata rights (or pro rata) in a term sheet or side letter guarantee an investor the opportunity to invest an amount in subsequent funding rounds that maintains their ownership percentage.

PRODUCT/MARKET FIT, TRACTION

A company's **traction** with customers indicates that there is actually demand for the product or service. This is sometimes referred to as (or as an important part of) **product/market fit**,[203] meaning that there is a validated market for the product at the stated price. Traction also shows that the company has actually built a working version of their product, and that they can sell it to businesses or generate consumer demand, for B2B or B2C offerings respectively.

PROTECTIVE PROVISIONS, PROTECTIVE PROVISIONS

Protective provisions are provisions in a set of investment documents which require the separate approval of a particular class of investor before the company can take certain actions. For example, the separate approval of holders of a majority of the Series A Preferred Stock might be required before the company can undergo a sale transaction.

---

203. There are a few schools of thought around what defines product/market fit. Holloway has a great post[204] about this, part of the *Holloway Guide to Raising Venture Capital*.
204. https://www.holloway.com/s/rvc-fundamentals-of-product-market-fit

QUALIFIED FINANCING

A **qualified financing** in a convertible note is usually defined as a fundraising of at least a fixed amount of money (for example, $1M), either including or excluding amounts raised under the note. These criteria cause the note to automatically convert into the type and number of shares being sold in the qualified financing. There are subtleties to how a qualified financing is defined.

QUALIFIED SMALL BUSINESS STOCK

Section 1202 provides a special incentive for investments in **qualified small business stock (or QSBS)**. QSBS is stock of a C corporation actively engaged in a "qualified" trade or business issued to an investor when the C corporation had less than $50M in gross assets (both before and after the investment). "Qualified" trades or businesses are generally not service-based businesses. Under Section 1202, if you hold the QSBS for more than five years, you get a tax break on your long-term capital gains tax rate.

REDEMPTION RIGHTS, REDEMPTION RIGHTS

Redemption rights (or put right) are the rights to have your shares redeemed or repurchased by the company, usually after a period of time has passed (3-7 years). It is also possible to prepare these provisions to allow redemption in the event the company fails to reach a milestone, or breaches a covenant.

REGISTRATION RIGHTS AGREEMENT

A **registration rights agreement** is an agreement of the company to register securities with the Securities and Exchange Commission so that the holder of the securities can sell them. When investors demand the company register the investors' shares, it is so the investors can sell those shares on the public market and get liquidity—the liquidity goes to the investors, not the company.

REPRESENTATIONS, WARRANTIES

Representations (or reps) and **warranties** can cover a broad range of topics in a financing transaction and they typically get more thorough as the amount of money gets bigger. In general terms, a representation is an assertion that the information in question is true at the time of the financing, and the warranty is the promise of indemnity if the representation turns out to be false. For example, a company might rep that they have no unpaid salaries, or that they are not currently being sued. We address two more specific reps below.

REVENUE LOAN

A **revenue loan** is a loan that has a monthly or periodic repayment amount that is a percentage of the company's gross or net revenue in the period with respect to which the payment is going to be made (for example, the preceding month or quarter). The payment amount is typically somewhere between 5-10% of the preceding period's gross or net revenue. In other words, the payment amount is not set and fixed like in a traditional loan. It goes up and down based on the performance of the business. A revenue loan may have a four-, five-, seven-, or ten-year term, and is considered repaid when the lender has received the negotiated multiple of the loan amount (anywhere from 1.5X-3X) and any other costs of the loan.

RIGHT OF FIRST REFUSAL

A **right of first refusal** gives the investors the right to buy the founder's shares if a founder is going to sell them to a third party.

RUNWAY

In startup lingo, **runway** refers to how much time in months the company has before it runs out of cash, calculated by dividing the amount of money they have in the bank by the burn rate (the amount of money they spend each month). For example, if the company is spending $25K a month and has $100K in the bank, it has four months of runway left.

S CORPORATIONS

Shareholders in **S corporations** can generally only be individuals who are U.S. citizens or lawful permanent residents. Shareholders cannot be other business entities or organizations. When a venture capital firm invests in an S corporation, that companies loses their S corporation status and convert automatically to a C corporation.

SECURITY

The term **security** is defined very broadly under U.S. securities law.[205] In general, a security is an investment in a common enterprise purchased with the expectation of profit, the value of which depends on the efforts of others.[206]

SIDE LETTER

The **side letter (or side letter agreement)** is an agreement between an investor and the company in which the company agrees to provide the investor with certain rights that are not otherwise present in the investment documents. This side letter usually includes terms like information rights, pro rata rights, and a most favored nations clause.

---

205. The Securities Act of 1933, as amended, states that a security is "any note, stock, treasury stock, security future, security-based swap, bond, debenture, evidence of indebtedness, certificate of interest or participation in any profit-sharing agreement, collateral-trust certificate, preorganization certificate or subscription, transferable share, *investment contract*, voting-trust certificate, certificate of deposit for a security, fractional undivided interest in oil, gas, or other mineral rights, any put, call, straddle, option, or privilege on any security, certificate of deposit, or group or index of securities (including any interest therein or based on the value thereof), or any put, call, straddle, option, or privilege entered into on a national securities exchange relating to foreign currency, or, in general, any interest or instrument commonly known as a 'security,' or any certificate of interest or participation in, temporary or interim certificate for, receipt for, guarantee of, or warrant or right to subscribe to or purchase, any of the foregoing."

206. https://en.wikipedia.org/wiki/SEC_v._W._J._Howey_Co

SUBSCRIPTION PROCEDURE

Subscription procedure refers to the documents you as an investor will be asked to sign. In a preferred stock financing, the documents you will be asked to sign will depend on what type of preferred stock is being sold. If it is a Series Seed Preferred round, you might just be asked to sign the Stock Investment Agreement. If the round is a Series A or beyond, you will probably be asked to sign a number of documents, including:

TERM SHEET

A **term sheet** is a summary of the key business terms of the proposed transaction. It should be short, easy to understand, and it should be free of legalese—save perhaps a sentence about the non-binding nature of the proposal. Term sheets are helpful in reaching agreement on the principal business terms as they are very short (1—2 pages) and concise, and easily understandable by those at all familiar with the terms.

VALUATION

Valuation is how much a company is worth; valuation and value may be used interchangeably, or valuation may refer to the process of determining a company's value. A public company's value is expressed by how much people are willing to pay for the shares on the stock market. For a private company, the company's value is determined in negotiations between the founders raising money and the investors.

VALUATION CAP

A **valuation cap** is a term included in a convertible note that sets the maximum valuation of a company at which an investor's note can be converted into stock of the company. An angel investor will typically want a valuation cap in a convertible note so that they are not converted at an unexpectedly high valuation.

VANITY METRICS

Vanity metrics are numbers that may sound exciting but don't translate in any direct way to the health of the business.[207] In a B2B scenario, a vanity metric would be how many people came by the sales booth at the conference. The meaningful metric is how many qualified sales leads came from the conference.

VENTURE CAPITALISTS

Venture capitalists (or VCs) generally invest \$1M or more (sometimes, *a lot* more) in a round of financing for a startup. They typically invest through a VC firm. Most VCs are looking to make \$3M–\$10M initial investments, with that number rising in follow-on rounds. They typically look for companies that have real traction with paying customers, though occasionally they will back successful serial entrepreneurs who have only an idea. They often like to invest when the company has achieved product/market fit, thereby dramatically reducing the risk of early failure. They invest when the company needs cash to accelerate its sales and marketing and scale up its engineering team to flesh out the early product. A company may raise many rounds of venture capital, and many VCs keep money aside to invest again in subsequent rounds for the winners in their portfolio (the "follow-on" investment).

VESTING SCHEDULE

In the majority of cases, vesting occurs incrementally over time, according to a **vesting schedule**. A person vests only while they work for the company. If the person quits or is terminated immediately, they get no equity, and if they stay for years, they'll get most or all of it.[209]

VOTING AGREEMENT

A **Voting Agreement** is an agreement between the voting stockholders of a company in which the parties agree to vote their shares in a particular fashion to ensure that certain persons or their designees are elected to the board of directors. The agreement must be signed by the stockholders, because under corporate law it is the shareholders who elect the directors of the company; if your agreement is just with the company your right will not be enforceable.

---

207. Thinking about vanity metrics always reminds Joe of this old article: "The Surprisingly Large Cost of Telling Small Lies.[208]"

208. https://boss.blogs.nytimes.com/2014/03/11/
     the-surprisingly-large-cost-of-telling-small-lies/

209. This definition comes from the *Holloway Guide to Raising Venture Capital*[210].

210. https://www.holloway.com/g/venture-capital/about

VOTING RIGHTS

The **voting rights** of stockholders come into play whenever the company is taking an action that requires stockholder approval. The typical items that require stockholder approval include, among other things: the election of directors; an increase in the company's equity incentive or stock option plan share reserve; an amendment to the company's charter (other than purely a change of the company's name).

WARRANT

A **warrant** is a contract entitling the warrant holder to buy shares of stock of a company. It is not stock itself. It is merely a contractual right to buy stock.

About the Authors

Joe Wallin is a Seattle-based corporate lawyer who represents startups, investors and lenders in startups, founders, and executives. Joe has been working in the early-stage company space since the late 1990s. He is a member of the Angel Capital Association's public policy advisory council, where he is actively involved in trying to make the law better for investors and founders. Joe has written for The Wall Street Journal, PandoDaily, GeekWire, and Xconomy, and blogs at The Startup Law Blog.

Pete Baltaxe has played many roles in the startup ecosystem. As a serial entrepreneur, he raised over $25M in seed financing and venture capital, and had two successful exits, an acquisition for 2Market and an IPO for RedEnvelope. He has advised startups on fundraising and product strategy, both individually and as part of accelerators like Techstars. Pete has also been an angel investor for ten years. As an executive in many startups over his 25-year career, Pete has seen first-hand how startups succeed and fail. He has felt the angst of the shortening cash runway and the thrill of the successful exit!

About Holloway

Holloway publishes books online, offering titles from experts on topics ranging from tools and technology to teamwork and entrepreneurship. All titles are built for a satisfying reading experience on the web as well as in print. The Holloway Reader helps readers find what they need in search results, and permits authors and editors to make ongoing improvements.

Holloway seeks to publish more exceptional authors. We believe that a new company with modern tools can make publishing a better experience for authors and help them reach their audience. If you're a writer with a manuscript or idea, please get in touch at hello@holloway.com.